# Foods Jesus Ate
# and How to Grow Them

# Foods Jesus Ate and How to Grow Them

## Allan A. Swenson

Skyhorse Publishing

Skyhorse Publishing books may be purchased in bulk at special discounts for sales promotion, corporate gifts, fund raising, or educational purposes. Special editions can also be created to specifications. For details, contact Special Sales Department, Skyhorse Publishing, 555 Eighth Avenue, Suite 903, New York, NY 10018 or info@skyhorsepublishing.com.

www.skyhorsepublishing.com

10 9 8 7 6 5 4 3 2 1

Library of Congress Cataloging-in-Publication Data

Swenson, Allan A.
    Foods Jesus ate and how to grow them / Allan A. Swenson.
        p. cm.
    Includes bibliographical references and index.
    ISBN-13: 978-1-60239-214-4 (pbk. : alk. paper)
    ISBN-10: 1-60239-214-5 (pbk. : alk. paper)
    1. Food in the Bible. 2. Jesus Christ. 3. Horticulture. I. Title.

BS680.F6S94 2008
220.8'6413—dc22    2007043877

Photos courtesy of stock.XCHNG

Printed in China

To a mentor and friend . . .
Rev. Marsh Hudson-Knapp

# Contents

Foods and Recipes .......................................... viii

Acknowledgments........................................... ix

Introduction ............................................... xi

Chapter 1. *Foods Jesus Ate, to Grow and Enjoy* .................. 1

Chapter 2. *A Scriptural Heritage* ............................. 13

Chapter 3. *Foods of the Bible to Nourish the Faithful* .............. 21

Chapter 4. *Fruits and Nuts of the Holy Land* .................... 105

Chapter 5. *Site and Soil for Abundant Growth* .................. 171

Chapter 6. *Container Gardening Rewards* ...................... 189

Chapter 7. *Plant a Row for the Hungry* ....................... 195

Chapter 8. *Neot Kedumim—World's Most Extensive Biblical Garden* . . 207

Chapter 9. *Biblical Gardens Around the World* .................... 219

Chapter 10. *Growing Adventures with Children* ................. 223

Chapter 11. *Biblical Food Celebration Service* .................. 237

Chapter 12. *Gardening Sources—Websites and Know How* ......... 247

Chapter 13. *Foods of the Bible Quiz* ........................... 259

Chapter 14. *Plan a Trip to the Holy Land* ..................... 267

Appendix A  *Seeds from the Holy Land* ........................ 272

Appendix B  *Biblical Garden Directory* ....................... 273

Appendix C  *Biblical Garden Update Form* .................... 279

Appendix D  *Concordances* ............................... 280

Appendix E  *Sources and Resources for Biblical Gardens
            by Rev. Marsh Hudson-Knapp* ........... 282

*Bibliography*................................................ 286

# Foods and Recipes

**BARLEY** 23–31
Barley and Shrimp Skillet Dinner 30
Barley Confetti Toss 30
Herbed Barley and Mushrooms 30
Barley Florentine 30
Barley Apricot Pilaf 31

**BITTER HERBS** 31–44
Mixed Green Salad with Red and Yellow
Pepper Vinaigrette 37
Red and Yellow Pepper Vinaigrette 37
Creamy Horseradish Dip 40
Horseradish Coleslaw 40
Easy Oven Stew 40
Horsey Burgers 40
Horseradish Sauce 41
Chicory and Roast Beet Salad with Blue
Cheese 43
Chicory and Bacon Salad 43
Belgium Endive Salad 44
Cream of Belgium Endive Soup 44

**CUCUMBER** 45–50
Refrigerator Dill Chips 47
Nontraditional Sweet Freezer Pickles 48
Cucumber Yogurt Salad Dressing 49
Thai Cucumber Salad 49
Yogurt and Cucumber Soup with Saffron 49

**FAVA/BROAD BEANS** 50–57
Tuscan Fava Bean Salad 55
Minestrone with Fava Beans 55
Mighty Veggie Minestrone 56
Creamed Fava Beans and Bacon 57

**GARBANZO BEANS/CHICKPEAS** 57–62
Garbanzo/Chickpea Mediterranean
Salad 61
Chickpea Antipasto Holiday Salad 61

**GARLIC** 62–66
Creamy Garlic Salad Dressing 65
Scampi with Garlic and Herbs 65

**LEEKS** 66–71
Cooked Leeks 69
Leeks in White Sauce 69
Leeks Vinaigrette 70
Braised Leeks 70
Leek and Potato Soup (Vichyssoise) 71
Swenson Leek Soup 71

**LENTILS** 71–78
Simple Lentil Salad 76
Hearty Italian Lentil Stew 76
High-Fiber Lentil Chicken Salad 77
Low-Fat Minestrone Lentil Soup 77

**MILLET** 78–82
Black Bean and Millet Salad 81
Millet Muffins 82

**MUSTARD** 82–87
Braised Mustard Greens with Smoked
Turkey 86

**ONIONS** 87–92
Onion and Celery Seed Relish 91
Grilled Green Onions 92

**WHEAT** 92–103
> Tasty and Easy Wheat Biscuits 100
> Basic Bread Bowls 101
> Honey Bread 102
> Whole Wheat Muffins 102

**ALMONDS** 105–110
> Almond Munchkin Mix 109
> Toasted Almonds 109
> Almond Shrimp Salad 109
> Roasted Almonds 110

**APPLES** 110–118
> Grandma's Apple Pie 117
> Apple and Wilted Lettuce Salad 117
> Apple Rhubarb Crunch 118

**APRICOTS** 118–123
> Apricot-Oatmeal Breakfast Cake 121
> Crisp & Flacky Orchard Apricot Pockets 122
> Apricot Nut Bread 122

**BRAMBLES** 123–129

**DATES** 129–135
> Date Muffins 134
> Aunt Martha's Date Balls or Cookies 135
> Date Bars 135

**FIGS** 135–140
> Stuffed Fresh Figs 139
> Fig Pudding 139
> Fig Raisin Cake 139

**GRAPES** 140–148
> Perfect Passover Pie 147
> Boston Lettuce Salad with Grapes and Walnuts 148

**MELONS** 148–158
> Watermelon Granita 157
> Watermelon Smoothie 157

**OLIVES** 158–163
> Mediterranean Salad 163
> American Creole Olive Salad 163

**POMEGRANATES** 164–169
> Chicken Salad with Almonds 169
> Zesty Pomegranate Let of Lamb 169

# Acknowledgments

**M**y heartfelt thanks to all the marvelous, dedicated, and faithful gardeners across America who have shared their wit and wisdom about biblical gardening with me, so that I may share it with you.

Thanks also to the well-focused friends at the National Garden Bureau, many different garden clubs and organizations, and the Garden Writers Association, as well as the many down-to-earth lifelong gardeners who have answered questions and provided guidance to my garden writing over the years.

May your faithful tending of biblical gardens continue, and may your visions for extending the faith of all grow greater as families learn to Grow with God in their gardens, with their families, friends, and neighbors everywhere.

# Introduction

The goal of this book is to provide you and your family with abundant knowledge about how to enjoy and grow the many foods mentioned in the Bible, while encouraging you to grow in your relationships with God, your children, families, friends, and neighbors as you come together through the garden.

Passages relating God's grace to plants abound in the Bible. In this book you'll learn much more about these delicious, nourishing fruits of the earth through Scripture, and find easy-to-follow how-to, hands-on tips for growing them productively and enjoying them tastefully.

From earliest descriptions of the Garden of Eden through books of the Old and New Testament and even the Apocrypha, we can read passages depicting flowers, trees, fruits, foods, and herbs. You'll find various scriptural references from King James, NIV, and other

editions and versions of the Bible and Apocrypha in this book. I've included Scriptures from different versions for a couple of reasons. In ancient Hebrew and Greek translations, before there was any plant or botanical nomenclature, early translators had no way to positively identify specific plants from the Scriptures, so different versions may interpret food references somewhat differently. Also, reading a range of translations and versions helps us to better understand our shared faith among many denominations.

As you read references to plants found in the Holy Land, you may wonder whether you can grow them yourself. The answer is a resounding and emphatic Yes. Since my first book, *Your Biblical Garden*, was published in 1981, I've spent decades doing further research to help people realize the wonders of biblical plants mentioned in Scriptures as well as other plants that didn't achieve mention but were part of the flora in the Holy Land.

Millions of people like you have discovered the pleasures of home gardening, which is today one of America's most popular family hobbies. According to recent polls, nearly one hundred million people garden in some form. With home gardening's increased popularity, more people have begun focusing on special types of plants that will give their gardens a different and distinctive look.

In this new millennium we've experienced a growing sense of spirituality in America. Church leaders I've interviewed often commented on this new feeling that has begun to grow among their home communities and in their church parishes and congregations. Many also report more openness and a reaching out to welcome and encompass more people.

After the terrible terror attack of September 11, 2001, people of many different faiths and denominations came together in a demonstration of their faith in God and their love of country. Today indeed, we are experiencing a greater understanding of different cultures and appreciation of the need to work together in our global society. Among church and synagogue members there is renewed attention to the Bible, and among gardeners, renewed interest in biblical plants—a welcome sign. Over the years, I have discovered that as more people look for special plants to make their gardens unique, they too realize that biblical plants have special meaning dating back thousands of years to the Holy Land.

Key foods eaten by Jesus and His Disciples in their day range from barley, beans, and cucumbers to garlic, leeks, lentils, melons, onions, and wheat. You'll discover new meaning in many scriptural references as you learn to cultivate almonds, apricots, brambles, dates, figs, grapes, mulberries, olives, and other fruits. You'll also find wonderful historic facts and gardening ideas, plus delicious recipes for these nutritious, wholesome foods.

As a nationally known author and active Christian writer, I've done careful research to provide the most extensive biblical food gardening book available today that is inspirational as well as a practical growing guide. Also included are tips for improving your garden soil, plus a special chapter on garden ideas for children. Other chapters feature the history of gardening in the Holy Land, biblical gardens to visit in the United States, food caring and sharing with needy families, and resources for seeds, plants, supplies, and knowledge at my favorite gardening websites. It is my fervent hope that this book will both inspire and motivate you and your family to grow with God in many important ways.

—Allan A. Swenson

# Chapter 1

# Foods Jesus Ate, to Grow and Enjoy

**F**oods that Jesus ate can be as close as your own home garden. You can dig in this year, sow seeds, and before you know it you'll have plants that were part of Jesus' diet in the Holy Land when he lived there more than 2,000 years ago. Think about the pleasure you can have growing these delicious and nutritious foods right in your own backyard. There are other advantages, too: You get to eat fresher and tastier food, share with your family and friends, and perhaps even have some very special church suppers featuring the foods that Jesus ate. This book will show you how.

The foods of the Scriptures were basic to the life of the people of the Holy Land. These are the foods that nourished Jesus, His Disciples, and the people of that area in biblical times and ever since. In fact, as we read the many Scriptures about these foods, we realize that they were probably well documented because of their importance in sustaining the people in the land that God had provided for them. Most scriptural food references are in the Old Testament because these were the basic foods of the people of the Holy Land, the forebears of Jesus—foods grown throughout the area to sustain the people there.

If a spiritually focused Florida doctor, Don Colbert, is correct, the well-remembered five loaves and two fishes should be on the menu for Americans as well. Dr. Colbert believes that eating the foods Jesus did, the way He did, may indeed be the best way to stay healthy, slim, and trim. In his book *What Would Jesus Eat* (Thomas Nelson, Nashville, 2005), he explores some of the Old Testament dietary laws and looks at foods mentioned in the Bible. "If you truly want to follow Jesus in every area of your life," says Colbert, "you cannot ignore your eating habits. The health of Americans is going down, and it is largely due to our bad food choices."

America is experiencing an obesity epidemic. People eat when they are stressed or on the run, and too many are eating super-sized fast food meals. "By getting them to look at the biblical side, it allows them to slow down and make the correct choice about their diet and lifestyle," Dr. Colbert says. I agree.

When you look carefully at what Jesus and His Disciples ate and the suggestions in the Bible, you too can see the messages about proper nutrition to guide us all. As Dr. Colbert notes, "Jesus ate primarily natural foods in their natural states, lots of vegetables, especially beans and lentils. He would have eaten wheat bread, a lot of fruit, drunk a lot of water and also red wine."

People of Jesus' time seemed to enjoy mealtimes as a chance to dine, relax, talk with each other, and listen to each other too. They would take their time eating, and the disciples would be lounging around and conversing while dining, not gulping down fast food as we do. Today, as people of faith we should appreciate and copy the lifestyle as well as the diet of the people of the Holy Land. Nearly every faith has some mealtime tradition. As Christians, we say grace before eating because food is a gift from God. We should remember that eating is about more than just our physical diet; it is also about our spiritual diet. A more holistic view of food, eating, faith, and living would benefit us all in our daily lives.

As we focus on foods that Jesus and His Disciples ate, it also helps to go back to their biblical roots. We might begin with this quotation from Hosea 2:23–24: "I will respond, declares the Lord. I will respond to the heavens, and they will respond to the earth, and the earth shall respond with grain, with wine, and with oil."

Indeed, grain, wine, and olive oil represent God's gift to His people on earth. As recorded in the Bible, God speaks to people through seasonal rain from the heavens vital for these three key crops, as we read in Deuteronomy 11:13–14: "If you obey the commandments that I enjoin upon you this day, loving the Lord your God and serving Him with all your heart and soul, I will grant the rain for your land in season, the early rain and the late, and you shall gather in your grain and your wine and your oil." And so it was.

As rain appeared in that unique Mediterranean climate of two seasons, rainy growing time and dry dormant time, crops grew. Many years later, similar crops were still feeding Jesus and the people.

Considering the myriad references to bread in the Scriptures, it is important to realize that wheat was a precious crop. Biblical scholars tell us that the ancients got about 50 percent of their calories from wheat, mostly in the form of bread. Even today in religious services by many denominations, blessing the bread blesses the entire meal.

As we read the Bible carefully, we can find 355 passages that mention bread in the King James Scriptures and about 300 in the New International Version. Here I've included early passages to underscore the importance of certain foods to Jesus and His Disciples and the people of the Holy Land.

Whichever edition or version of the Bible that you read, you too will find dozens of scriptural references to foods of all types. As you do your own research about foods you may wish to grow, be aware that varieties of these foods available for growing today are often very different, but they do still trace their roots to the Holy Land in the time of Jesus. Perhaps there were only a few types of melons then, but you have a wide range of melons thanks to the contributions of plant breeders that have given us varieties that grow more abundantly, even in northern, short-growing season areas.

# Focus on Scripture

## Bread

Genesis 3:19—"In the sweat of thy face shalt thou eat bread, till thou return unto the ground; for out of it wast thou taken: for dust thou art, and unto dust shalt thou return."

Genesis 14:18—"And Melchizedek king of Salem brought forth bread and wine: and he was the priest of the most high God."

Genesis 18:5—"And I will fetch a morsel of bread, and comfort ye your hearts; after that ye shall pass on: for therefore are ye come to your servant. And they said, So do, as thou hast said."

Genesis 19:3—"And he pressed upon them greatly; and they turned in unto him, and entered into his house; and he made them a feast, and did bake unleavened bread, and they did eat."

Genesis 25:34—"Then Jacob gave Esau bread and pottage of lentiles; and he did eat and drink, and rose up, and went his way: thus Esau despised his birthright."

Genesis 27:17—"And she gave the savoury meat and the bread, which she had prepared, into the hand of her son Jacob."

Genesis 31:54—"Then Jacob offered sacrifice upon the mount, and called his brethren to eat bread: and they did eat bread, and tarried all night in the mount."

Genesis 37:25—"And they sat down to eat bread and they lifted up their eyes and looked, and, behold, a company of Ishmaelites came from Gilead with their camels bearing spicery and balm and myrrh, going to carry it down to Egypt."

Genesis 39:6—"And he left all that he had in Joseph's hand; and he knew not ought he had, save the bread which he did eat. And Joseph was a goodly person, and well favoured."

Genesis 41:54—"And the seven years of dearth began to come, according as Joseph had said: and the dearth was in all lands; but in all the land of Egypt there was bread."

Genesis 41:55—"And when all the land of Egypt was famished, the people cried to Pharaoh for bread: and Pharaoh said unto all the Egyptians, Go unto Joseph; what he saith to you, do."

Genesis 43:25—"And they made ready the present against Joseph came at noon: for they heard that they should eat bread there."

Genesis 43:31—"And he washed his face, and went out, and refrained himself, and said, Set on bread . . ."

Genesis 45:23—"And to his father he sent after this manner; ten asses laden with the good things of Egypt, and ten she asses laden with corn and bread and meat for his father by the way."

Genesis 47:12—"And Joseph nourished his father, and his brethren, and all his father's household, with bread according to their families."

---

If you wish, you can continue research about the importance of bread as a basic food. For example, in Nave's Topical there are many more cross-references to bread:

- Called the staff of life, Ezekiel 4:16; 5:16; 14:13
- About kinds of bread, leavened (made with yeast), Leviticus 7:13; 23:17; Hosea 7:4; Amos 4:5; Matthew 13:33
- Unleavened (made without yeast), Genesis 19:3; Exodus 12:8, 13:7, 23:15, 29:2; Numbers 6:15; Judges 6:19; 1 Samuel 28:24; 2 Kings 23:9; Luke 22:7; 1 Corinthians 5:8
- Made of wheat flour, Exodus 29:2; 1 Kings 4:22, 5:11; Psalms 81:16

- Made of barley, Judges 7:13
- Kneading bread, Genesis 18:6; Exodus 8:3, 12:34; 1 Samuel 28:24; 2 Samuel 13:8; Jeremiah 7:18; Hosea 7:4
- Made into loaves, Samuel 10:3, 17:17, 25:18; 1 Kings 14:3; Mark 8:14

Leaven is a substance (such as yeast) that produces fermentation in dough and causes it to rise. Unleavened bread is made without any such ingredient and in Scriptures was often served to guests, as we see in Genesis 19:3, Judges 6:19, and 1 Samuel 28:24. When the Jews were rushing to escape from Egypt they didn't have time to let bread "rise" and so made unleavened bread with barley and wheat flours. Thus began the Feast of Unleavened Bread, as described in Exodus 12:8, 12:15, 12:20, 13:3, and 13:6–7.

In the ancient Mediterranean, wine was also an important part of the diet, providing a major source of calories, sugar, and iron. In that area with sparse rainfall, the drinking water was often rainwater that had been stored in a cistern for months. Historians note that by adding wine to the water, residents improved the taste and lowered the bacteria content. Water mixed with wine was a standard drink, as we discover in Psalms 104:15: "wine gladdens the human heart."

Grapes were (and still are) a vital crop in the Holy Land. Each spring, leaves and delicate white flowers appear on the vines. Grapes appear and ripen in mid- to late summer, depending on variety. In olden days, entire families moved into the vineyard watchtower around harvest time. This way they could pick the grapes as soon as they were ready and dissuade thieves from stealing the crop. Once harvested, the next step was to tread the grapes in the winepress and store the fresh juice in jugs to ferment.

Oil references in the Bible usually mean olive oil. Olive trees thrive in that land's rocky, well-drained hills. Olive trees have extraordinarily long lives; some live for a thousand years and bear fruit for centuries. Olive oil was one of the blessings of the Holy Land. It was valued for cooking, healing, and spiritual purposes, and especially for light in ancient oil lamps.

Green olives are typically harvested in the fall, but the ripe, black olives that are full of oil are usually picked in November and December. To make oil, olives are first crushed by a large, rotating stone, then the pulp is put in round, woven baskets and the oil squeezed out.

To survive, ancient people in the land of Jesus needed all three basics: the grain, the wine, and the oil. As farmers today still realize, to achieve adequate harvests, we must rely on God's gift of good growing weather, a balance between rain and sun, heat and cold, that was and is beyond human control.

It is not surprising that many religious services have been handed down that involve blessing bread, blessing wine, and kindling lights. The Sabbath table, no matter where in the world, holds a reminder of the ancient Jewish origins in a narrow, rocky strip of the Eastern Mediterranean, of the ancient farmer's plea for the ecological balance that meant survival, and of our own ultimate dependence on the earth we share with so many people of different faiths and denominations today.

From original research and contacts around America and the world, thanks largely to the miracle of the Internet, I have been able to assemble some of the best ideas, growing tips, and advice from devout, talented biblical gardeners and a wide range of horticultural authorities and experts.

One of my most trusted advisors early on was the Rev. Marsh Hudson-Knapp, a down-to-earth friend and man of spiritual and biblical gardening vision. With thanks to him and many others who guided me, I have tried to plant the seeds of productive biblical gardening throughout our country. A trip to Vermont to visit Rev. Marsh and the biblical garden at the First Congregational Church of Fair Haven, United Church of Christ, he serves was monumentally rewarding. Rev. Marsh helped me focus on what is the theme for

this book: growing with God, in your garden, with your family, friends, neighbors and in life itself.

# Food Plants of the Old Testament

Perhaps it is best, as in the Bible, to start at the beginning as God created the good earth and His people. We all undoubtedly remember that infamous "tree of the knowledge of good and evil" that was planted in the midst of the Garden of Eden, as noted in Genesis 2:17. For generations, tradition said that it was an apple tree. Today, reading Scriptures and various translations and versions again, many botanists agree that it was really an apricot. Never fear, you'll find details about growing both apples and apricots in this book.

Actually, the very first tree mentioned by name is the fig. As we know, Adam and Eve used fig leaves as clothing when they became ashamed of their nakedness, as told in Genesis 3:7. Later, the prophets understood the fig as a symbol of peace. Rev. Marsh reminded me of that important message in Micah 4:3–4: When Micah spoke of the great day of peace, he declared, "They shall beat their swords into plowshares . . . neither shall they learn war anymore; but they shall sit every man under his vine and fig tree."

The lentil appears next in biblical history. Do you remember tricky Jacob who talked his older brother Esau into trading his birthright as oldest son for a bowl of lentil soup (Genesis 25:29)? For years I obediently ate lentil soup because "it is good for you," as I was told. The fact is, lentils are both nourishing and delicious when prepared well.

Each year, our Jewish brothers and sisters celebrate their deliverance by observing the Feast of Passover. One part of the Seder meal involves eating bitter herbs, which are a symbolic reminder of how bitter life was for them when they were slaves in Egypt. Today, you can grow these biblical plants including endive, chicory, lettuce, and even dandelion, which many scholars believe are among those bitter herbs mentioned in Exodus 12:8.

When Jesus' ancestors began to grumble against God and Moses about the difficulty of their life in the wilderness, which had become discouraging, many longed for the fruits and spices they had enjoyed back in Egypt. In Numbers 11:5 you can find their complaint, "We remember the fish we ate back in Egypt for nothing, the cucumbers, the melons, the leeks, the onions and the garlic." In this book you'll learn about these foods in more detail with tips for growing and using them, too.

Other food is mentioned in the Scriptures, for reasons known to God, when He told Moses to make the end of each branch of the menorah like an almond (Exodus 28:33). Perhaps, my friend Rev. Marsh suggests, this was because the almond blossom served as a herald of spring to our ancestors, and as a promise of hastening events. He also calls attention to Aaron's rod, that almond branch brought by Moses' brother Aaron on the Exodus journey. It was placed in the tent of God's presence, and the next time someone went into the tent it had bloomed and produced almonds, according to Numbers 17:1–8.

Barley was a vital food grain in biblical times, as it is today. Barley reminds us of a later scene from the story of Ruth. Naomi and her daughter-in-law Ruth returned to Israel after both of their husbands had died. To obtain food, Ruth went into the barley fields to collect leftovers from the harvest. There, in one of the Bible's beautiful love stories, she met her husband-to-be, Boaz (Ruth 1:22).

Later, during the reign of King David, his son Absalom organized a rebellion. Some of David's men remained faithful and retreated with the king into the wilderness. The people of Manahaim fed them, among other things, beans (2 Samuel 17:27–28). Biblical scholars believe these were probably broad beans, which archaeologists have said were

very common as a food crop in those times.
Although broad beans (a.k.a. fava beans)
are not native to the New World, they are
available in some areas of this country. If
you cannot find broad/fava beans locally,
Lima beans may be a more readily available substitute.

Popular fruits of biblical days often
were copied in art and otherwise. The special garments worn by the priests who led
worship at the temple were made of flax that was threshed, combed, and
woven into fine linen. These garments were then decorated with pomegranates, which scholars tell us, based on Exodus 39:24–26, were symbols of
fruitfulness and of great value. In addition, beautiful olivewood, probably
from the Russian olive, was also used in carvings of the cherubim inside the
temple, as we read about in 1 Kings 6:23, 6:31–33.

Through Isaiah, God also promised times of restoration and blessing
when even "the asses that till the ground will eat salted provender," today
known as garbanzo beans, a.k.a. chickpeas.

# Food Plants of the New Testament

The New Testament reminds us not only of the blessings we find in plants,
but also of our responsibilities. The first letter of Peter urges us to deeply
root ourselves in God and God's Word. In time, "The grass withers and the
flower falls, but the Word of the Lord abides forever." The passage reminds
us of our own vulnerability and dependence on God.

Jesus made the same point when he taught about grapes. He advised that
a branch cut off from the vine will not only fail to bear fruit, but will wither,
die, and be thrown into the fire to burn. On the other hand, those which stay
deeply connected to the vine, though they may be pruned at times, will bear
much fruit, and prove to be Christ's true disciples (John 15:1–8).

Other advice comes from Luke 6:44–45 about an important way to tell
Jesus' true followers from the false: by their fruit. We read, "For figs are
not gathered from thorns, nor are grapes picked from a bramble bush. The
good man out of the good treasure of his heart produces good, and the evil

man . . . evil." In your garden you can grow with the Scriptures and enjoy both grapes and brambles. (I abide with biblical scholars who say brambles are best explained as blackberries or raspberries.) Later in this book you'll find advice for growing these delicious fruits.

Jesus taught that the wheat and the tares, a.k.a. useless weeds, grow together all the way to the harvest, but that the tares then will be thrown into the fire, while the wheat will be gathered into the barn and treasured (Matthew 13:24–30). Earlier, John the Baptist gave the same warning when he sought to prepare people for the coming of Christ. In Matthew 3:12 you find, "His winnowing fork is in his hand, and he will clear the threshing floor, and gather his wheat into the granary, but the chaff he will burn with unquenchable fire."

Jesus showed how God can make miracles out of even small gifts. We can all recall one of the most quoted passages in the Bible: when Jesus took the few barley loaves of bread and fish from a small boy and fed a huge multitude with them (John 6:8).

At times people reach out to Jesus as He reaches out to us. On Palm Sunday, when Jesus made his triumphal entry into Jerusalem, people waved branches of the palm tree, welcoming Jesus as the long-awaited Messiah (John 12:12). Date palms remain one of the favored and long-lasting fruit crops in the Holy Land, and many other parts of the world. You'll discover some secrets about them and ways to grow your own replica palm tree as a reminder of this favored food of biblical times.

Get ready to dig in. Growing with God to produce the tasty foods that Jesus ate can be your next exciting and fun gardening adventure.

# Chapter 2

# A Scriptural Heritage

**A**s you embark on your new growing horizons to plant, cultivate, harvest, and enjoy the foods that Jesus ate, it is helpful to begin with an overview of history from the Bible and the Holy Land. Then, as you read the scriptural passages about biblical foods and plants throughout the book, think about the wisdom we have been given in the Bible, and think back to what life must have been like when Jesus walked the land with His Disciples.

Throughout history, biblical foods, herbs, and plants were grown in the gardens of religious orders. Many more have been growing in local churchyards, faithfully tended by devout and dedicated gardeners all across America as well as other parts of the world. (You'll find many biblical gardens that you can visit and contact in a special chapter in this book.)

## Gardening Then and Now

From Deuteronomy 8:7–8 we can visualize the land of the Bible: "For the Lord thy God bringeth thee into a good land, a land of brooks of water, of fountains and depths that spring out of valleys and hills; a land of wheat, and barley, and vines, and fig trees, and pomegranates; a land of oil olive, and honey."

Some understanding of the ecology and environment of the Holy Land in Jesus' time helps us to appreciate what the people of those days faced as they grew food for their own families. With that perspective, you can use this book as a ready resource about biblical gardening from our shared spiritual heritage and the plant roots that grew eons ago in the Holy Land, where our faith also took root and grew through these 2,000 years.

The Holy Land has always been a crossroads of the world, linking Europe, Asia, and Africa. Throughout antiquity, caravans traveled through that area with goods for trade, including plants and seeds. Over centuries, pilgrims and travelers visited and transplanted plants of the Bible to the far corners of the world. At other times, wars brought people to the Holy Land. Armies carried foods from afar that were then planted. Plants originally native to India, Africa, China, and much of Europe were carried on caravans across hundreds and hundreds of miles. Orchards and vineyards, grain fields, and vegetable gardens were planted for food. As people moved and warred and traded, it was also natural that this interchange of plant varieties would take place.

Ancient Romans traded throughout their Empire, which stretched not only from Western Europe but, more importantly, through the Middle East into Africa. During the Crusades, plants were taken home for use in the countries from which the Crusaders, pilgrims, and merchants had come. As merchants traveled and traded, they brought foods and plants with them, which were then grown in the countries they visited. Today, there is even more interest in the foods of the world; seeds of many exotic food varieties are available from catalogs. Order free mail order catalogs and select the biblical foods you wish to grow. Start with a few and expand your garden year by year to taste.

# Holy Land Ecology and Seasons

It helps to focus on Holy Land seasons to better understand these biblical plants. We who live in North America and Europe naturally plan our gardens based on four seasons. In the Holy Land there are two seasons, the dry dormant time and the rainy growing season. These seasons are different from what we might expect. The "winter" is actually the growing season because in the time of rain, plants are given the moisture they need to grow well. It is a time when seeds sprout and rush to produce plants, which in turn bloom, set seeds, and die as annual plants do. Even perennials must bloom and mature in this short season when moisture arrives.

The Holy Land, a crossroads of three continents, Europe, Asia Minor, and Africa, has flora that are unique in the world. The Holy Land was part of the Fertile Crescent, which history records as one of the earliest centers of civilization. Scientists estimate that as few as 15,000 years ago, the Holy Land was indeed a literal Garden of Eden. Lush vegetation abounded and fertile valleys, wooded mountains, and tropical oases provided abundant sustenance for those who lived there.

In more recent times, archaeological digs have provided ample evidence of the abundant and wide range of vegetation that once existed there. When Moses led the children of Israel in their flight from slavery in Egypt through the wilderness, their goal was the Promised Land. Even then the land had an abundance of plants as we understand from our reading of the Bible. Over the years, wars and overgrazing, overcultivation, and land misuse have wreaked havoc in large areas. Fortunately, efforts have been made to bring back productivity there. Perhaps if we heed messages in the Bible, we can learn lessons about conservation.

Scriptures give us some guidance as we embark on creating our own biblical gardens today. Too often we do not pay enough attention to protecting and preserving our environment. Fortunately, a greater focus

on recycling, conservation, and natural gardening seems to have come alive. That is a good sign. It may prove worthwhile to note that conservation and care of the environment were early topics in the Bible. If humans had focused on this wisdom in the Scriptures, perhaps we would not have seen the destruction of the land in so many parts of the world.

As you contemplate your biblical gardening projects, reflect on some of the things mankind has done to destroy our environment and vow to avoid them. By cutting trees, continual planting of one crop only, and neglecting to replace soil nutrients taken out of the land by plants, we often have caused serious depletion of natural resources. For proof, look at the dust bowls created in our own Midwest during the last century. Wars and unrestricted farming also ravaged the Holy Land. Most of the forests that once graced the land are gone, and very few of the Cedars of Lebanon of biblical fame remain. The Bible gives useful advice on care of the land, if we follow it.

In Exodus 23:10–11 we can find good advice about conservation and proper land use: "And six years thou shalt sow thy land, and shalt gather in the fruits thereof: But the seventh year thou shalt let it rest and lie still. . . ."

From Leviticus 24:3–5 we also receive an admonition to allow land a time of rest: "Six years thou shalt sow thy field, and six years thou shalt prune thy vineyard, and gather in the fruit thereof; But in the seventh year shall be a sabbath of rest unto the land, a sabbath for the Lord: thou shalt neither sow thy field, nor prune thy vineyard. That which groweth of its own accord of thy harvest thou shalt not reap, neither gather the grapes of thy vine undressed: for it is a year of rest unto the land."

From Deuteronomy 8:15–16, we learn how other parts of the land and its adjacent areas must have been in great contrast: "Who led thee through that great and terrible wilderness, wherein were fiery serpents, and scorpions, and drought, where there was no water; who brought thee forth water out of the block of lime; who fed thee in the wilderness with manna, which thy fathers knew not, that he might humble thee, and that he might provide thee, to do thee good at thy latter end."

These scriptural descriptions seem to aptly explain part of that land of ancient times. There were harsh deserts that had to be crossed, and they still exist today, inhospitable to plants except those that have adapted to difficult growing conditions of baking sun and sparse rainfall. However, there is a time when plant life bursts forth even in deserts. Anyone who has seen the short but colorful flush of spring in America's Southwestern deserts will understand what a few drops of rain in spring can do. Seeds indeed do await their time to sprout, rush to bloom, and scatter their seeds to set the scene for new plants with the rain of the following year. Desert life is a harsh one for mankind and plants.

# Holy Land Climate Zones

There are three basic climatic zones in the Holy Land: the Mediterranean Zone, the Irano-Turanian Steppe Zone, and Desert Zone. Each has its distinctive features, but the variances in vegetation are not as clearly defined. Adjacent valleys may reflect plant life of the Mediterranean Zone while the mountains between support vegetation of the steppe. The transition of one zone of lush, verdant growth may change gradually to a less productive area. Sometimes the change is abrupt, with plant life differing dramatically within less than a mile, from verdant, blooming, beautiful scenes to drastic desert conditions. There is extreme diversity and contrast in a very small area.

The Mediterranean Zone is characterized by a dry, not overly hot summer and winter months of rainfall. The Irano-Turanian Steppe Zone has long periods of dryness and a scant 10 inches of rainfall annually. The Desert Zone is hot and arid with negligible rainfall. Atlases give you a good picture of such zones; the *Rand McNally Millennium World Atlas* has some good maps, but best of all is the *Westminster Historical Atlas to the Bible*. It has maps that depict the Holy Land during the Roman era, the Period of the Judges, various parts of Palestine in biblical times, plus interesting historic information about the land and the people who have inhabited it for the past millennia.

The Mediterranean Zone provides the most favorable conditions for plant growth. Rainfall ranges from 20 to 40 inches per year and occurs during the winter months. Temperatures rarely fall below freezing in this zone, but the dry period of summer serves as the dormant or resting period for most plant life.

Rain begins in late September to early October and marks the beginning of the growing time. Scattered showers appear which develop into heavier rains during December and January and slacken during April. This warm, rainy winter season is the peak growing period for most crops and flowers. Horticulturists explain that summer dews which collect during cool nights provide some moisture for plants, perhaps about 10 inches of rainfall during the seemingly dry summer season.

Type of soil, amount of rainfall, and temperature range are also key factors that determine the type of plant growth that appears. Both coniferous forests of pine and deciduous oak trees are still present, along with the native terebinth and carob trees.

The Irano-Turanian Steppe Zone is a dividing zone that separates the Mediterranean Zone from the Desert Zone. These steppes of the Holy Land are distinguished by their dryness. Rainfall is scarce, seldom reaching 10 inches annually, and only during the winter season from December to March. Other months are almost totally dry.

> This presence or lack of water is the key that influences plant life. Although few plants can tolerate such difficult growing conditions, annuals can sprout, bloom, and reseed themselves in a short period. If you are planning a visit to the Holy Land, the winter season is the time to see the desert bloom.

Bulbous flowers send up their pre-formed leaves and blooms once rain gives them the signal. Wild annual flowers sprout and bloom quickly. It is a remarkable sight as the land comes alive for a brief but dramatically colorful profusion of bloom, and then as swiftly returns to its aridity.

The third Holy Land area is the Desert Zone, which for most of the year is devoid of apparent plant life. During scorching summer, no plants appear, but roots and seeds lie secretly awaiting a brief chance at life and beauty. This Desert Zone has climatic conditions similar to those of the Sahara-Arabian Desert, but in the Holy Land the desert is bordered on

the west by the Sinai, which includes most of the Negev Desert. To the south it circles around the Mediterranean and Steppe areas and links into the expanses of the vast Arabian Desert.

As you consult the Bible about plants of all types, you'll only find mention of two seasons. In the Song of Solomon, 2:11–13, you will find this passage: "For lo, the winter is past, the rain is over and gone; the flowers appear on the earth; the time of the singing of birds is come, and the voice of the turtle is heard in our land; the fig tree putteth forth her green figs, and the vines with the tender grape give a good smell. Arise, my love, my fair one, and come away."

Go ahead, search further, even through the Talmud, the Jewish Holy Book. Don't be surprised that you only find reference to the two seasons: the growing period through harvest, and the time of the resting of the land. In effect you will learn from both the Talmud and the Bible that there are the days of sun and the days of rain. If you search other parts of the Mediterranean Sea basin, Greece, Turkey, Italy, Egypt, and North African nations for climate variations, you'll find that they have basically the same two-season year. However, the Holy Land is distinctive. It has the least rainfall of any country in the region.

# Growing Biblical Heirloom Plants

Today, enthusiastic gardeners are turning their attention to plants with historic importance and spiritual significance. Heirloom plants are being rediscovered and brought back to cultivation. Several mail-order firms including Burpee, Seeds of Distinction, Select Seeds, Heirloom Roses, and others are finding and offering marvelous traditional flowers and vegetables. We have all enjoyed nutritious food in America, but now as backyard gardeners we can find some of the older varieties, pure strains that were used to develop modern hybrids. Avid gardeners tell me some of these old-time varieties have appealing and distinctive tastes, although they are not especially productive and may not have hybrid plant disease resistance. Heirloom melons, cucumbers, and special bitter herb plants can be found and are worth trying. I've included a list of many reliable firms that offer free catalogs with biblical plants at the end of this book.

Another point about plant identification to keep in mind: the Old Testament, or Hebrew Bible, originated in the form of songs, ballads, and poetry handed down from generation to generation by word-of-mouth tradition. Appropriately, the moral and religious messages were of far greater importance than accurate plant identifications. The Bible was never intended by its writers, translators, or religious leaders to serve as a botanical or even natural science text or reference. Today as in the past, debate among biblical scholars and botanists alike continues concerning the true identity of certain specific flowers, fruits, trees, and other plants mentioned in scriptural passages. Considering the number of different translations of the Bible, especially from the ancient Greek and Hebrew into various modern languages, confusion is to be expected.

To understand this point, consider that the widely accepted Authorized Version of the King James Bible sometimes confuses the biblical plant names and common English ones. For example, aspens have been called mulberries and mulberries called sycamores. Add to that the different translations in the New International Version, the New English Bible, Today's English Version, the Goodspeed, Jastrow and Moffatt, and other versions, and we have every right to scratch our heads.

Despite the lack of exact definition of some plants, most have actually been rather clearly and accurately identified. I've spent two decades doing research and interviews with experts for my earlier biblical plant books and this one. Thanks to e-mail and the Internet, it has been possible to compare the old Scriptures and translations with the plants that are native today in the climates and soils of the Holy Land.

Now, with this basic background about the land, the climates, and growing conditions in the Holy Land, it's time to focus on your land.

# Chapter 3

# Foods of the Bible to Nourish the Faithful

This is an exciting new millennium, a time of great growing opportunities in our gardens and our lives. Many millions of families enjoy the beauty of flowers that grace their home landscapes. Many others love to treat themselves to tasty, nutritious, home-grown food.

With the Bible as our guide, we can truly dig in to cultivate bounty from God's good earth. As we do, we can grow deeper in our love for God and in our appreciation of His blessings. We can also cultivate worthwhile new family relationships that will sprout, grow, and be rewardingly productive. My mission as an avid gardener and enthusiastic Christian writer is to help families grow together. It is time we all dig in and, with God's help, get America growing stronger, too.

As you pick the best spot, improve your growing ground, sow your seeds, and add other productive plants, you'll find that through biblical food gardening you can cultivate the best in people, too. That's especially important with children—you'll learn great growing ideas in Chapter 10 to help nourish your children's bodies and minds.

We're all stewards of the land and our good planet Earth. There are many lessons to be learned as we garden. As we pursue our goal in life, it is often wise and worthwhile to consider the lessons we can get from the Scriptures and from the good earth of our gardens. The Scriptures mention a variety of healthy, nutritious foods that Jesus and His disciples ate. We can grow many tasty foods in our home gardens, our churchyard, in the schoolyard, in community gardens, and even in pots, tubs, and planters on porches, balconies, and rooftops in cities.

We can and should rededicate ourselves to making every square yard more attractive and productive garden spots. As the desert can bloom in the Holy Land, city lots can come alive, bloom, and bear in urban areas as well.

As we sow, so shall we reap. We can make this and every year a productive one. We can reawaken ourselves, brighten lives, and build new friendships in abundance. You'll find ways to do that, from the innovative Plant a Row for the Hungry program that has taken root across America to feed thousands of needy, hungry people, to church suppers, to growing and preparing delicious treats for your own families.

We each can do much to make this world a better place, a more productive and beautiful place. The Bible offers a daily living guide, not just for religious matters, important as they are, but for growing matters as well. In the Bible we find useful descriptions of plants and advice to care for the land. We must focus on restoring the goodness to our land and lives. It has been said that mankind must preserve and tend the land, and the land will supply bounty in response. It is time we paid closer attention to these time-honored teachings.

Looking back at America's history, we see that our Christian heritage in this land of opportunities led our country to become the most productive, sharing nation on earth. In this book, from the ground up, you'll find some of the worthy wit and wisdom of our heritage and from the Bible to encourage you to grow better. Dig in, plant good seeds and ideas, cultivate your gardens and family, your friends and neighbors. The food and wisdom you harvest will reward you well.

As we begin taking a closer look at the key foods mentioned in the Bible, it may help to understand the format followed throughout this chapter.

For each featured food, you'll first find an introduction with key facts about the food. Next you'll find scriptural references, which may be from King James, NIV, or other versions depending on which most accurately portrays the foods in the Bible. Then you'll find more details of historic perspective. Finally, you'll come to the hands-on, how-to growing ideas, tips, and advice. You may want to stick a Post-it on those pages to make it easy to refer to the growing tips during your own gardening season.

# Barley

Barley is the common name for any of a genus of cereal grain native to Asia and one of the most ancient cultivated plants. As you will note from the many passages, barley has deep roots in biblical Scriptures. It was grown by the ancient Egyptians, Greeks, and Romans, and even by the Chinese. Today, barley is the world's fourth largest grain crop, after wheat, rice, and corn. Commercially, barley is sown in the spring in the United States, but around

the Mediterranean Sea and in parts of California and Arizona it is sown in the fall.

Barley belongs to the genus *Hordeum*, of the family Gramineae. Two-rowed barley is classified as *Hordeum distichon*, six-rowed barley as *Hordeum vulgare*, and irregular barley as *Hordeum irregulare*. To grow barley, obtain seeds from mail order firms that feature this crop. Another good source is the unprocessed, natural barley sold at health food stores. You also can look up barley on the Internet to find supplies of seeds to grow.

# Focus on Scripture

## Barley

Exodus 9:31—"And the flax and the barley was smitten: for the barley was in the ear, and the flax was bolled."

Leviticus 27:16—"And if a man shall sanctify unto the Lord some part of a field of his possession, then thy estimation shall be according to the seed thereof: an homer of barley seed shall be valued at fifty shekels of silver."

Numbers 5:15—"Then shall the man bring his wife unto the priest, and he shall bring her offering for her, the tenth part of an ephah of barley meal; he shall pour no oil upon it, nor put frankincense thereon; for it is an offering of jealousy, an offering of memorial, bringing iniquity to remembrance."

Deuteronomy 8:8—"A land of wheat, and barley, and vines, and fig trees, and pomegranates; a land of oil olive, and honey . . ."

Judges 7:13—"And when Gideon was come, behold, there was a man that told a dream unto his fellow, and said, Behold, I dreamed a dream, and, lo, a cake of barley bread tumbled into the host of Midian, and came unto a tent, and smote it that it fell, and overturned it, that the tent lay along."

Ruth 1:22—"So Naomi returned, and Ruth the Moabitess, her daughter in law, with her, which returned out of the country of Moab: and they came to Bethlehem in the beginning of barley harvest."

Ruth 2:17—"So she gleaned in the field until even, and beat out that she had gleaned: and it was about an ephah of barley."

Ruth 2:23—"So she kept fast by the maidens of Boaz to glean unto the end of barley harvest and of wheat harvest; and dwelt with her mother in law."

Ruth 3:2—"And now is not Boaz of our kindred, with whose maidens thou wast? Behold, he winnoweth barley to night in the threshing floor."

Ruth 3:15—"Also he said, Bring the vail that thou hast upon thee, and hold it. And when she held it, he measured six measures of barley and laid it on her: and she went into the city."

Ruth 3:17—"And she said, These six measures of barley gave he me; for he said to me, Go not empty unto thy mother in law."

2 Samuel 14:30—"Therefore he said unto his servants, See, Joab's field is near mine, and he hath barley there; go and set it on fire. And Absalom's servants set the field on fire."

2 Samuel 17:28—"Brought beds, and basons, and earthen vessels, and wheat, and barley and flour, and parched corn, and beans, and lentils, and parched pulse . . ."

2 Samuel 21:9—"And he delivered them into the hands of the Gibeonites, and they hanged them in the hill before the Lord and they fell all seven together, and were put to death in the days of harvest, in the first days, in the beginning of barley harvest."

1 Kings 4:28—"Barley also and straw for the horses and dromedaries brought they unto the place where the officers were, every man according to his charge."

2 Kings 4:42—"And there came a man from Baalshalisha, and brought the man of God bread of the first fruits, twenty loaves of barley, and full ears of corn in the husk thereof. And he said, Give unto the people, that they may eat."

2 Kings 7:1—"Then Elisha said, Hear ye the word of the Lord; Thus saith the Lord, Tomorrow about this time shall a measure of fine flour be sold for a shekel, and two measures of barley for a shekel, in the gate of Samaria."

2 Kings 7:16—"And the people went out, and spoiled the tents of the Syrians. So a measure of fine flour was sold for a shekel, and two measures of barley for a shekel, according to the word of the Lord . . ."

2 Kings 7:18—"And it came to pass as the man of God had spoken to the king, saying, Two measures of barley for a shekel, and a measure of

fine flour for a shekel, shall be tomorrow about this time in the gate of Samaria."

1 Chronicles 11:13—"He was with David at Pasdammim, and there the Philistines were gathered together to battle, where was a parcel of ground full of barley; and the people fled from before the Philistines."

## History and Nutrition Highlights

Barley was a staple cereal of ancient Egypt, where it was used to make bread. According to Deuteronomy 8:8, barley is one of the "Seven Species" of crops that characterize the fertility of the Promised Land of Canaan. In ancient Greece, barley's significance dates back to the earliest stages of the Eleusinian Mysteries. The mixed drink of the initiates, prepared from barley and herbs, was referred to in the Homeric hymn to Demeter. Greeks historically dried barley groats and roasted them before preparing the porridge, according to Pliny the Elder's *Natural History*.

In Jesus' time barley was primarily used to make bread, as described in the famed quotation of the young boy with the five loaves of barley bread (John 6:9). It was also used in soups and stews, especially among the poor.

America, barley is a short-season, early-maturing crop grown commercially in both irrigated and in dry land environments. Because this grain adapts well to different types of environments, it is grown in many regions throughout the United States, primarily North Dakota, Montana, Idaho, Minnesota, Washington, South Dakota, California, Oregon, Colorado, and Wyoming.

Just as in the lifetime of Jesus, today grain foods are considered an important part of a healthful diet. In fact, they make up the base of the U.S. Department of Agriculture Food Guide Pyramid, which recommends that we eat six to eleven servings of grain foods every day. For example, typical servings would include 1 cup of ready-to-eat cereal flakes, 1 slice of bread, and 1/2 cup cooked pearl barley, rice, or pasta. The American Dietetic Association recommends at least three servings a day of whole-grain foods (foods made of whole barley flour, whole-wheat flour, oatmeal, etc.).

Barley, like all grains, contains substances that are important for good health. These include fiber, antioxidants, phytochemicals, and vitamins and minerals. Like all plant foods, barley is naturally cholesterol-free and low in fat. For example, a 1/2-cup serving of cooked pearl barley contains less than 1/2 gram of fat and only 100 calories, according to the USDA Nutrient Database. Barley contains several vitamins and minerals including niacin (vitamin B3), thiamine (vitamin B1), selenium, iron, magnesium, zinc, phosphorus, and copper.

It seems the ancients knew instinctively that barley is a valuable staple. Today, health and nutrition professionals recommend that we eat about 20 to 35 grams of fiber every day. A 1/2-cup serving of cooked pearl barley contains 3 grams of total dietary fiber. In most grains, fiber is found only in the bran, which is the outer layer of the kernel. When most grains are processed, the bran or outer layer is typically removed and its fiber is lost. However, barley contains fiber throughout the entire kernel, which means that a processed barley product such as flour, flakes, or pearl barley made from hulled or covered barley retains at least 50 percent of its original fiber content even after the bran is removed. Laboratory studies show that the insoluble fiber found in barley can be extremely effective in maintaining regular intestinal function. In addition, extensive research on barley's soluble fiber has revealed that it can help lower blood cholesterol levels and reduce the risk of heart disease.

# Growing and Harvesting Tips

Barley is one of the sturdiest grains, drought resistant and hardy, and can be grown on marginal land. Salt-resistant strains are being developed to increase its usefulness in coastal regions. Basic varieties of barley belong to three distinct types: two-rowed barley, six-rowed barley, and irregular barley, but commercially the six-rowed type is favored in the United States.

Barley appreciates good soil and plentiful sunlight but will tolerate poor conditions. It is a hardy survivor that thrives in cold and even drought. Once you pick your growing plot, hand-turn or rototill the ground. Actually, your first challenge in growing barley may be in finding seed. Check seed catalogs, agricultural feed stores, and online sources. Use your favorite search engine to seek out "barley seed sources."

Plant barley in the spring after the ground has warmed up and started to dry out. Sow barley generously, hand scattering to apply about one grain per square inch of soil. Then rake or roll. Barley grain will crowd out most weeds, which saves cultivating time. You can apply liquid fertilizer to boost plant growth, especially in poorer soils. Be certain to read and heed the directions for the type of fertilizer you buy. Too much overfeeds plants and wastes money. With animal manures, your best bet is to incorporate raw manures into compost before using. Otherwise, dried natural fertilizers are readily available from commercial chain stores, Lowe's, Home Depot, Wal-Mart and others.

Once beautiful nodding seed heads turn golden in the fall, it is time to harvest. The easiest way to harvest barley is to cut it with a sickle, then tie it in sheaves to dry. When the seeds turn hard, thresh the sheaves with a flail to get the seeds out. You can leave some barley standing in the garden to provide a striking picture of this biblical-era food. Then, when the plant color fades late in the season, simply till them under. The grain will reseed itself and grow another crop next year on the same spot.

Try growing a sample patch of barley or wheat as a test and see how it does. As a gardener, you can enjoy seeing some barley and wheat grow, but are better rewarded with wholesome barley from natural food stores who also have many delicious recipes. Both require too much space to grow sufficient crops for substantial food use. If you plan to do significant cooking with these traditional biblical foods, your best bet is to purchase natural barley and wheat in health food stores.

# Cooking Tips and Recipes

Rich in scriptural history and food value, barley makes a natural choice for healthful dining and provides a significant source of soluble and insoluble dietary fiber. This wholesome, nutritious grain adds a delightful nutty flavor, pleasant chewy texture, and fiber to hot and cold dishes of all kinds. Along with trying the recipes offered here, you can broaden your biblical culinary horizons with hundreds more delicious barley dishes. Experiment with apple and barley pudding, baked barley, barley corn bread, muffins, salads, and more.

Some main-dish recipes posted on the Internet include Turkey Barley Stir-Fry, Cheesy Barley Bean Bake, and Curried Barley and Chicken Bake. For side dishes, try Herbed Barley and Fruit Pilaf, Barley Mushroom Pilaf, and Barley-Stuffed Tomatoes. Soups include Barley Lentil Soup, Barley Cheddar Chowder, or Barley Kielbasa Stew. Salads may include Barley Walnut Vegetable Salad, Paradise Barley Fruit Salad, and Barley Bean Picnic Salad.

Dozens of tasty barley recipes are on the Internet from the Barley Growers Association. There just isn't room in this book for many different recipes of all types of biblical foods. I've tried to include those that my family likes best.

## BARLEY AND SHRIMP SKILLET DINNER

*This one-pan meal is a true seafood sensation for two! Serve with a fresh romaine lettuce salad and thick slices of crusty sourdough bread.*

*Makes 2 generous servings.*

- 2 teaspoons olive oil
2/3 cup regular pearl barley
1 clove garlic, minced
1/4 teaspoon ground turmeric
2 tablespoons chopped parsley
1 1/2 cups cherry tomatoes, cut in halves
1 1/2 cups bottled clam juice or chicken broth
1/2 cup dry white wine
6 to 8 ounces scallops or shrimp, or a combination of both
1/2 cup frozen green peas, defrosted

▶ Heat oil in wide skillet over medium heat. Add barley, garlic, and turmeric. Cook, stirring, until barley is golden, about 3 or 4 minutes. Stir in parsley, cherry tomatoes, clam juice, and wine. Bring to a boil. Reduce heat, cover, and simmer for 35 minutes. Arrange seafood and peas over barley. Cover and cook 10 to 15 minutes longer or until barley is tender. Add more liquid if barley seems dry. Spoon into bowls. You can also enjoy this bounty of barley side dishes, each of which serves 4 people amply. My thanks to Alberta Barley Commission.

They have many more tasty recipes at their website: www.albertabarley.com.

## BARLEY CONFETTI TOSS

Combine 3 cups hot cooked pearl barley with 1/2 cup diced tomato, 1/4 cup each chopped red, green, and yellow bell pepper, 2 tablespoons minced onion, 2 tablespoons minced fresh basil, 1 teaspoon minced fresh garlic, and 1 tablespoon red wine vinegar. Toss gently and serve.

## HERBED BARLEY AND MUSHROOMS

Sauté 1/2 cup sliced fresh mushrooms in 2 teaspoons olive oil. Add 2 tablespoons minced green onion, 1/4 teaspoon crumbled dried rosemary, 3 cups chicken, beef, or vegetable broth, and 1 cup pearl barley. Bring to boil. Cover, reduce heat to low, and cook 45 minutes or until barley is tender and liquid is absorbed.

## BARLEY FLORENTINE

Place 3 cups chicken broth, 1 cup pearl barley, 1 teaspoon dried basil, and 1/2 teaspoon onion powder in saucepan. Bring to boil. Cover, reduce heat to low, and cook 40 minutes or until barley is tender and most of liquid is absorbed. Stir in 1 cup thinly sliced fresh spinach leaves, 2 teaspoons fresh lemon juice, and a dash of nutmeg. Continue to cook 5 minutes longer.

## BARLEY APRICOT PILAF

Combine 1 3/4 cups chicken broth, 1 cup orange juice, 1/4 cup white wine, 1 cup pearl barley, 1/4 cup chopped dried apricots, and 1/4 cup raisins in saucepan. Bring to boil. Cover, reduce heat to low, and cook 45 minutes or until barley is tender and liquid is absorbed. Sprinkle pilaf with 1/2 cup toasted slivered almonds and 1 teaspoon grated nutmeg.

# Bitter Herbs

The identity of the bitter herbs mentioned in the Bible has been debated for years. Many identify them as dandelion, endive and chicory (two closely related plants), lettuce, and sorrel. Other biblical scholars believe that bitter herbs included many different plants. Of course, they are mostly associated with the Passover meal, a seven-day feast that includes a dinner of lamb served with unleavened bread and bitter herbs.

Studious authorities believe that the dandelion was one of the herbs. In fact, dandelions are valued as food all around Europe. America is perhaps the only country that turns its collective nose up to the taste and nutritious value of dandelions. The lowly dandelion is native to southern Europe and many parts of the world and supposedly gets its name from the French *dent de lion* because the pointed leaves resemble a lion's

tooth. Other names for this plant include bitter cress and wild lettuce. Dandelions grow abundantly in the Sinai Peninsula and Egypt.

I'm not convinced that sorrel is truly one of the biblical bitter herbs. However, if you prefer to add sorrel to your own list of biblical herbs, follow growing directions for lettuce and endive included here. You'll find more details about dandelions because elsewhere in the world they remain a basic and valued food. As one of the deeply rooted biblical plants it is worth a try using one of the tasty cultivars or the special Mediterranean varieties available today from mail order firms.

# Focus on Scripture

## Bitter Herbs

Exodus 12:8—"And they shall eat the flesh in that night, roast with fire, and unleavened bread; and with bitter herbs they shall eat it."

Numbers 9:11—"The fourteenth day of the second month at even they shall keep it, and eat it with unleavened bread and bitter herbs."

# History

We should remember that when the people of Israel were preparing to leave Egypt, God told Moses and Aaron that the Israelites were to "eat the meat roasted over the fire, along with bitter herbs" (Exodus 12:8). Then, in the first month of the second year after they left Egypt, God spoke to Moses in the desert of Sinai. As we know from Numbers 9:11, Moses was told that the people of Israel were to celebrate Passover "on the fourteenth day of the second month at twilight. They are to eat the lamb, together with unleavened bread and bitter herbs."

As mentioned above, modern Israelites eat the Seder or home Passover meal to remind them of the bitterness of Egyptian bondage prior to the Exodus as explained forcefully in Exodus 12:8 and Numbers 9:11. Such herbs included watercress, radishes, endive, and horseradish. Some have suggested that these "bitter herbs" consisted of such plants as chicory, bitter cresses, hawkweeds, sow-thistles, and wild lettuces, which grow abundantly in the peninsula of Sinai, in Palestine, and in Egypt. Now, horseradish often accompanies the Seder meal.

When you read the Bible you'll find numerous references to a wide variety of herbs. Considering the climate in the Holy Land and the historic records from other writings, most of these herbs are well suited to dry, desert-like conditions found in the Middle East.

Today we Americans think of herbs as plants grown for seasoning, fragrance, or medicine. However, the bitter herbs of biblical passages actually may have been leafy vegetables, juicy salad greens that the Jewish population had developed a taste for during their long stay in Egypt. After all, ancient Egyptians ate lettuce, endive, chicory, and dandelion leaves, all of which can have a bitter taste at times.

When researching the herbs for a biblical garden, one often finds different names in different versions of the Scriptures. That is because there have been many different translations of the same verse. One translation may attempt to specifically identify an herb. However, another translation may refer to it more simply as "bitter herb." When early translations and other versions of the Bible were being produced, there was no botanical nomenclature. Those doing the writing had to rely on their own knowledge and best interpretation of which plant or herb was mentioned in the original Hebrew or Greek.

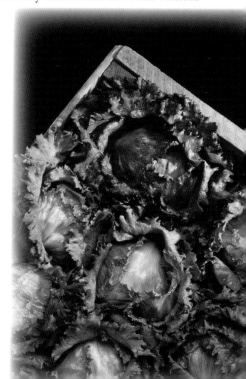

# Lettuce

Lettuce is both a historic and significant "bitter herb" and as such deserves attention for biblical gardens. The leaves of garden lettuce, *lactuca sativa*, are often bitter when unbleached as gardeners note with some head lettuce varieties. Of course, new varieties have been improved and you can find dozens of types in seed racks and from mail order catalogs. Today, lettuce is an American favorite, one of the top ten vegetables grown in our gardens. Plant breeders have given us many tasty varieties for growing pleasure. You can have different types growing from spring into fall, mainly in cooler seasons.

## History and Nutrition Highlights

Lettuce traces its tasty roots back more than 25 centuries to the royal gardens of Persia and beyond. It became popular in Europe where salads have long been respected parts of most meals.

In Europe, romaine lettuce is called "cos" and is named after the Greek island of "Kos" in the Aegean Sea. Romaine lettuce was named by the Romans who believed it had healing properties. Emperor Caesar Augustus erected a statute hailing lettuce because he thought it had cured an illness he had. In China, lettuce is typically eaten cooked. Both the English and Latin name of the genus are derived from 'lac,' the Latin world for milk, referring to the plant's milky juice.

> Americans eat more than thirty pounds of lettuce per person each year, about five times what we ate in the early 1900s. Curiously, iceberg lettuce was called crisphead until the 1920s when California began shipping large amounts in ice to keep it cool, hence the new name, iceberg.

According to the American Cancer Institute and the American Cancer Society, foods rich in vitamins A and C antioxidants offer protection against some forms of cancer. Along with other phytochemicals, antioxidants reduce the risk of cancer of the respiratory system and intestinal tract. Lettuce, except iceberg, is also a moderately good source of vitamin C, calcium, iron, and copper. The spine and ribs of the leaves provide dietary fiber, while vitamins and minerals are concentrated in the delicate part of the leaf. For optimal nutritional value, lettuce should be eaten while it is fresh and crisp.

## Growing and Harvesting Tips

Lettuce is a fairly hardy, cool-weather vegetable that thrives when the average daily temperature is between 60°F and 70°F. It should be planted in early spring or late summer. At high temperatures, growth is stunted, the leaves may be bitter, and a seed stalk forms or "bolts," elongating rapidly. Some varieties of lettuce withstand heat better than others.

You have a wide choice when it comes to growing lettuce. There are five distinct types: leaf, which is also called loose-leaf lettuce; cos or romaine; crisphead; butterhead; and stem (which may be also called asparagus lettuce).

Leaf lettuce is the most widely adapted type. It produces crisp leaves loosely arranged on the stalks. It is the most commonly planted salad vegetable. Cos or romaine forms an upright, elongated head, a tasty addition to salads and sandwiches. Butterhead varieties are generally small, loose-headed types with tender, soft leaves, and delicate sweet flavor. Stem lettuce forms an enlarged seed stalk mainly used for creamed and Oriental recipes.

As you consider which lettuces to grow, there are some facts to note. Crisphead varieties, the supermarket iceberg types, are adapted to northern conditions but require the most care. In warmer areas they should be grown from transplants, which you can buy or start indoors early and transplant outdoors as soon as the soil can be worked. These are extremely sensitive to heat, so plant them early and pick before summer. Plant again in summer for a fall crop.

Good leaf lettuce varieties include early Black-seeded Simpson; Grand Rapids, with frilly edges; Oakleaf, which is resistant to tip burn and is good for hot weather; plus Red Leaf and Ruby, the darkest red of all (also resistant to tip burn). Red varieties add color to mixed salads.

Among cos or romaine types, try Cimmaron, with a unique dark red leaf, Green Towers (early with large leaves), and Paris Island, a long-standing variety.

For heading or crisphead lettuce, try Great Lakes, a favorite that holds well in warm weather, or Ithaca which tolerates heat, resists bitterness, and is slow to bolt.

If you wish to try stem or asparagus lettuce, consider Celtuce.

Leaf, cos, and butterhead lettuce can be planted anytime in the spring when soil is dry enough to rake the surface. It pays to make two or more successive plantings at 10- to 14-day intervals to harvest a continuous supply of lettuce. Because lettuce does not withstand hot summer days well, spring planting should be completed at least a month before the really hot days of early summer begin. Then, for luscious lettuce in the fall, try plantings in late summer that will mature during cool fall weather.

Lettuce loves water, so regular watering is essential for germination and good seedling growth and best plant development. You can also try heat-tolerant varieties among loose-leaf types. Try growing them in the shade of taller crops, but be sure to side-dress with fertilizer and watch water when plants are in close growth with others.

Plant seeds 1/4 to 1/2 inch deep with about 10 seeds per foot in single, double, or triple rows 12 to 18 inches apart. Thin seedlings to 4 inches apart for leaf lettuce and 6 to 8 inches apart for cos or butterhead types. Save and eat the tiny seedlings you remove. Transplant crisphead seedlings 10 to 12 inches apart.

Be aware that lettuce has shallow roots, so cultivate or till carefully. Frequent light watering encourages leaves to develop rapidly, producing high-quality lettuce. Consider useful organic mulches to moderate soil temperature, thwart weeds, and hold moisture in the soil.

Cut leaf lettuce whenever it is big enough to use. Try cutting every other plant at ground level to give remaining plants more space for growth. Leaf lettuce reaches a maximum size of 6 to 12 ounces in 50 to 60 days. Butterhead varieties form small, loose heads of 4 to 8 ounces at 60 to 70 days. The innermost leaves are a real delicacy. Cos varieties have an upright growth habit and form a long, medium-dense head. After harvest, simply wash, drip dry, and place lettuce in a plastic bag in the refrigerator. Lettuce keeps best at 32°F and high humidity.

# Cooking Tips and Recipes

## MIXED GREEN SALAD WITH RED AND YELLOW PEPPER VINAIGRETTE

*Try a mix of two or three different lettuce varieties of different colors for both taste and texture. A leaf lettuce like Black-seed Simpson or oakleaf combines well with crisp romaine or other crisphead lettuce, accented with other herb leaves. Gourmets agree that often the best way to appreciate a tossed green salad is with a simple vinaigrette dressing so that the flavor doesn't overpower the tasty lettuce.*

*Makes 4 1-cup servings.*

■ 4 cups mixed fresh greens, combining leaf lettuce with crisp varieties, such as romaine, red leaf, and oakleaf
4 tablespoons Red and Yellow Pepper Vinaigrette (see recipe below)
2 tablespoons crumbled blue cheese or goat cheese (optional)

▶ Wash and dry lettuce leaves. Tear into bite-sized pieces. Place in an oversized bowl with room for tossing. Place in refrigerator until ready to toss and serve. Can be prepared up to 2 hours in advance. Pour 4 tablespoons of vinaigrette over the greens and toss well with two large forks to coat. Add crumbled cheese if desired and toss to combine. Serve immediately.

## RED AND YELLOW PEPPER VINAIGRETTE

*Makes 1 cup vinaigrette.*

■ 1 small yellow bell pepper, finely chopped, about 1/2 cup
1 small red bell pepper, finely chopped, about 1/2 cup
4 tablespoons red wine vinegar
2 tablespoons extra virgin olive oil
2 teaspoons warm water
Pinch of sugar
1/2 teaspoon salt
Freshly ground black pepper to taste

▶ In a medium bowl, whisk together all ingredients until combined well. This vinaigrette will keep, tightly covered, in the refrigerator for 3 days.

# Horseradish

Horseradish has won acclaim for the unique hot taste it gives to many meals. Horseradish is a member of the mustard family. The bite and aroma of the horseradish root are almost absent until it is grated or ground. During this process, as root cells are crushed, volatile oils known as isothiocyanates are released. Vinegar stops this reaction and stabilizes the flavor. For milder horseradish, vinegar is added immediately.

## History

Egyptians wrote about enjoying horseradish around the time of the Exodus. Horseradish was named by some biblical scholars as one of the "five bitter herbs" that Jews were told to eat at Passover, and is still part of this religious observance. Greeks extolled horseradish in ancient writings, and from 1300 to 1600 A.D. it spread throughout Central Europe to Scandinavia and England.

Treasured by Europeans for its unique hot taste, horseradish was brought by immigrants to the New World and cultivated there. For example, German immigrants to Illinois began growing horseradish in the late 1800s, passing their growing methods from generation to generation. The cold winters provide the required root dormancy, and long summers provide excellent growing conditions. Each May, horseradish is saluted at the International Horseradish Festival in Collinsville, Illinois, the area where 60 percent of the world's supply is grown. Events include a root toss, a horseradish-eating contest, and a horseradish recipe contest. Begun in 1988, the festival was designed to create national awareness for the herb.

## Growing and Harvesting Tips

Horseradish is a true perennial in the garden. According to Tony Bratsch, horticulture educator with University of Illinois Extension, home gardeners can get those large roots that are easier to peel and process by adapting the techniques that commercial growers use. Select a permanent garden spot for your horseradish bed.

Start by planting horseradish in the fall or very early spring. Till the area thoroughly and deeply, because the roots grow down deep. Use root pieces, called sets, that are finger width in diameter and about 12 to 18 inches long. Lay sets horizontally, with the large end, the head, slightly elevated. Cover sets with 6 to 8 inches of soil, to form a ridge 1 to 2 feet wide. One or two plants are usually plenty for the home gardener. After leaves appear, fertilize with compost or 10-10-10.

During the growing season, crowns with multiple shoots form above the ground. The original set grows in diameter with many side roots forming underground. Your goal is to grow the original set as large as possible, which you can do by either suckering or lifting.

Suckering is done by removing all but one or two leaf shoots at the head end as they develop. Lifting is simply digging through the ridge and gently lifting the crown end with a hoe to break roots forming at the crown. This practice forces side roots to form at the tail end, and should be done a couple of times during early and mid-season. Both methods will result in greater swelling of the initial root, producing a large 1- to 2-pound main root at harvest. Once the top leaves are frozen in late fall, you can pick horseradish roots. Dig the large central root and as much of the secondary root system as possible. Save side roots for planting next year's crop. Roots can be stored in the refrigerator wrapped in plastic to conserve root moisture. You can leave horseradish in your outdoor garden ground and dig as needed throughout the winter and even into spring.

## Cooking Tips and Recipes

You can process horseradish by peeling and dicing the root pieces, and then grinding in a blender. One basic recipe for prepared horseradish is to fill a blender half full with diced horseradish, add a small amount of water and ice, and grind to desired consistency. To preserve and enhance the flavor, add 2 or 3 tablespoons white vinegar (not cider vinegar) and 1/2 teaspoon salt or 1 tablespoon sugar. Vinegar stops the heat-building enzyme activity caused by crushing. Therefore, for a milder sauce, add the vinegar immediately. For a hotter sauce, wait a few minutes after grinding before adding the vinegar. Place in clean jars and leave 1/2 inch head space. Cover tightly. Store in the refrigerator or freezer. When you are really cold this winter, heat up your life with horseradish.

## CREAMY HORSERADISH DIP

*Makes 6 to 8 servings.*

■ 2 tablespoons bottled horseradish
2 cups cottage cheese
1 tablespoon ketchup
1 teaspoon pepper
Dash of salt

▶ Mix all ingredients together well in a bowl. Cover and chill for 4 hours so flavors will blend. Serve with your favorite crackers.

## HORSERADISH COLESLAW

*Makes 6 servings.*

■ 16-ounce bag fresh-cut coleslaw mix (or shredded fresh carrots and cabbage)
3/4 cup of your favorite coleslaw dressing
1/4 cup creamy horseradish dip

▶ Pour dressings over slaw and mix well. Let marinate a few hours before serving.

## EASY OVEN STEW

*If desired, top with biscuits, pastry, or breadcrumbs moistened with a little olive oil rather than the corn chips.*

*Makes 6 servings.*

■ 1 pound chuck or other lean beef, cut into 2-inch squares
3 tablespoons flour, seasoned
4 tablespoons cooking oil
3 tablespoons prepared horseradish (see directions above)
2 cups tomatoes, chopped
2 medium onions, quartered
2 medium potatoes, peeled and cubed
2 medium carrots, quartered
1 cup lightly crushed corn chips, measured after crushing

▶ Coat beef in seasoned flour and brown in cooking oil in Dutch oven or large skillet. Add horseradish, tomatoes, onions, potatoes, and carrots. Place 1/2 cup corn chips in a casserole dish, add stew, and top with remaining chips. Cover and bake at 350°F for 1 hour. Serve with sourdough bread.

## HORSEY BURGERS

*Makes 4 servings.*

■ 1 pound ground beef
4 tablespoons prepared horseradish (see directions above)
4 tablespoons prepared mustard
1/2 cup breadcrumbs
1 egg

Salt and pepper
4 hamburger buns

▶ Mix together meat, horserad-ish, mustard, egg, and breadcrumbs. Add salt and pepper to taste. Form into 4 patties. Grill until done. Place on buns and serve.

## HORSERADISH SAUCE

*Makes about 1 cup.*

■ 2 teaspoons mayonnaise

1 cup sour cream
3 tablespoons ground horseradish
1/4 teaspoon salt
1 scant teaspoon sugar

▶ Stir together all ingredients until smooth. Cover and chill for 4 hours or overnight. Use as a dip or with corned beef—a tasty treat, especially when made from your own freshly ground horseradishes.

# Chicory and Endive

Chicory is a curious perennial herb. It is the root of *Cichorium intybus* and, when cultivated, goes under the various common names of radicchio, Belgian endive, French endive, coffeeweed, and wiltloof.

The first written record of chicory was on Egyptian papyrus dating to 400 B.C. From Egypt it spread through the Mediterranean where the roots were baked, ground, and used as coffee. Much later, this additive also became popular in America's southern states. It also is a staple in Cajun food such as New Orleans' red-eye gravy. The wild chicory eventually became naturalized in North America and is now a common roadside plant with appealing blue flowers.

True endive is a species of chicory that is mainly grown and used as a salad green. It has a slightly bitter taste, attributed to its herbal properties. Curly endive and broad-leaved escaroles are true endives.

## History

Chicory has long roots, both literally and figuratively. Not only is it a tap-root plant, but its historic roots trace back to ancient Egypt more than 5,000 years ago. No wonder it was one of the plants mentioned in the Bible; undoubtedly it was part of the diet of the Jewish people when they were slaves in Egypt. It was and is today grown in the Nile River valley where it is called succory, and eaten by Egyptians as a vegetable and in salads.

Greek writers Pliny, Virgil, and Ovid mentioned this food. Even Dioscorides noted chicory in his herbal writings in the 1st century. Records reveal that Emperor Charlemagne included it in his gardens and meals. In England, Nicholas Culpeper wrote about it in the 17th century, and here in America it was noted in the famed Monticello gardens of President Thomas Jefferson.

Common chicory, with its blue or lavender flowers, has become naturalized across North America. Over the years, chicory roots have been baked, ground, and used as a coffee substitute not just in the Mediterranean, the plant's original locale, but are still used as a coffee substitute in the southern United States.

## Growing and Harvesting Tips

Endive has curly, finely cut leaves. Recommended varieties include green curled Lorca; Ruffec, which resists cold and wet conditions; and Salad King. Others include Frisan, which is heat resistant for Southern areas. Among so-called escarole with typical wide, crumpled leaves, you can try Batavian full-hearted Grosse Bouclee, which resists bolting, and Tosca, a smaller variety. Both endive and escarole are considered coarse in texture and have a strong flavor; some people today do consider these bitter herbs, which fits their deeply rooted heritage in the Bible.

Witloof chicory, the endive type, produces tall, leafy plants with healthy, strong roots. Head-like clusters of blanched leaves are 5 to 6 inches long and used in salads. To blanch endive, follow the same methods as you would to blanch leeks, mounding soil around the bottom part of the plant and along rows to deny plants light.

These and related varieties are cultivated like lettuce, so follow those procedures (described above) for abundant crops. You can find different varieties at heirloom and regular mail-order firms. Give these a try in your biblical garden and on your dining table. You may be surprised and pleased to add this other bitter herb to your family's special meals.

## Cooking Tips and Recipes

If you can't grow this special herb, Belgian endive is available year-round in supermarkets, with a peak season from November through April. Curly endive and escarole are available all year long, with the peak season from June through October.

Whether you grow or buy endive, rinse it in cold water before using. One easy treat is to toss Belgian endive leaves with sliced pear and crumbled blue cheese. Also try combining curly endive, radicchio, and olives; or cook escarole with white beans and chopped garlic, another biblical food.

## CHICORY AND ROAST BEET SALAD WITH BLUE CHEESE

*For this recipe you can substitute half a 15-ounce can of whole beets cut into wedges for the fresh; and there is no need to roast the canned beets.*

*Makes 6 servings.*

■ 3 beets (about 3/4 pound), trimmed
2 cups (3/4-inch) cubed French bread, about 3 ounces
Cooking spray
6 cups torn chicory, a.k.a. curly endive
Blue cheese dressing

▶ Preheat oven to 425°F. Leave root and 1 inch of stem on fresh garden beets; scrub with a brush. Place beets on a baking sheet and bake at 425° for 1 hour or until tender. Cool slightly. Trim off beet roots; rub off skins. Cut each beet into 8 wedges.

Place bread cubes on a baking pan; lightly coat bread cubes with cooking spray. Bake at 425° for 7 minutes or until golden. Combine croutons with chicory in a large bowl. Add dressing and toss to coat. Top with beets. Serve immediately.

## CHICORY AND BACON SALAD

■ 2 shallots, minced
2 tablespoons Dijon mustard
2 1/2 tablespoons red wine vinegar
1/4 teaspoon freshly ground pepper
1/2 cup olive oil
2/3 pound thick-cut bacon, cut into 1/2-inch pieces
1/2 loaf French bread, crust removed, cut into 1/2-inch cubes
1 head chicory (curly endive), torn into large pieces
Salt

▶ In small bowl, whisk together shallots, mustard, vinegar, and pepper. Gradually whisk in olive oil in a thin stream. In medium skillet, cook bacon over medium heat until browned and crisp, about 10 minutes. Remove with a slotted spoon and set aside. Pour off all fat except 1/4 cup. Add bread cubes to the hot bacon fat and sauté over medium heat, tossing lightly until slightly browned, about 5 minutes. Remove and set aside. Return bacon to skillet and toss until heated through. Remove from heat and stir in the dressing. Place chicory in large bowl and add the dressing, bacon, and bread, toss well, and add salt if desired.

## BELGIUM ENDIVE SALAD

*Let your own taste guide you as you adapt recipes for your family. For a variation, use as many chopped hard-boiled eggs as you like instead of the beets, but leave out the mustard and add some curry powder to the sour cream. Or add some chopped green onion, or use 4 to 6 ounces cubed or chopped cheese of your choice instead of the beets. Be innovative—this is a very flexible recipe.*

*4 to 6 servings.*

■ 2 heads Belgian endive, cored
2 cooked beets, grated or chopped
1 apple, chopped in cubes
3 tablespoons sour cream
1 teaspoon mustard
Salt and pepper to taste

▶ Wash endive and remove the bitter core, then finely chop the leaves. Coarsely grate or chop beets. Mix sour cream with mustard and add salt and pepper. Combine with rest of ingredients.

## CREAM OF BELGIUM ENDIVE SOUP

*Serves 4 or more.*

■ 2 Belgian endives, cored
1 white onion, diced
1 garlic clove, diced
2 tablespoons butter
2 large potatoes, peeled and diced
2 cups chicken broth
1 cup milk, half-and-half, or cream, per your diet
Salt and pepper to taste
Chopped chives
Dill sprigs for garnish

▶ Mince the Belgian endives, reserving a few small leaves for garnish. Sauté onion, garlic, and minced endives in butter for 3 minutes. Add potatoes and chicken broth and simmer for about 15 minutes or until potatoes are soft. Use a blender or food processor to process until smooth. Add milk, salt, and pepper, and blend. Serve hot or cold. Garnish with the small endive leaves, chives, and dill.

# Cucumber

Cucumber is the common name for a trailing or climbing annual herb of the gourd family that is native to Asia and is widely cultivated in North America and Europe for its fruit. Cucumbers were one of the favorite foods in the Middle East and received their proper attention in the Bible. Today, thanks to plant hybridizers, there are many excellent varieties for eating fresh in salads or making delicious different types of pickles. Different varieties of cucumbers vary in length from about 4 to 20 inches. Cucumbers are scientifically known as *Cucumis sativus* and belong to the same family as watermelon, zucchini, pumpkin, and other types of squash.

## Focus on Scripture

### Cucumbers

Numbers 11:5—"We remember the fish, which we did eat in Egypt freely; the cucumbers and the melons, and the leeks, and the onions, and the garlic"

Isaiah 1:8—"And the daughter of Zion is left as a cottage in a vineyard, as a lodge in a garden of cucumbers, as a besieged city."

Baruch 6:70—"For as a scarecrow in a garden of cucumbers keepeth nothing: so are their gods of wood, and laid over with silver and gold."

Jeremiah 1:70—"For as a scarecrow in a garden of cucumbers keepeth nothing: so are their gods of wood, and laid over with silver and gold."

# History and Nutrition Highlights

The cucumber has been cultivated for at least 3,000 years in Western Asia, and was probably introduced to other parts of Europe by the Romans. The cucumber is also listed among the products of ancient Ur, and some authorities say that it was produced in ancient Thrace. From India, it spread to Greece and Italy where the Romans were especially fond of it. The fruit is mentioned in Numbers 11:5 as having been freely available in Egypt, even to the enslaved Israelites: "We remember the fish, which we did eat in Egypt freely, the cucumbers, and the melons, and the leeks, and the onions, and the garlic." The Israelites later came to cultivate the cucumber themselves, and Isaiah 1:8 briefly mentions their method of agriculture: "The Daughter of Zion is left like a shelter in a vineyard, like a hut in a field of melons, like a city under siege." The shelter was for the person who kept the birds away, and guarded the garden from robbers.

Other historic reports say that Roman emperor Tiberius had the cucumber on his table daily during summer and winter. Pliny the Elder describes the Italian fruit as very small, and also writes about several other varieties of cucumber.

Historians say that Charlemagne had cucumbers grown in his gardens in 9th-century France. Reportedly, Christopher Columbus brought cucumbers to Haiti in 1494, and they have been popular in America for centuries.

Although cucumbers are mostly water and do not have special nutritional value they brighten many meals. In Jesus' day as now, cucumbers were eaten fresh and preserved by pickling. Be aware that cucumbers do not lend themselves to freezing.

# Growing and Harvesting Tips

Cucumbers must be grown in warm temperatures and full sunlight and will not stand frost. Plants can be highly prolific, mature quickly, and are best suited to large gardens but can be grown in small areas if caged or trellised. Cucumbers do best in loose, sandy loam soil, but can be grown in any well-drained soil. Till soil to a depth of 8 to 12 inches.

Cucumbers require plenty of fertilizer. Scatter 1 cup of a complete fertilizer such as 10-10-10 for each 10 feet of row, and work the fertilizer into the soil.

Some good varieties include Burpless hybrid, maturing at about 65 days, and the original sweet, long, Chinese-type hybrid, maturing at about 65 days. Straight 8 matures earlier and is an all-American prize, a long-time favorite with excellent flavor. Salad Bush hybrid is another early AAS winner with uniform 8-inch fruit on compact plants; tolerant to a wide variety of diseases.

Cucumbers are usually started by planting seeds directly in the garden after danger of frost has passed and soil has warmed in spring. A second planting for fall harvest may be made in mid- to late summer. Plant seeds 1/2 to 1 inch deep, cover lightly with soil, and thin seedlings to one plant every 12 inches in the row. Using black plastic mulch warms the soil in the early season and can give significantly earlier yields and also prevents weeds so plants get more moisture and nutrients. To save space in small gardens, train vines on a hoop, trellis, or fence. Wire cages also can be used to support the plants. Apply about 1/2 cup of fertilizer for each 10 feet of row or 1 tablespoon per plant when the vines are about 10 to 12 inches long. Soak the plants well with water weekly if it does not rain.

Pick cucumbers at any stage of development before the seeds become hard. Best size depends upon the use and variety. They may be picked when they are no more than 2 inches long for pickles, 4 to 6 inches long for dills, and 6 to 8 inches long for slicing varieties. A cucumber is of highest quality when it is uniformly green, firm, and crisp.

# Cooking Tips and Recipes

Here are some simple ways to enjoy cucumbers: Pick cukes when young and tender, and use 1/2-inch-thick slices as petite serving "dishes" for chopped vegetable salads. Or try mixing diced cucumbers with sugar snap peas and mint leaves, and toss with rice wine vinaigrette. A cold gazpacho soup can be prepared in 5 minutes: Simply purée cucumbers, tomatoes, green peppers, and onions, then add salt and pepper to taste. You can also add diced cucumber to tuna fish or chicken salad recipes.

### REFRIGERATOR DILL CHIPS

*Pickled cucumbers add spice and texture to sandwiches and meals. For highest-quality pickles, use cucumbers that are no more the 24 hours from the vine. Always use "pure" or pickling salt; table salt contains additives that make a cloudy brine and off-color pickles.*

*Makes 1 pint.*

■ 2 to 2 1/2 cups sliced cucumbers, about 1/4 inch thick
2 1/2 teaspoons pickling salt
2 springs fresh dill weed, about 6 inches long, or 1 tablespoon dry dill seed or 1 head fresh dill
2 cloves garlic
1/2 cup white distilled vinegar
1/2 cup water

▶ Prepare a 1-pint jar, lid, and screw band. Wash in hot soapy water, rinse well, and drain. Combine sliced cucumbers and 1 1/2 teaspoons pickling salt. Toss well. Cover with cold water and let stand for 2 to 3 hours. Drain.

Put the dill, garlic, and remaining 1 teaspoon pickling salt in the clean, hot jar. Add the cucumber slices, leaving 1/2 inch head space (the space between the rim of the jar and its contents). Push slices down and firmly pack. Combine water and vinegar and bring to a boil. Pour hot vinegar solution over cucumbers.

Use a spatula to release air bubbles. Insert the spatula down the side of the jar and gently push the cucumber slices toward the center so that the vinegar solution gets between the slices. Pour on more hot vinegar solution if necessary, still leaving 1/2 inch head space. Wipe the rim. Put on the lid and screw the top in place. Refrigerate for 6 weeks before eating.

## NONTRADITIONAL SWEET FREEZER PICKLES

*From the University of Illinois, this is not your typical pickle recipe. No special equipment or ingredients are needed. This recipe produces a crisp, sweet pickle that goes well in salads, on sandwiches, or on the side. The secret to the crisp texture is the sugar, so do not reduce the sugar in the recipe. This recipe works well with slicing, pickling, seedless, or hothouse cucumbers.*

*Makes 2 quarts.*

■ 2 quarts cucumbers, peeled and thinly sliced (use any variety of cucumber)
1 medium onion, thinly sliced
1 tablespoon salt (table salt, canning salt, or kosher salt can be used)
1 1/2 cups sugar
1/2 cup white distilled vinegar

▶ Mix cucumbers, onions, and salt in a large bowl and cover with plastic wrap. Set the bowl on the counter for 2 hours. Pour into a colander and drain water from cucumber mixture. Combine sugar and vinegar. Stir well and pour over cucumbers. Pack into freezer containers or zip-closure bags. Freeze immediately. Pickles are ready to eat in 3 or 4 days. They will keep in the freezer for up to one year.

## CUCUMBER YOGURT SALAD DRESSING

*This is a delicious, heart-healthy, low-calorie salad dressing, which can be used as a dip for steamed or raw vegetables or as a topping for baked potatoes or steamed carrots. Store in a covered container in the refrigerator for up to 2 weeks.*

*Makes 1 1/2 cups.*

■ 1 medium cucumber, peeled, seeded, and coarsely chopped (about 2/3 cup)
2/3 cup plain, nonfat yogurt
2 tablespoons minced red onion
1 tablespoon toasted sesame oil or vegetable oil
2 teaspoons rice vinegar or white vinegar
1/4 teaspoon salt (optional)
2 teaspoons chopped fresh dill or 1/2 teaspoon dried dill

▶ Combine all ingredients in a blender or food processor and puree until creamy and smooth. Chill for about 2 hours before serving.

## THAI CUCUMBER SALAD

*Here's a unique treat to expand your international flavor horizons.*

*Makes 4 servings.*

■ 1/4 cup sugar
1 teaspoon salt
1/2 cup rice vinegar
4 pickling or slicing cucumbers, thinly sliced lengthwise and seeded1 shallot, thinly sliced
10 whole cilantro leaves
1/4 cup red pepper, julienned (about 1 inch long)

▶ Combine sugar, vinegar, and salt, and heat in a small saucepan until sugar has dissolved (about 5 minutes). Do not boil. Set saucepan in cold water to cool the vinegar mixture. When cool, pour over cucumbers, add shallots and cilantro and garnish with red peppers.

## YOGURT AND CUCUMBER SOUP WITH SAFFRON

*This soup is wonderfully refreshing on a summer day.*

*Makes about 4 servings.*

■ 2 peeled/seeded cucumbers
2 cups plain yogurt
1 1/2 tablespoons chopped fresh dill
2 teaspoons chopped fresh mint

1 cup chicken stock
Pinch white pepper
Salt to taste
1 teaspoon saffron

▶ Coarsely grate the cucumbers and place in a plastic bowl. Add remaining ingredients except the saffron. Rub the saffron between your fingers into a small glass. Add 1 teaspoon hot tap water and stir with a spoon to release the yellow-orange color. Add to the other ingredients and stir. Cover and refrigerate overnight. Stir before serving and adjust salt if necessary. Serve cold.

# Fava/Broad Beans

The fava or broad bean traces its history by various names by which it has been known through time: fava bean, faba bean, broad bean, horse bean, field bean, or tic bean, depending on the area. Broad/fava beans, among the most ancient plants in cultivation, have been extensively cultivated all around the Mediterranean Sea and remain popular there. Along with lentils, peas, and chickpeas, fava beans were part of the eastern Mediterranean diet from around 6000 B.C. or earlier.

The broad bean, is in the Order *Fabale*; family, *Fabaceae*; Genus, *Viciae*; Species, *V. faba*. Although usually classified in the same genus as the vetches (*Vicia*), some botanists treat the fava as a separate monotypic genus, *Faba sativa Moench*.

# Focus on Scripture

## Fava Beans

2 Samuel 17:28—"Brought beds, and basons, and earthen vessels, and wheat, and barley, and flour, and parched corn, and beans, and lentils, and parched pulse..."

Ezekiel 4:9—"Take thou also unto thee wheat, and barley, and beans, and lentils, and millet, and fitches, and put them in one vessel, and make thee bread thereof, according to the number of the days that thou shalt lie upon thy side, three hundred and ninety days shalt thou eat thereof."

## History and Nutrition Highlights

Fava beans have been found in some of the earliest known human settlements. They probably originated in the Near East in late Neolithic times. By the Bronze Age they had spread to Northern Italy, have been found in lakeside dwellings in Switzerland, and have been dated to the Iron Age at Glastonbury in Britain. Favas were widely cultivated and mostly eaten by the common people in ancient Egypt, as the upper classes considered them unworthy food.

Unlike the Egyptians and Greeks, the Romans held the faba bean in high esteem. The Elder Pliny praised faba beans and spoke of bean meal as being mixed with wheat or millet flour in the baking of bread to make loaves heavier. In ancient Greece and Rome, fava beans were used in voting; a white bean for a yes vote and a black bean for no. Fava beans have been a part of cuisines all around the Mediterranean for centuries.

Fava beans are the common bean of Europe, where they are standard fare; indeed, they are the only "Old World" bean. Fava beans were overlooked in America for years but interest in the Mediterranean diet and specialty foods of that part of the world has led to their increasing popularity.

Fava beans are high in fiber (85 percent of the recommended daily value), high in iron (30 percent of a day's requirement), and very low in sodium.

They have no cholesterol and are low in fat. However, a warning is in order about fava beans, according to botanical experts: Favism is an inherited disorder of certain individuals, particularly those of southern European origin. These people have an enzyme deficiency expressed when fava beans are eaten, especially raw or partially cooked. Symptoms are similar to those of influenza and commonly include acute toxic hepatitis. Males are more commonly affected than females. Fava plant pollen in the respiratory tract also affects these people. Be aware of this situation and take necessary precautions, including questioning your medical advisor if necessary.

## Growing and Harvesting Tips

Happily, fava beans are among the easiest beans to grow. California is justly famed for production of much of our nation's foods, and new food trends often start there. The fava bean has spread its roots from there to home gardens around the country. Today, you may hear of fava bean varieties such as horse, broad, English dwarf bean, tick, pigeon, bell, faba, feve, and Windsor beans (a current favorite in America).

Fava beans are classified as legumes because they produce a "bean," and because they fix nitrogen from the air into the soil. That fact makes them useful at rejuvenating older garden sites. Fava beans may grow 6 feet high by late May, and make excellent green manure. Because they are very tolerant of heavy, clay soils, their extensive root system breaks up soil to 2 feet deep and brings up soluble nutrients from lower soil levels.

Fava beans are best grown in the cooler spring or fall weather, as they don't do well in hot climates. The bushy, erect plants grow 2 to 7 feet tall, with stout stems and pinnate leaves between 10 to 25 cm long, each with two to seven leaflets of a distinct gray-green color. Curiously, unlike most vetches, fava bean leaves do not have tendrils for climbing over vegetation. White or purplish flowers with distinctive black centers are borne in clusters on short, thick stalks in the leaf axils. The large-seeded varieties bear one or two pods at each node, but the small-seeded types produce from two to five pods. Horticulturists note that there can be 15 pods per stalk on the large types and 60 pods on plants of the small-seeded varieties.

Fava beans grow inside large, 7- to 9-inch thick pods with a white blanket-like padding inside the pod to protect the beans. The larger Windsor beans, *Vinca faba,* grow in a rather short pod that contains three to four beans. Long-pod beans are generally smaller and grow in a long, narrow pod containing six to eight beans. The beans themselves look like small to medium-sized lima or butter beans.

Although they have been in cultivation in many parts of the world for thousands of years, favas are relatively new to American gardeners. You may need to search for seeds. The following are a selection of those you can find on the Internet.

Victory Seed Company offers Aquadulce, a favorite Old World variety that can stand very cold conditions, to about 15°F, and can be planted in the fall or winter for spring harvest. Their Broad Windsor matures in about 85 days on 36- to 48-inch plants that are upright and non-branching. Seeds of Change has organic fava bean seeds including medium size Sweet Lorane fava beans that survive winter temperatures down to 10°F. Heirloom Seeds offers Aquadulce, a good choice for an extra-early crop and respected Nichols Seeds in Oregon offers the Broad Windsor favas, along with many other types of rare and hard-to-find vegetable varieties. This firm rates high marks for its range of unique and international vegetable seeds. Check Internet sources for some old-time favas like Supersimonia, and Super Aquadulce.

Pick a sunny area. Fava beans can grow on a wide range of soils, from loams to clays, and under a variety of drainage conditions. They tolerate a wide range of pH from 4.5 to 8.3, although low pH may delay the development of root nodules, which prevents the plant from converting atmospheric nitrogen to plant-available forms. Be aware, however, that favas don't tolerate extended periods of saturated soils or drought, especially at flowering time (seed production will be reduced drastically).

Because these beans are heavy feeders, add compost prior to planting. Fava bean enthusiasts suggest a side dressing of fertilizer to give these plants a fast start as soon as they germinate.

Plant outdoors after the last frost date for your area. To produce the best crops, remember that the fava bean is a cool-season annual legume and is usually planted in early spring for vegetable use in summer. The seeds should be planted about 1 to 2 inches deep in well-prepared soil, 3 to 5 inches apart. Germination takes place in 7 to 14 days. Since they will grow into small bushes, the sprouted seeds should be thinned to 8 to 10 inches apart, allowing 2 to 3 feet between rows. Plant them in blocks, or two to three rows together, to help prevent the plants from falling over. Because these beans can grow tall and don't have tendrils, consider using supports such as fences or poles.

Water well after planting and a second time 2 to 4 days later if there has been no rain. You can also side-dress the rows with general-purpose fertilizer when flowers form to produce large, well-filled pods. Thin seedling to proper distance, as noted on the seed packet, about 3 inches apart in rows 3 feet apart.

Cold tolerance among fava bean cultivars varies, but most varieties winter-kill at temperatures below 15°F and even the most winter-hardy will die at temperatures below 10°F, although many varieties winter well on the coasts and in the southern U.S.

In addition to their value as a new bean treat, favas can also produce large amounts of biomass, making them useful as a green manure crop. As legumes they capture nitrogen from the air, so when plants are worked back into the soil as organic matter they enhance the tilth of many clay and sandy type soils, and the leguminous nature adds large amounts of nitrogen to the soil benefiting existing perennial crops.

Planted in early spring, fava beans will be ready to start harvesting by the end of July. Watch for maturity as beans develop within their pods. Favas can be eaten while small, just as the pods begin to fill, as you would green or snap beans. They are primarily used as a green shelled bean and cooked in salted water. Harvest them for fresh eating as shelled beans when the beans swell the green pods; pods that are green, thick, and have a glossy sheen should be well filled with large beans. As a dry bean, or as saved seed, they can be harvested as the pods begin to turn black, darkening from the ground up over a period of several weeks.

## Cooking Tips and Recipes

If you don't grow fava beans, you can often now buy them in natural and health food stores, farmer's markets, and in some supermarkets in areas where favas are popular. You may need more beans than you think: 5 pounds of unshelled favas will make about four servings. Some recipes note that 1 pound of unshelled beans equals 1 cup of shelled beans, depending on bean size.

If you are using dried fava beans rather than fresh shelled beans, soak favas overnight, then bring to a boil and simmer 75 minutes. As a rule of thumb, you can figure a cup of dry fava beans nearly doubles in size when soaked and cooked.

Fresh-picked fava bean pods can be kept in the refrigerator for a day or two. To shell the beans, pull on the stem of the pod and unzip them, on both sides. Drop the beans in boiling water for 30 seconds, then remove and plunge them into ice water. This should loosen the beans' waxy outer covering, or pericarp, around each seed, which you can then peel off (these outer skins become tough when cooked). Drain, and the beans are ready for use in recipes.

To cook fresh fava beans, put them in boiling salted water in a covered saucepan with a little parsley or winter savory, and cook until tender: about 8 minutes when young, 20 to 25 minutes when more mature. For simplicity, serve with melted butter and parsley, or with garlic, olive oil, and lemon.

Along with the following recipes using fresh fava beans, you might check out local Italian restaurants for preparation ideas. You may find fresh favas mashed or pureed and spread on crostini, or used in dishes ranging from vegetable stews to grilled meats and fish to chicken. A favorite traditional Italian appetizer is peeled cooked fava beans sprinkled with olive oil and salt along with salami, prosciutto, and slices of Parmesan or pecorino cheese. Consider adding fava beans to spring vegetable stews, ragouts, and soups, or substitute them for lima beans in a vegetable side dish.

## TUSCAN FAVA BEAN SALAD

*To see whether you will like growing and cooking fava beans, try this recipe using canned favas, courtesy the Progresso food firm (or substitute fresh shelled beans from your garden).*

*Makes 5 1-cup servings.*

■ 1 can (19-oz) Progresso fava beans, drained and rinsed
2/3 cup chopped red onions
1 cup chopped tomato
12 cup chopped celery
1/4 cup chopped fresh cilantro
1/4 cup olive oil

3 tablespoons red wine vinegar
1 1/2 teaspoons dried thyme leaves
1 clove garlic, minced
1/8 teaspoon salt

▶ Combine all ingredients in a large bowl, stir well, and refrigerate until serving time.

## MINESTRONE WITH FAVA BEANS

*This may be the perfect early spring soup, thick enough to be satisfying, fresh enough to entice, according to Ed Giobbi in* **Pleasures of the**

**Good Earth.** *Try his tasty recipe and others from that fine book.*

*Makes 4 to 6 servings.*

■ 2 cups shelled fava beans
2 tablespoons olive oil
1 small onion, coarsely chopped
1 stalk celery, coarsely chopped
1 tablespoon finely chopped flat-leaf parsley
1 carrot, coarsely chopped
1 cup coarsely chopped tomatoes
5 cups water
1/4 cup white rice
2 cups chopped spinach
Salt

▶ Cook fava beans in pot of boiling salted water 2 minutes. Drain and rinse under cold running water. Remove outer skins, discard, and reserve beans.

Heat olive oil in soup pot over moderate heat. Add onion and celery and sauté until onion begins to brown, 7 to 10 minutes. Add parsley, carrot, and tomatoes, and cook, stirring, several minutes. Add water and peeled beans, cover, and cook over low to moderate heat until beans are tender, about 50 minutes. Add rice, cover, and cook 10 more minutes.

Add spinach, cover, and cook over low heat until rice is tender, about 10 to 12 minutes. Season to taste with salt and serve hot.

## MIGHTY VEGGIE MINESTRONE

*Minestrone has become one of the most popular Mediterranean soups. This recipe is from neighbors who were inspired by a trip to italy.*

*Makes 6 to 8 servings.*

■ 1 1/2 pounds fresh fava beans
1 1/2 pounds fresh, unshelled green peas
2/3 pound ripe tomatoes
2/3 pound white or golden onions
1 1/2 pounds zucchini
1 tablespoon of basil leaves
2 tablespoons minced parsley
1 head of lettuce
1 1/2 tablespoons olive oil
1 quart beef broth
Salt and pepper to taste

▶ Shell fava beans and green peas and keep them separate. Peel and chop tomatoes. Slice onions. Wash and slice unpeeled zucchini. Clean, rinse, and mince basil and parsley.

Place veggies in a pot: first, place the tomatoes at the bottom, cover them with onions, layer sliced zucchini over them, then lettuce and green peas. Sprinkle half the parsley and add the fava beans. Sprinkle vegetables with olive oil, cover the pot, and let cook over medium heat. Do not stir for about 10 minutes until the vegetables at the bottom of the pot release their water.

Add the beef broth, a pinch of salt, and a pinch of pepper. Stir, cover the pot, and let cook on a very low heat for about an hour. Don't add any water while the minestrone is cooking. When done, add the remaining parsley and serve.

## CREAMED FAVA BEANS AND BACON

*This recipe—"Feves au Lard Fume"—from Richard Olney's* **Simple French Food** *is almost compulsively edible. After all, how bad can bacon, cream, and egg yolks be?*

*Makes 4 servings.*

- 5 pounds young fava beans, in pods
- 1/4 pound lean bacon strips
- 1 tablespoon butter
- 1 stalk fresh savory (or pinch finely crumbled dried savory)
- About 3 tablespoons water
- Salt
- 1/2 cup whipping cream
- 3 egg yolks
- Freshly ground black pepper
- Lemon juice
- Chopped parsley

▶ Shell beans and remove skins from all except those pods that are tiny and bright green. Cut bacon in 1/2-inch sections, parboil for a few seconds to remove excess salt, and drain. Cook bacon in heavy saucepan over low heat 2 to 3 minutes. Bacon should remain limp. Add fava beans, savory, just enough water to moisten slightly, and salt to taste. Cover tightly and cook over high heat for a few seconds. Turn heat to low again so beans stew in their own steam rather than boiling. Cook, shaking pan gently from time to time, until beans are tender, 15 to 20 minutes.

Remove from heat and cool 1 minute or so. Mix cream, egg yolks, and pepper to taste and stir gently into fava beans. Return to low heat, stirring until sauce is only lightly bound, coating spoon thinly. Sauce should not approach a boil. Squeeze in a few drops lemon juice to taste, sprinkle with chopped parsley, and serve.

# Garbanzo Beans/Chickpeas

If chickpeas, also known as garbanzo beans, aren't a regular part of your diet, you're missing out on one of nature's truly perfect foods. Nutritionists tell us that these tasty cream-colored, mild-flavored, marble-size legumes not only contain hefty amounts of protein, but very little fat and provide us with slow-burning complex carbohydrates, fiber, and B vitamins. They may not be well known to most Americans, but they are gaining deserved popularity, especially among folks tuned in to natural foods and vegetarian specialties. They have been a staple in the Mediterranean area for centuries.

# Focus on Scripture
## Garbanzo Beans/Chickpeas

2 Samuel 17:27–29—"[They] brought beds, and basons, and earthen vessels, and wheat, and barley, and flour, and parched corn, and beans, and lentiles, and parched pulse, and honey, and butter, and sheep, and cheese of kine, for David, and for the people that were with him, to eat: for they said, The people is hungry, and weary, and thirsty, in the wilderness."

Ezekiel 4:9—"Take thou also unto thee wheat, and barley, and beans, and lentiles, and millet, and fitches, and put them in one vessel, and make thee bread thereof, according to the number of the days that thou shalt lie upon thy side, three hundred and ninety days shalt thou eat thereof."

## History and Nutrition Highlights

During the exile of the Jewish people, the Prophet Isaiah (Isaiah 30:24) offered hope that the people and animals would be blessed by God. "The oxen likewise and the young asses . . . shall eat clean provender, which hath been winnowed with the shovel and with the fan."

As reported in 2 Samuel, beans were among the highly nutritious foods sent to feed King David's hungry army to restore their strength. It is likely that chickpeas were included in their wholesome diet.

Today we realize that beans and other pulses are packed with soluble fiber, which helps lower LDL and reduces blood pressure. The same fiber also helps keep blood sugar levels stable, staves off hunger (a bonus for every dieter), and has even been shown to reduce the insulin requirements of people suffering from diabetes. If you look up other facts about beans and garbanzos, you'll discover that garbanzos aren't really "beans" as we gardeners know true beans (*Phaseolus vulgaris*). Scientifically known as *cicer arietnum*, these beans were a staple of the holy land diet during Jesus' time and remain a favored food there. The chick pea is one of the more nutritious members of the bean family, rich in protein, calcium, iron and B vitamins. Some mail order firms like Salt Spring Seeds offer several varieties or garbanzos so you may wish to experiment with growing several types.

Garbanzos are a legume and more like a vetch. They have been overlooked in American gardens for years, but now that more people are enjoying international veggies and Mediterranean diets, these tasty beans are better appreciated and seeds more readily available from mail order firms.

Now garbanzos are the most widely consumed legume in the world. Originating in the Middle East, they have a firm texture with a flavor somewhere between chestnuts and walnuts. Garbanzo is the name used in Spanish-speaking countries. The English name chickpea comes from the French *chiche*, which comes from the Latin *cicer*.

Also sometimes called cici beans, chickpea plants grow between 10 to 24 inches tall and have small feathery leaves on both sides of the stem. Chickpeas have been a favorite food for centuries in Southern Europe, Northern Africa, and Afghanistan.

Important as they are today in balanced diets, they were even more important as a staple food in biblical times. They were and are a wonderful source of protein, which was a scarce commodity in primitive societies.

Botanical experts believe that chickpeas probably originated in the Middle East. Today they are prized in several of the world's cuisines, Middle Eastern, Indian, Italian, Spanish, and Latin American among them. Their delicate nutlike flavor makes them eminently adaptable to all sorts of recipes, from salads, soups, and dips to pasta or grain dishes. Chickpeas can also be roasted for snacks and are the basis for falafel, a Middle Eastern dish in which the mashed beans are formed into balls and deep-fried or baked.

If you want to try eating them first before growing them, buy some at your local supermarket. You'll find them available either precooked in cans, or dried in bags. If you have trouble finding them among the beans and pulses, check the aisles with Italian and Latin American or international foods. Chick peas are usually available in bulk at natural food stores and expanding health food sections in supermarkets.

# Growing and Harvesting Tips

Garbanzos are a cooler-weather crop and can be sown like peas early in spring. The plants are best thinned to about a foot apart because of their spreading habit. They don't need staking. They require little attention beyond the occasional weeding or hoeing and are quite drought-tolerant.

Garbanzo seeds are often hard to find, but some specialty firms offer varieties of them, along with detailed growing instructions. One such supplier is Salt Spring Seeds, Box 444, Ganges P.O., Salt Spring Island, BC, V8K 2W1, Canada; email dan@salteaspoonringseeds.com. Or, check some of the online seed sources mentioned in the previous section on favas. For these seeds, check the reliable mail order firms listed at the end of this book. You'll find many firms that offer international food seeds few know about but which I've found to be reliable sources.

Garbanzo beans are adapted to warm, semiarid conditions and culture is similar to that for dry beans. Once you have your chickpea seeds, plant them in early spring so they'll have time to grow during the warm summer weather and be available to harvest as a summer crop. Follow growing methods you would use for peas. Space rows 8 to 12 inches apart or, if in a hill system, allow for 6 plants per square foot. Water regularly and tend as you would basic bean crops. You can harvest them when they have matured and pods are green, and use them as fresh shelled beans, or wait until pods yellow and dry and save them as dried beans.

# Cooking Tips and Recipes

Whether garden grown or store bought, check over dried chickpeas before cooking. Spread them on a white kitchen towel so that you can easily see and discard any dirt, debris, or damaged specimens. Then place the chickpeas in a strainer or colander and rinse them under cold water.

Dried chickpeas have tough skins and should be soaked before cooking. As typical of all kinds of dried beans, place chickpeas in a large pot, as they will double in size soaking. Add enough water to cover them by 2 inches. Let stand six hours at room temperature or overnight in the refrigerator. Discard any chickpeas that float to the top after soaking and pour off the soaking water. Be aware that these beans will usually double in size during the cooking process from dry to fully cooked.

Add fresh water or broth to cover the chickpeas by about 2 inches. Bring liquid slowly to a boil, skimming off the scum that rises to the surface. When the liquid boils, reduce heat, partially cover the pot, and simmer until the chickpeas are tender (about 20 to 30 minutes). For salads, remove them from the heat while they are cooked but slightly firm. For soups and purees, cook them until they are very soft. Stir occasionally during cooking, and add more water, if necessary. The chickpeas are done when they can be easily pierced with the tip of a knife. It takes less time to cook fresh chickpeas, so refer to the recipes in your favorite cookbooks. These days, health food stores often offer many tempting recipes to entice customers. You'll also find these stores a wonderful source of natural food cookbooks.

To enjoy these unusual delights, try some simple recipes first. As you learn to grow them, you'll probably want to expand your culinary horizons, enjoying them harvested as fresh young shelled beans as well as dried.

With thanks to several Italian friends who savor these veggies, I have included recipes from their cherished family cookbooks.

## GARBANZO/CHICKPEA MEDITERRANEAN SALAD

*You'll note the salad has a variety of biblical foods included.*

*Makes 6 1-cup servings.*

■ 1 1/2 cups coarsely chopped fresh tomatoes, or canned diced ones
1 1/2 cups coarsely chopped cucumber
1 cup cubed mozzarella cheese
1/2 cup sliced ripe olives
1 can (19 ounces) chickpeas, drained and rinsed or about 2 cups dried chickpeas soaked and cooked for use.
1/3 to 1/2 cup Italian salad dressing to taste
1/4 teaspoon dried basil leaves

▶ Mix all ingredients in large bowl. Toss gently and serve immediately.

## CHICKPEA ANTIPASTO HOLIDAY SALAD

*Here's another easy treat with chickpeas for a family.*

*Makes 4 to 6 servings.*

■ 1/4 cup canned chicken broth
2 tablespoons extra-virgin olive oil
2 tablespoons red wine vinegar
2 teaspoons favorite mustard
1 garlic clove, minced
1/2 teaspoon black pepper
1/4 teaspoon oregano
1/2 cup thinly sliced red onions
4 cups stemmed spinach
1/2 cup shredded carrots

1 can (10 1/2 ounces) chickpeas, rinsed and drained
1 1/2 cups bottled roasted red peppers, cut into strips
1 1/2 cups thinly sliced fennel
1/2 cup sliced red radishes
2 plum tomatoes, cut into wedges
3 to 4 ounces roast turkey breast, sliced
1 ounce sliced provolone cheese, cut into quarters

▶ In a small bowl, whisk together chicken broth, olive oil, vinegar, mustard, garlic, black pepper, and oregano. Then stir in onions and let the mixture marinate while you assemble the rest of the salad. Arrange spinach on a platter. Sprinkle with carrots. Mound chickpeas, roasted peppers, fennel, radishes, tomatoes, turkey, and cheese in separate piles on spinach. Spoon onions and dressing over salad. Makes a wonderful one-dish meal with warm multigrain bread.

## Garlic

Garlic, that wonderful, aromatic herb and food of Scriptures, was worshipped by the ancient Egyptians, chewed by Greek Olympian athletes, and thought to be essential for keeping vampires at bay. What a nice reputation! However, garlic does indeed have valuable properties. Perhaps that's why it has regained appeal and is more widely used today than in yesteryear.

## Focus on Scripture

### Garlic

Numbers 11:5—"We remember the fish, which we did eat in Egypt freely; the cucumbers, and the melons, and the leeks, and the onions, and the garlick."

# History and Nutrition Highlights

The word garlic comes from Old English *garleac,* which means "spear leek." Dating back over 6,000 years, this fragrant herb is native to Central Asia, and has long been a staple in the Mediterranean region, as well as a common seasoning in Asia, Africa, and Europe. Botanical scholars tell us that Egyptians worshipped garlic and placed clay models of garlic bulbs in the tomb of Tutankhamun. In fact, garlic was so highly prized, it was even used as currency in ancient times. Moreover, folklore says that garlic repelled vampires, and protected against "the evil eye."

Common garlic is a member of the onion family and as such dates so far back in antiquity that it is difficult to trace the country of its origin. De Candolle, in his treatise on the *Origin of Cultivated Plants,* considered garlic indigenous to the southwest of Siberia and concluded that it spread from there to southern Europe, became naturalized, and eventually became a wild plant in Sicily. For centuries garlic has been widely cultivated in the Latin countries around the Mediterranean. Dumas has described the air of Provence as being "perfumed by the essence of this mystically attractive bulb." Good for him and his nose!

Garlic has left a long historic and aromatic trail. Supposedly, garlic was placed by the ancient Greeks on the piles of stones at crossroads as a supper for Hecate. Greek historian Pliny alleged that garlic and onion were invoked as deities by the Egyptians at the taking of oaths. Garlic was consumed widely by ancient Greeks and Romans, as we may read in Virgil's *Eclogues.* Homer also makes garlic part of the entertainment that Nestor served up to his guest Machaon. There is a curious superstition that if a bit of a garlic bulb is chewed by a man running a race, it will prevent his competitors from getting ahead of him. Another fable says that Hungarian jockeys will sometimes fasten a clove of garlic to the bits of their horses so that other racers catching them will fall back when they smell the strong garlic odor.

Historically, many writers praised garlic as a medicine, a concept that is supported by much evidence today. Scientists report that garlic is useful in zapping bacteria, keeping your heart healthy, and warding off coughs and colds. In fact, there seem to be many benefits associated with taking garlic regularly. You can find more information from the Garlic Information Centre (www.garlic.mistral.co.uk). They report 12 studies published around the world that confirm that garlic in several forms can reduce cholesterol.

The largest study published recently was conducted in Germany where 261 patients from 30 general practices were given either garlic powder tablets or a placebo. After a 12-week treatment period, mean serum cholesterol levels dropped by 12 percent in the garlic treated group and triglycerides dropped by 17 percent compared to the placebo group.

Despite historic praise for garlic, food snobs in the United States turned their noses up and backs on garlic until the first quarter of the 20th century. However, garlic was favored in ethnic dishes among working-class neighborhoods. By the 1940s America had embraced garlic, finally recognizing its value as not only a minor seasoning, but as a major ingredient in a variety of recipes.

## Growing and Harvesting Tips

Garlic is kin to onions, shallots, and leeks. Garlic plant leaves are long, narrow, and flat like grass. The bulb, the only part eaten, consists of numerous bulblets known as cloves, grouped together between scales and enclosed within a whitish sac. Flowers form at the end of a stalk rising directly from the bulb. They are whitish and grouped together in a globular head, and may have small bulbils.

Garlic likes sun and can grow well in a variety of soils, from sandy loam to clay, but does best in a rich, moist, sandy soil. Prepare your growing areas as you would for onions. Dig or rototill well, eliminating all lumps, and incorporate some lime in the ground. Divide bulbs into individual "cloves," probably 10 to 12 cloves per bulb. Then, plant the cloves, stem-side down, about 2 inches deep and 6 inches apart with 1 foot between rows. It is helpful to give the cloves a dressing of wood ashes to aid their growth and development.

Garlic does well with high amounts of fertilizer; apply 3 pounds of 10-10-10 fertilizer per 100 square feet or follow soil test recommendations for your particular garden soil. Keep soil evenly moist, as dry soil will cause irregularly shaped bulbs. Avoid heavy clay soil, which can create misshaped plants. Add organic matter, such as well-rotted manure or compost to the soil on a yearly basis to keep it friable.

You can set garlic in the fall as growers do in northern areas. One of my favorite seed and plant sources is Johnny's of Maine. Other mail order firms also ship various types of garlic with specific culture directions in time for late fall as well as early spring planting. Check catalogs for different types of garlic to spice up your meals.

When planted early in the spring, February or March, mature bulbs should be ready for lifting in August, when leaves begin to wither, and up to the middle of September. Harvest when the tops start to dry and dig them up rather than pulling them to avoid stem injury. Allow tops to dry. After bulbs have dried, remove tops and roots to within an inch of the bulbs. It is essential that garlic be well cured before going into storage. Mature bulbs are best stored at 32°F.

You can also enjoy the curly green stalks, cutting them to add to stir fries. By removing them you stop flower heads from forming so that the plant can put its energy into produce the garlic bulbs.

# Cooking Tips and Recipes

Garlic adds flavor and nutritional value to food. Look through cookbooks to find more recipes worth trying. Here are some we like.

## CREAMY GARLIC SALAD DRESSING

*This is a recipe we've used for years to praise from family and friends. It came from the Donatelli family in New Jersey.*

*Makes 2 1/2 cups.*

- 1 pint mayonnaise
4 ounces water
1 ounce lemon juice
1 ounce (about 6 to 8 cloves) finely chopped garlic
1/2 teaspoon chopped parsley

▶ Salt and pepper to taste
Combine ingredients and mix well.

## SCAMPI WITH GARLIC AND HERBS

*Thanks to the Mossbergs and their fishermen family members for this treat when it is shrimping time in Maine*

*Makes 6 to 8 servings.*

- 2 tablespoons butter
2 garlic cloves, peeled
1 onion, sliced
1 bunch parsley, chopped
Salt and pepper to taste
30 to 40 medium shrimp, slit lengthwise
1/3 cup bread crumbs
1 tablespoon fresh thyme, minced

1 tablespoon fresh marjoram, minced
6 medium tomatoes, halved
1/2 cup extra-virgin olive oil
2 cups mixed salad greens, washed
1 bunch chives

▶ Preheat oven to 450°F. Combine butter, 1 clove garlic, 1 slice onion, half of the parsley, salt, and pepper in a food processor and puree until smooth. Place shrimp on a large baking sheet. Sprinkle with 2 tablespoons bread crumbs and spread with herbed butter mixture.

Combine remaining bread-crumbs, garlic, and parsley with thyme, marjoram, salt, and pepper. Place tomatoes on the baking sheet, sprinkle with seasoned bread crumbs, and drizzle with 1 tablespoon olive oil. Bake for 15 minutes.

Toss greens with remaining olive oil and onion, and season with salt and pepper to taste. Serve scampi and tomato halves on each plate, and garnish with other greens and chives.

# Leeks

Leeks have enjoyed a long and rich history that can be traced back through antiquity. Thought to be native to Central Asia, leeks have been cultivated in the Mediterranean area and the Holy Land and in Europe for thousands of years.

Leeks (*Allium porrum*) belong to the onion family, but are milder than either onions or garlic and don't form bulbs or produce cloves. Instead they develop an edible 6- to 10-inch-long round stem as much as 2 inches in diameter. The leek has leaves that are round and hollow.

# Focus on Scripture

## Leeks

Numbers 11:5—"We remember the fish, which we did eat in Egypt freely; the cucumbers, and the melons, and the leeks, and the onions, and the garlick . . ."

# History

This vegetable was prized by ancient Greeks and Romans. Supposedly the Roman emperor Nero ate leeks every day to make his voice stronger. In the Holy Land, leeks are still boiled for use like onions and often used as the basis for soups. These are ages old basic cooking methods from time honored family traditions.

The Romans are thought to have introduced leeks to the United Kingdom, where they were able to flourish because they could withstand cold weather. Leeks have attained an esteemed status in Wales, and today they serve as the country's national emblem. The Welsh regard for leeks can be traced back to a battle that they successfully won against that Saxons in 1620. During that fight, Welsh soldiers placed leeks in their caps to identify themselves from their enemies. Today, leeks are an important vegetable in many northern European dishes and are grown in most European countries.

# Growing and Harvesting Tips

Check your mail order catalogs for the varieties recommended for you're area. After your first growing trial, experiment with other leek and onion varieties to expand your dining horizons.

Leeks perform best in sunny locations with well-drained, fertile garden soil. You can easily grow them from seeds or transplants, much the same as onions. Leeks require about 120 days from seed to maturity. In northern areas set them out as transplants in early spring if you want to harvest by midsummer. In southern areas, leeks perform best when seeded or transplanted in late summer or early fall for harvesting during early winter. Soil should be prepared for leeks by adding liberal amounts of organic matter and manure. They won't thrive in clay soil, but you can improve your garden ground as noted in our special chapter on soil.

You can use both the leaves and stems of leeks. After they reach sufficient size, you can begin picking, which opens space for remaining leeks to mature better.

Good soil is the key to growing leeks. Leeks need nutrient-rich, well-drained soil with a pH between 6.0 and 7.0. A good, crumbly loam is what leeks truly prefer. But, they will do well in almost any garden soil as long as it is well aerated and 12 inches or more deep.

Dig in and plant leek seeds at a rate of 8 to 10 seeds per linear foot and cover them 1/2 inch deep with soil. If temperatures are high, cover seeds with compost or organic matter and mulch the seeded area with organic matter. After 4 to 6 weeks, thin plants so that they are 4 inches apart. Keep soil moist during early development; but as plants mature, it is best to let the soil dry somewhat.

For nicer-looking leeks, when stems are about 1 inch in diameter they may be blanched by piling dirt around the plants which excludes light from the stem. Some gardeners tie brown wrapping paper or black plastic around the stems to exclude light. Others may pile a 5- to 6-inch layer of organic matter around the plant. Blanching produces a pure-white leek of high quality.

Leeks will need to be watered during the growing season. Keep soil evenly moist and use mulch, especially to blanch the stems. Leeks also benefit from bi-monthly or monthly applications of a fertilizer, following the amounts for the type you purchase for vegetable nutrition.

Leeks, like parsnips, are extremely hardy in the cold and will remain usable well into the spring. When planted in the spring, leeks will be ready for harvest during early summer. Leeks are mature when they are approximately 24 inches tall or about ¾ to 1 inch in diameter, which can be about 70 to 110 days from germination. Long-season leeks can be harvested after the first frost and throughout the fall and winter, while short-season leeks should be harvested during the summer. To harvest properly, loosen the soil around the leek and lift it from the ground. Leeks can be left in the ground and harvested as needed where winters stay above 10°F.

# Cooking Tips and Recipes

Before preparing leeks, clean them thoroughly to remove any soil that may have gotten caught within the overlapping layers of this root vegetable. First, trim the rootlets and a portion of the green tops and remove the outer layer. For all preparations except cutting into cross-sections, make a lengthwise incision to the centerline, fold it open, and run the leek under cool water. If your recipe calls for cross-sections, first cut the leek into the desired pieces, then place them in a colander and run under cool water.

You can add finely chopped leeks to salads or make vichyssoise, a cold soup made from pureed cooked leeks and potatoes. You can also add leeks to broths and stews for extra flavoring, or add sliced leeks to your favorite omelet or frittata recipe.

Cooking time will vary according to the leek's diameter and age. Avoid overcooking, which makes them tough. Leeks have acquired fame in soups and stews, but exhibit their versatility served au gratin, creamed, or sautéed alone or with other fresh vegetables.

## COOKED LEEKS

*You can add wine, herbs, or cream to this recipe, which makes a nice side dish to serve with roast meats.*

■ 8 leeks
Water, stock, or a mixture
4 tablespoons butter
Salt and pepper to taste
Fresh parsley, minced, for garnish

▶ Preheat oven to 350°F. Clean leeks; remove all withered leaves, and trim the roots carefully. Without cutting entirely through the root, slit the leeks lengthwise to remove all of the dirt. Trim to a total length of about 8 inches. Save the trimmings for stock.

Place the leeks in a baking dish in a single layer. Pour in enough water or stock to come about halfway up the leeks. Dot with butter and salt and pepper to taste. Set the baking dish over high heat on the stovetop and bring to a boil. Cover and braise in oven for 30 to 40 minutes or until the whites of the leeks are tender. Leave the cover slightly open to evaporate some of the liquid. Sprinkle with butter or minced parsley and serve.

## LEEKS IN WHITE SAUCE

■ 2 to 3 leeks
2 tablespoons butter

1 1/2 to 2 tablespoons flour
About 1 cup milk
Salt and pepper

▶ Wash leeks and remove roots
and some of the green ends. Cut
into slices about 2 to 3 inches long.
Cook in boiling, salted water until
soft but firm. Drain and place in
serving bowl.

While the leeks are cooking,
make white sauce by melting butter
in a saucepan over moderate heat.
Whisk in flour and stir briskly over
the heat till the sauce thickens,
adding up to 1 cup of milk slowly
and stirring continuously with a
whisk so no lumps form; stir until
the sauce begins to boil. Add salt
and pepper to taste. Remove from
heat and pour over leeks. Keep
warm till ready to serve.

## LEEKS VINAIGRETTE

*Here's another taste treat you can
make with just a few leeks.*

■ 3 to 4 leeks
1 teaspoon French mustard
1 tablespoon wine vinegar
1/4 cup olive oil
1 garlic clove crushed with 1 teaspoon salt
Chopped herbs—parsley, chives,.
tarragon, oregano to taste
Freshly ground pepper

▶ Trim the leeks and cut them
lengthwise almost to the root end.
Wash thoroughly, then tie them
together with string. Drop into
boiling, salted water and simmer
till tender, about 10 to 12 minutes.
Drain. Mix mustard, garlic and salt,
pepper, and vinegar. Add the oil
gradually, stirring until the ingredients are well blended. Stir in the
chopped herbs. Marinate leeks in
the dressing for at least 2 hours and
chill before serving.

## BRAISED LEEKS

*This is a flavorful and easy to pre-
pare treat. Serve warm on toast or
chilled with French dressing as an
hors d'oeuvre.*

■ 3 to 4 leeks
2 tablespoons butter
1 small white onion, minced
2 cups broth
Salt and pepper

▶ Cut the tops off the leeks and
remove the roots. Cut stalks in half
lengthwise and wash. Tie leeks
with string to keep them together.
Heat butter in a pan over low heat,
adding the onion. Sauté gently until
light brown. Add the leeks, broth,
salt, and pepper. Cover and simmer
until leeks are tender, about 10 to 15
minutes.

## LEEK AND POTATO SOUP (VICHYSSOISE)

*This is one of our favorite recipes. It combines the flavor of leeks with potatoes, another nutritious food that fed the Irish well for generations, as my wife reminds me, remembering her family roots.*

■ 1 bunch leeks
3 medium potatoes, peeled
1 to 2 tablespoons butter
4 cups chicken stock or broth made from bouillon cubes
1/4 to 1/2 pint cream
Salt and pepper
Chopped chives, parsley, or tarragon

▶ Wash leeks and slice white parts only. Peel and slice the potatoes. Melt the butter in a pan, add the leeks and potatoes, and cook very slowly for 5 to 10 minutes without browning. Add stock, bring to a boil, cover, and simmer gently for 30 minutes till vegetables are very soft. Blend in food processor until smooth. Cool, then mix in the cream and season to taste. Chill. Sprinkle with chives, parsley, or tarragon before serving.

## SWENSON LEEK SOUP

*Makes 6 servings.*

■ 4 cups sliced leeks
3 cups peeled, diced potatoes
6 cups chicken broth
1 cup whipping cream
3 tablespoons sherry
Chives

▶ Combine the first 3 ingredients. Cook 20 minutes. Blend in a blender or food processor. Add the rest and serve hot or cold.

# Lentils

Lentils were a staple food in the time of Jesus. The lentil plant originated in the Near East and has been part of the human diet since Neolithic times, as its name (*Lens culinaris*) indicates. Scientists say it was one of the first crops domesticated in the Near East. Having 25 percent protein, lentils are the vegetable with the highest level of protein other than soybeans. For this reason they

are a very important part of the diet in many parts of the world. There are numerous types of lentils with colors ranging from yellow to red-orange to green, brown, and black as well as small and large varieties. Lentils are still widely used throughout the Mediterranean regions and the Middle East.

Lentils didn't receive the same number of mentions as other grains in the Bible, but they were one of the essential foods, fairly easily grown and basic to a balanced diet in the time that Jesus lived and taught.

---

# Focus on Scripture

## Lentils

Genesis 25:34—"And Jacob gave Esau bread and stew of lentils; then he ate and drank, arose, and went his way. Thus Esau despised his birthright."

2 Samuel 17:28—"[They] brought beds and basins, earthen vessels and wheat, barley and flour, parched grain and beans, lentils and parched seeds . . ."

2 Samuel 23:11—"And after him was Shammah the son of Agee the Hararite. The Philistines had gathered together into a troop where there was a piece of ground full of lentils. So the people fled from the Philistines."

Ezekiel 4:9—"Also take for yourself wheat, barley, beans, lentils, millet, and spelt; put them into one vessel, and make bread of them for yourself. During the number of days that you lie on your side, three hundred and ninety days, you shall eat it."

---

## History and Nutrition Highlights

Lentils are botanically known as *Lens culinaris esculenta*. They have been [repeats introduction]found on archaeological digs dating back 8,000 years. The word "lentils" comes from the Latin *lens,* and the seeds of this bean cousin are shaped like the double convex optic lens, which actually gained its name from the lentil.

Lentils grow two to a pod and are dried after harvesting. There are hundreds of varieties, with as many as fifty or more cultivated for food, all with their own distinctive flavor, ranging from nutty to slightly peppery.

Archaeologists have found lentil seeds dating to the Bronze Age. Lentils are grown commercially in most European countries, Asia, North Africa, and North America. Small lentils tend to be more flavorful and are preferred in the Middle East. Although lentils are one of the most ancient of all cultivated foods, they have not been popular in America until recently.

Lentils are believed to have originated in central Asia. For millennia lentils have been favored with barley and wheat as three foods that originated in the same regions and spread throughout Africa and Europe during migrations of various tribes. Lentils have been found in Egyptian tombs dating from 2400 B.C. The Egyptians were thought to have introduced the lentil to the Greeks and Romans. Hippocrates wrote about them in ancient Greece. Even farther back in time, lentils were probably cultivated in the gardens of Babylon in 800 B.C. Lentils were mentioned in the Bible both as the item that Jacob traded to Esau for his birthright and as a part of a bread that was made during the Babylonian captivity of the Jewish people.

Lentils are full of nutrients, fiber, complex carbohydrates, and folic acid, and are a low-calorie, low-fat, and cholesterol-free food. Lentils' high protein content is more easily digested than that of larger beans. Lentils are also an important source of iron. Eating lentils with foods rich in vitamin C, such as tomatoes, green peppers, broccoli, and citrus fruits or juices, helps the body absorb iron more efficiently. According to nutrition experts, the soluble fiber in lentils aids the digestive system. This type of fiber also decreases serum glucose and cholesterol, and decreases insulin requirements for people with diabetes. A study published in the *Archives of Internal Medicine* confirms that eating high fiber foods, such as lentils, helps prevent heart disease.

Lentils are relatively tolerant to drought and are grown throughout the world. About half of the worldwide production of lentils today is in India, and Canada is the largest export producer of lentils in the world, with Saskatchewan the most important producing region.

# Growing and Harvesting Tips

Lentils are a brushy, easily grown annual plant of the legume family, taking the same time as peas to mature. Different varieties typically grow from 1 to 2 1/2 feet in height. Lentil plants are short with finely divided leaves, flowers of red, pink, purple, or white, and carry pods that each contain two seeds. Green varieties have green or tan seed coats and green cotyledons. Red lentils have tan or pink seed coats, and pink or red cotyledons.

The three most common types of lentils for growing and cooking are brown, red, and green. Brown lentils, also called Egyptian lentils, are milder in flavor and hold their shape well after cooking. Red lentils are less common and have a slightly sweeter taste than brown ones. Green lentils, also known as French lentils, are the finest but most expensive lentils. They are the richest tasting and remain quite firm after cooking, which makes them excellent for salads. Another interesting lentil is Beluga, which is black; when cooked they glisten, looking like beluga caviar.

Here are some recommended varieties from a reliable supplier: Black Beluga matures in 110 days and is a very rare and wonderful lentil from Asia, known for its deep, shiny black color and exceptional flavor. They are used to make a beautiful black lentil soup. These lentils are 1/2 centimeter wide with a mild, earthly flavor and soft texture. Canary matures in 96 days and is a medium-sized lentil for cooking, yellow in color and about 1/2 to 3/4 centimeter wide with a mild flavor and fine texture. French Green, with a 105-day maturity, is a very rare heirloom and a most unusual one at that, mottled green with green and black highlights, very delicious and beautiful. Finally, Red Chief, maturing at 110 days, is a medium-sized lentil for cooking, deep orange to red in color and about 1/2 to 3/4 centimeter wide with a mild, earthly flavor and soft texture. They hold their shape well when cooked. You can contact Victory Seed Company at P.O. Box 192, Molalla, OR 97038 or email at info@victoryseeds.com as a key source for lentils and other biblical foods (including fava beans).

Plant lentils early in the growing season, when you'd plant green peas. You should sow as early in spring as the soil can be worked, while it is still moist but warm enough to encourage germination.

Although lentils prefer a sandy soil in a warm, sunny, sheltered position, many believe that the plant produces the most seeds when grown on poorer soils. Some varieties are quite hardy, surviving the cooler growing conditions, so they are worth a test in your garden as you experiment with biblical plants to grow and eat.

Sow seeds 1 to 1 1/2 inches deep in moist soil. Seeding depth can be increased in soils with a low water-holding capacity. Once established, lentils grow under quite dry conditions. Young immature pods may be used as a vegetable.

Lentils should be grown and harvested much like dry beans except that harvest is typically mid-July when the seeds mature and the soil dries. There must be a period of two to three weeks of sunny, dry weather at harvest time to dry the pods. Because dry soil is a requirement, plan to stop watering several weeks before harvest, usually in July for most varieties. To shell the mature dry seeds, remove from pods as you do with other types of beans and store in glass jars or other containers you can seal from moisture

## Cooking Tips and Recipes

Whether you grow lentils for your biblical garden explorations or prefer to buy them, they are easy to prepare. There is no need to soak lentils; they have a short cooking time, especially for small varieties with the husk removed, such as the red lentil. Lentils are used throughout Europe to prepare an inexpensive and nutritious soup, often combined with some form of pork. Cooking time is similar to rice. Sort them, removing any debris, then rinse and bring to a boil, using 3 cups of liquid for each 1 cup of lentils. Turn down the heat to simmer and cover. Green lentils usually take 30 minutes to cook, while red ones require 20 minutes. Test tenderness as you try different types. Place in containers, label, date, and refrigerate or freeze to use in recipes.

Lentils readily absorb a variety of different flavors from other foods and seasonings, are high in nutritional value, and are available throughout the year. If you prefer not to grow lentils, they are generally available in prepackaged containers as well as bulk bins at health food stores and in supermarkets. Canned lentils also can be found in some grocery stores and most natural foods markets. Unlike many canned vegetables, which lose much of their nutritional value, there is little difference in the nutritional value of canned lentils and those you cook yourself.

Store dry lentils in an airtight container in a cool, dry, and dark place, and they will keep for up to 12 months. After long storage, their color may fade slightly but taste will not be noticeably altered. Cooked lentils will keep fresh in the refrigerator for about three days if placed in a covered container.

Combine cooked lentils with chopped sweet peppers to make a delicious cold salad and season with your favorite herbs and spices. Or, combine cooked lentils, small broccoli florets, and leeks, and add olive oil mixed with garlic and ginger.

## SIMPLE LENTIL SALAD

*A tasty salad that features several biblical foods.*

*Makes 4 to 6 servings.*

■ 3 cups brown lentils
1 large onion stuck with 2 cloves
2 garlic cloves, peeled
1 medium carrot, cut into 4 pieces
1 celery stalk, cut into 4 pieces
1 bay leaf
6 small green onions thinly sliced
French dressing
Salt
Freshly ground pepper
Tomato wedges
1/4 cup minced parsley

▶ Put lentils in large saucepan, add water to cover plus 3 inches, and bring to boiling point. Lower heat to very low. Add the onion, garlic, carrot, celery, and bay leaves. Simmer covered for about 30 minutes or until the lentils are tender but not mushy. Be certain they retain their shape. Drain and remove the vegetables. Turn lentils into a bowl while hot. Add green onions and the French dressing.

Mix well. Season with salt and pepper to taste. Cool lentils, then cover the bowl and refrigerate for 2 hours to blend the flavors. Serve garnished with tomato wedges and parsley.

## HEARTY ITALIAN LENTIL STEW

*This dish can be made as a soup or stew, depending on the amount of water added. Extra then can be saved in the refrigerator for enjoyment over the next week or two. We also save surplus in quart freezer containers.*

*Makes 8 servings if served as a stew, somewhat more if thinned to a soup.*

■ 1 tablespoon extra-virgin olive oil
1 medium carrot, finely chopped (about 1 cup)
1 small onion, finely chopped (about 1 cup)
1 cup diced fennel
1 1/2 cups green or small brown lentils
1/2 cup finely chopped flat-leaf parsley
1/2 teaspoon basil
1/2 teaspoon marjoram

1/2 to 1 teaspoon chopped dried chives
Salt and freshly ground black pepper, to taste
1/3 cup small pasta (small elbows or bowties)

▶ In a small Dutch oven or 3-quart saucepan, heat oil over medium-high heat. Stir in the carrot, onion, and fennel and cook 3 minutes, stirring occasionally to soften vegetables slightly. Add the lentils and 6 cups water. Then, stir in parsley, basil, marjoram, and chives and bring to a boil. Reduce heat and simmer uncovered for 30 minutes. Then, stir in the salt, pepper, and pasta. Cook until pasta is done and the lentils are soft, about 10 to 15 minutes. Add water, stirring gradually until mixture is desired consistency. Adjust seasonings if desired.

## HIGH-FIBER LENTIL CHICKEN SALAD

*Having raised backyard chickens for years, this is a favored recipe.*

*Makes 8 1-cup servings.*

■ 2/3 cup green or brown lentils
1 1/2 cups water
1/4 cup light mayonnaise
2 tablespoons green onions, chopped
1/8 teaspoon hot red pepper sauce

1 cup cooked chicken, diced
1/2 cup celery, diced
1/2 cup cucumber, diced
1/4 cup green bell pepper, diced
2 ounces chopped pimiento
4 cups mixed salad greens
1 tablespoon fresh parsley, chopped

▶ Rinse lentils in cold water and drain. Bring water to a boil in a heavy nonstick pan over medium-high heat. Reduce heat and add lentils. Cover and simmer about 20 minutes or until lentils are tender. Drain and refrigerate until cooled.

Combine next 3 ingredients in a small bowl, mixing well. Then, combine cooled lentils, chicken, and next 4 ingredients in a medium bowl. Pour in dressing and mix. Cover and refrigerate for at least 1 hour. Arrange salad greens on individual plates, top with chicken salad and sprinkle with parsley.

## LOW-FAT MINESTRONE LENTIL SOUP

*Here's a heartier soup to try for big appetites.*

*Makes 8 to 10 1-cup servings.*

■ 2 tablespoons olive oil
2 cups chopped onion
2 tablespoons tomato paste
1/4 cup chopped fresh parsley

4 cloves garlic, chopped
3 carrots, diced
1 cup celery, diced
1 cup green or brown lentils, rinsed
2 bay leaves
8 sprigs parsley and 6 sprigs fresh
thyme tied together
9 cups water or vegetable broth
2 cups cooked pasta
Salt and pepper

▶ Heat oil in a large pot over high heat. Add onion and sauté until browned, stirring frequently. Add tomato paste, chopped parsley, garlic, carrots, and celery and cook for 3 minutes. Add lentils, bay leaves, parsley and thyme sprigs, and water and bring to boil. Lower heat and simmer partially covered for 30 minutes. Season with salt and pepper. Remove bay leaves and parsley and thyme sprigs and discard. Add pasta, heat through, and serve.

# Millet

In biblical times millet was commonly used to make porridge and flatbreads. The millets are a group of cereal crops or grains that have been widely grown around the world for food for generations. The most widely cultivated species are: pearl millet, foxtail millet, proso millet (also known as common millet), broom corn millet, hog millet (or white millet), and finger millet. Millet belongs to the family Poaceae. Common millet, or proso, is classified as *Panicum miliaceum*. Pearl millet is *Pennisetum americanum*. Unlike wheat and barley, millet has lost popularity since Jesus' time. However, it's worth giving millet a try. If you can't grow it, you can find millet in health food stores and natural food aisles in supermarkets.

## Focus on Scripture

### Millet

Ezekiel 4:9—"Also take for yourself wheat, barley, beans, lentils, millet, and spelt; put them into one vessel, and make bread of them for yourself. During the number of days that you lie on your side, three hundred and ninety days, you shall eat it."

Ezekiel 27:17—"Judah and the land of Israel were your traders. They traded for your merchandise wheat of Minnith, millet, honey, oil, and balm."

# History and Nutrition Highlights

Millet is one of the world's oldest foods and perhaps the first cereal grain used by humans. Archaeologists say that broomcorn and foxtail millet were important crops beginning in the Early Neolithic period of China. Botanists tell us that millet was the common grain in China before rice became popular. Some of the earliest evidence of millet cultivation in China was found dating to 7000 to 5000 B.C. in pit-houses, storage pits, and pottery remnants, including a 4,000-year-old well-preserved bowl containing foxtail millet and broomcorn millet. We also know that millet was consumed in northern Europe at least since the Iron Age and archeologists have found that the plant was grown by lake dwellers of Switzerland during the Stone Age.

In Western India, millet flour has been used with sorghum flour for hundreds of years to make flat bread, a local staple which was also common in the Holy Land in Jesus' time. The Hunzas, who live in remote Himalayan mountain foothills, are renowned for their longevity, which health experts believe is due in part to millet as a staple in their diet. The protein content in millet is very close to that of wheat; both provide about 10% protein by weight. Millet is rich in many beneficial nutrients, including fiber, calcium and B vitamins, especially niacin, B6, folacin, thiamin, and riboflavin. According to nutritionists, it is particularly high in the minerals iron, magnesium, phosphorous, and potassium. It contains no gluten, so it cannot rise. However, when combined with wheat it can be used for raised bread. Alone, it is suited for flatbread.

This tiny grain grows in ears or heads atop stalks that range from 1 to 10 feet high. It is an important food staple in most of the former Soviet republics, western Africa, and Asia. Because it ripens in 60 to 80 days, grows in less-fertile soils, and resists drought, it is widely cultivated in poorer agricultural areas. An estimated 64 million acres of pearl millet is grown in Africa and India, equivalent in acreage to the total U.S. corn crop. Millet usually contains less protein than wheat or rye but more protein than rice. It is highly nutritious and is considered one of the most digestible grains available. It has a sweet, nut-like flavor.

Millet was introduced to the U.S. circa 1875 and was grown and consumed like corn by the early colonists. Although most people know this grain as bird feed, in recent years it has begun to make a comeback in kitchens of the Western world. Perhaps you can recapture this tasty grain of biblical heritage.

## Growing and Harvesting Tips

Millet seeds look like tiny, pale yellow beads. Millet has a short growing season and can develop from a planted seed to a mature, ready to harvest plant in as little as 65 days. Millet grows well on poorly drained and dry soils and fits well in hot climates with short rainfall periods and cool climates with brief warm summers. Millet is better adapted to dry, infertile soils than most other crops. Most millet has strong, deep rooting systems and short life cycles and can grow well and rapidly when moisture is available.

Pearl millet grows similarly to sorghum. As a warm season crop it should be planted in early summer when soils have warmed up to at least 65°F. Best planting time is early June. Seeding depth should be 1/2- to 1-inch deep. Pearl millet responds well to good soil fertility, but does not have a high nutrient demand.

Flowers and seeds grow in a spike at the end of the stem, somewhat like a cattail head. Plants mature 4 to 5 feet tall, although height can vary from 3 to 6 feet depending on variety and growing conditions. Grain heads will mature a few weeks prior to the plant leaves drying, so when planted around June 1 you can plan to harvest in late September.

Like any grain crop, pearl millet will yield best in fertile, well-drained soils. However, it also performs relatively well on sandy soils under acidic soil conditions and when soil moisture and soil fertility are low. Pearl millet appears to have relatively fast root development, sending extensive roots both laterally and downward into the soil to take advantage of available moisture and nutrients. The crop does best when there are plenty of hot days.

Millet also attracts wild songbirds including gold finches and juncos. Plants will continue to stand after a frost, so a delayed harvest is possible, but it is best to harvest as soon after seed maturity as plant dry down allows to avoid loss to birds.

The seed hulls are of different colors depending on variety. Seed heads are on a spike-like panicle 6 to 14 inches long and are extremely attractive.

Because of a hard, indigestible hull, the grain must be hulled before it can be used for human consumption. Hulling does not affect the nutrient value because the germ stays intact through this process. Once out of the hull, millet grains look like tiny, pale yellow beads.

# Cooking Tips and Recipes

There are many ways to prepare millet. A good general guideline is to use 3 parts water and 1 part grain. Simply add grain to boiling water and simmer covered for approximately 30 minutes or until water is completely absorbed, as you do with rice. Remove from heat and let steam covered for 10 more minutes. Note: millet has fluffier texture when less water is used and denser when cooked with extra water. You can enhance the flavor by lightly roasting grains in a dry pan 3 to 4 minutes before cooking. Presoaking millet will shorten cooking time by 5 to 10 minutes.

Millet is delicious as a cooked cereal and in casseroles, breads, soups, and stews. If you like salads, try sprouting millet. In a tightly sealed glass container millet can be stored for a year.

## BLACK BEAN AND MILLET SALAD

*As a lover of black beans, I like to experiment with them in a variety of recipes. This is a simple and delicious dish, perfect for a light summer dinner.*

*4 to 5 servings*

- 1 cup millet, uncooked
3 cups water
2 cups black beans, cooked
2 large tomatoes, chopped
1 medium onion, (or substitute green onions), chopped
1 medium cucumber
Dressing

1/3 cup water
3 tablespoons lemon juice
1 tablespoon balsamic vinegar
2 teaspoons garlic, minced
1 teaspoon sea salt
1/2 teaspoon allspice
1/4 teaspoon black pepper
1 teaspoon cumin

▶ Cook millet in 3 cups of water until water is absorbed, about 30 minutes. Then fluff with fork and let cool. In a large bowl, combine millet, black beans, tomatoes, and onion. Peel several strips of skin from the cucumber, remove seeds, and cut into 1/2-inch slices. Add cucumber to the salad. Mix all dressing ingredients and pour over the salad. Toss to blend well. Cover and refrigerate until the salad is well chilled, then serve on lettuce leaves or stuff into pita bread.

## MILLET MUFFINS

***Start the day with these tasty muffins.***

*Makes 12 muffins.*

■ 1 1/2 cups millet flour
1/2 cup soy flour

1 tablespoon baking powder
1/4 teaspoon orange flavoring
1 cup water or orange juice
1/4 cup vegetable oil
1/4 cups honey

▶ Combine all dry ingredients in a medium bowl. Next, mix all the liquid ingredients together and then add to dry ingredients. Put mixture in well-oiled muffin tins. Bake at 375°F for 15 to 20 minutes or until done.

# Mustard

Mustard, including mustard greens, leaf mustard, and white mustard, is a quick-to-mature, easy-to-grow, cool-season vegetable for greens or salads. Curiously, this popular topping for America's favorite food, the hot dog, has a long and deeply rooted history. Prepared mustard dates back thousands of years to the early Romans, who used to grind mustard seeds and mix them with wine into a paste not much different from the prepared mustards we know today.

Mustard is a member of the Brassica family of plants, which bears tiny, round, edible seeds as well as tasty leaves. Our word mustard comes from the Middle English *mustarde*, meaning condiment; which in turn comes from the Old French *mostarde*. *Mosto* derives from

the Latin *mustum*, the word for grape must, or young, unfermented wine. That was the liquid mixed with ground mustard seed by French monks who made the condiment.

From scriptures we understand even more about the significance of the mustard seed and plant. The mustard seed exemplifies something that is small and insignificant, but which, when planted, grows in strength and power.

# Focus on Scripture

## Mustard

Matthew 13:31—"Another parable put he forth unto them, saying, The kingdom of heaven is like to a grain of mustard seed, which a man took, and sowed in his field . . ."

Matthew 17:20—"And Jesus said unto them, Because of your unbelief: for verily I say unto you, If ye have faith as a grain of mustard seed, ye shall say unto this mountain, Remove hence to yonder place; and it shall remove; and nothing shall be impossible unto you."

Mark 4:31—"It is like a grain of mustard seed, which, when it is sown in the earth, is less than all the seeds that be in the earth . . ."

Luke 13:19—"It is like a grain of mustard seed, which a man took, and cast into his garden; and it grew, and waxed a great tree; and the fowls of the air lodged in the branches of it."

Luke 17:6—"And the Lord said, If ye had faith as a grain of mustard seed, ye might say unto this sycamore tree, Be thou plucked up by the root, and be thou planted in the sea; and it should obey you . . ."

## History and Nutrition Highlights

A few amusing tidbits about this spicy plant . . . You probably have heard that losers and quitters can't cut the mustard, i.e., live up to the challenge.

You may not have heard Pliny the Elder's sage wisdom: "With a few spoonfuls of mustard, a cold and lazy woman can become an ideal wife." Perhaps the reason ballpark mustard is so popular is because pitchers apply mustard to their fastballs to get those strike-outs. The disabling and even lethal chemical weapon known as mustard gas is a synthetic copy based on the volatile nature of mustard oils.

Mustard is a Northern Hemisphere plant and its seeds have been found in Stone Age settlements. Cultivated for thousands of years, mustard was the primary spice known to Europeans and was used long before pepper, which originated in India. Once trade routes were established, ancient people from India to Egypt to Rome chewed mustard seeds with their meat for seasoning.

Mustard was part of the oldest Mediterranean cultures. At first, mustard was considered primarily a medicinal plant rather than a culinary one. In the sixth century B.C., Greek scientist Pythagoras used mustard as a remedy for scorpion stings. One hundred years later, Hippocrates used mustard in a variety of medicines and poultices.

By the first century A.D. mustard was on nearly every Roman table, prized for the way it enhanced fish and meats. The greatest philosophers of the era attributed it with an ability to enflame the senses, which won mustard acclaim. This belief survived for centuries, and was still current much later in Denmark. Apothecaries made a fortune by preparing a concoction made of mustard seeds, ginger, and mint, which love-starved husbands gave to their wives in the hope of making them more receptive to their amorous advances.

Mustard's popularity declined by the early eighteenth century. The House of Maille, founded in 1747, was doing well in Paris, but general interest had ebbed. However, the market was revived, and the city of Dijon secured its place in history as the capital of mustard when, in 1856, Burgundian Jean Naigeon substituted verjuice for the vinegar in prepared mustard. The use of verjuice resulted in a mustard that was less acidic than France had tasted before, and the smooth, suave condiment we call Dijon assumed its place in history.

Pope John XXII was so fond of mustard that he created a new Vatican position, *grand moutardier du pape*, which translates to "mustard-maker to the pope."

In 1866, Jeremiah Colman, founder of Colman's Mustard of England, was appointed as mustard-maker to Queen Victoria. Colman perfected the technique of grinding mustard seeds into a fine powder without creating the heat which brings out the oil. The oil must not be exposed or the flavor will evaporate with the oil.

Mustard is a member of the cruciferous vegetable family. It shares the same cancer-preventing benefits of broccoli, cabbage, and kale.

Because it was a basic flavoring, ancient texts from Roman writers as well as the Scriptures mention mustard. It is probably more popular in the Holy Land and Mediterranean area today than in other parts of the world. No doubt it enjoyed popularity during Jesus' time.

# Growing Tips

There are about 40 species of mustard plant. The ones used to make the commercial mustard products are the black, brown, and white mustards. White mustard, which originated in the Mediterranean basin, is what we know as the bright yellow hot dog mustard. Brown mustard originated in the Himalayas and is the basic Chinese restaurant mustard. Black mustard is popular in the Middle East and Asia Minor, where it originated. Some of the best mustard varieties today include Florida Broadleaf; with 45 days to harvest it has large leaves and is slow to bolt. Another good variety is Green Wave, with dark green, heavily curled leaves; it does well in warm temperatures and is very slow to bolt.

Mustard is a cool-season vegetable that naturally flowers during the long, warm days of summer. Plant early in the spring, about 3 weeks before the frost-free date, and again 3 weeks later. You should also plant from midsummer on for a fall harvest. Fall plantings are usually of higher quality because they mature under cooler conditions in most locations. Sow seeds 1/3 to 1/2 inch deep and thin seedlings to 3 to 5 inches apart. Thinnings can be eaten. Be aware that mustard grows rapidly and without stopping, so fertilize, weed, and water during dry periods. Pull and compost when hot weather arrives and preferably before flower stalks develop.

# Cooking Tips and Recipes

It really isn't worthwhile to try growing enough mustard plants to produce sufficient seeds to make your own mustard. However, mustard greens have been eaten since biblical times and are a prized food in many parts of the United States. Young leaves add zest and variety to salads and can be used as a flavorful garnish for meat dishes or cheese platters.

Mustard greens can be eaten raw or cooked. The whole plant can be cut at once or individual outer leaves can be picked for a cut-and-come-again harvest. The leaf texture becomes tough and the flavor strong in summer. The young leaves, four to five inches long, are mild-flavored and can be eaten raw in salads. The older leaves taste better when prepared as cooked greens. Avoid yellow, over mature mustards with seeds or yellow flowers attached.

Freezing is the best way to preserve an overabundance of mustard greens. Like other vegetables, mustard greens must be blanched before freezing. To do so, simply dip the greens in scalding water and then into an ice water bath before freezing.

## BRAISED MUSTARD GREENS WITH SMOKED TURKEY

*This traditional southern American preparation of mustard greens involves long, slow cooking with salt pork, bacon ends, or ham hocks. This cooking method is high in both salt and fat. Tradition is difficult to break; however, similar results can be achieved by substituting smoked turkey parts and using garlic-infused oil rather than bacon fat. The following recipe has been modified for your health in the twenty-first century.*

*Makes 6 servings.*

■ 1 smoked turkey leg or wing
Water
3 pounds young mustard greens
2 tablespoons olive oil
2 cloves garlic
1 teaspoon crushed red pepper flakes (optional)
1/2 cup chopped onions

▶ In a large pot, cover the smoked turkey leg with water and bring to a boil. Boil for about five minutes, pour off the water, cover with fresh water, and continue boiling until the turkey leg is tender (about one hour). Pierce with a fork to test for doneness. When cool, remove meat from the bone and chop, if desired, or leave whole. Set aside.

While the turkey is cooking, prepare the mustard greens.

Pick through the greens, removing yellow, wilted greens and large tough stems and veins. Fill the sink with cool water and wash greens in three changes of water. Fresh greens hold soil and dirt. Swishing greens through the cold water removes the clinging grit. Drain.

While the greens drain, place a large Dutch oven over medium heat. Add the olive oil. When the oil is hot (not smoking), add the garlic, red pepper flakes, and chopped onions. Stir and cook for about 30 seconds. Add 2 cups water or the cooking liquid from the turkey leg. Bring to a boil. Add the washed greens to the boiling pot, one handful at a time. Use a long-handled fork to push the greens down into the cooking water. If all the greens do not fit into the pot, cover for 2 to 3 minutes—the greens will cook down and shrink. Continue adding handfuls of greens until all have been added to the pot. Cook until the greens are tender. Young mustard greens will cook in about 20 minutes. Older, tougher greens will take longer, up to 45 minutes.

Sample the greens after 20 minutes. If they are tender, add the chopped smoked turkey. Continue cooking until the turkey is heated, about 10 minutes. Taste, adjust seasoning, and serve.

# Onions

"I will not move my army without onions!"—Gen. Ulysses S. Grant
"It's hard to imagine civilization without onions."—Julia Child
"Onions can make ev'n heirs and widows weep"—Benjamin Franklin

Onions are one of the world's most versatile vegetables. History records them far back in time and although they only show up in one biblical passage they have become a staple in many different cuisines. Ancient legends say the workers who built the pyramids were fed with vast quantities of onions.

Onions can be eaten raw in salads, cooked, or pickled in a variety of ways, and are used as a flavoring or seasoning. Dehydrated onion products provide popular flavorings for soups and stews.

## Focus on Scripture

### Onions

Numbers 11:5–6—"We remember the fish we ate in Egypt for nothing, the cucumbers, the melons, the leeks, the onions and the garlic; but now our strength is dried up, and there is nothing at all but this manna to look at."

# History

Bulbs from the onion family have been a food source for millennia. In Palestinian Bronze Age settlements, traces of onion remains were found alongside fig and date stones dating back to 5,000 B.C. Archaeological evidence suggests cultivation probably took place around 2,000 years later in ancient Egypt. This happened alongside the cultivation of leeks and garlic and it is likely that workers who built the pyramids were fed radishes and onions.

Egyptians worshipped onions, believing their spherical shape and concentric rings symbolized eternal life. The onion made its way to Greece where athletes ate large quantities of onion because they thought it would lighten the balance of blood. Roman gladiators were rubbed with onion juice to firm up their muscles. In the Middle Ages onions were such an important food that people would pay for their rent with onions and even give onions as gifts. Christopher Columbus introduced the onion to the New World on his 1493 expedition to Haiti.

Onions are one of the earliest crops mentioned in written text, in Numbers 11:5, where they are described as part of the Egyptian diet. Six types of onions were known at the time of Pliny the Elder's *Natural History*.

Because onions are small and their tissues leave little trace, there is no conclusive proof of their exact origin. Many archaeologists, botanists, and food historians believe onions were first grown in central Asia. Other research suggests that onions originated in Iran and West Pakistan. Ancient writings tell us that onions grew in Chinese gardens as early as 5,000 years ago. They were mentioned in some of the oldest Vedic writings from India and Sumerians were growing onions as early as 2500 B.C.

Onions were probably one of the earliest cultivated crops because they are less perishable than other foods of the time, are transportable, are easy to grow, and can be grown in a variety of soils and climates. In addition, onions prevent thirst and could be dried and preserved for later consumption when food was scarce.

# Growing and Harvesting Tips

In warm areas, onions can be planted as winter crops and are milder in taste and odor than onions planted during the summer in cooler regions. Yellow Bermuda and white Spanish onions are among the mildest cultivated onions.

Onion is the common name for any of a genus of biennial herbs of the lily family. The true onion is a bulb-bearing plant with long, hollow leaves and thickened bases. White or pink flowers borne in umbels have 6 sepals, 6 petals, 6 stamens, and a solitary. Onions can be divided into two categories: spring/summer fresh onions and fall/winter storage onions. Fresh onions are available in yellow, red, and white from March through August. With its delicate taste, the spring/summer onion is an ideal choice for salads and other fresh and lightly cooked dishes.

Fall/winter storage onions are available August through April in stores. They too are available in yellow, red, and white, and have multiple layers of thick, dark, papery skin. Storage onions have an intense flavor, higher percentage of solids, and are the best choice for savory dishes that require longer cooking times or more flavor.

Onions range in size from less than 1 inch to more than 4.5 inches in diameter. Onions are a cool-season vegetable that can be grown successfully throughout most of temperate North America from sets, transplants, or seeds. Onions start bulb formation when the day length is of the proper duration and different varieties of onions require different day lengths to initiate bulbing.

Common varieties fall into one of two classes: long-day for northern gardens and short-day for southern areas. When you shop for varieties, note that those grown in the South are not adaptable to the North and vice versa. Onions have shallow roots and can't compete with weeds and grasses.

Timely shallow hoeing and cultivation are important, especially when the onions are small. Most gardeners find mulching along rows smothers weeds well and conserves moisture.

Yes, you can grow onions from seed. There are perhaps more unique and heirloom varieties available from mail order forms as seeds. However, veteran gardeners strongly advise growing onions from sets, the tiny pre-formed onions available by mail order and at most garden centers and chains. Growing green onions from sets is probably the simplest method because you have a fairly wide choice of types and sets root quickly and begin grow-ing sturdily faster than seeds. You can also transplant young onion seedlings, which produces large, dry, attractive onions. Transplants can be purchased in bundles, usually 60 to 80 plants, from local garden stores and through seed and nursery catalogs

Be aware that sets are seldom sold under variety names, but rather by color: yellow, white, or red. Yellow sets are sometimes sold as the varieties Ebenezer or Stuttgarter. You are better assured of getting desired onion varieties by mail order. When sets arrive, divide into two sizes before plant-ing. Sets larger than a dime in diameter are best used for green onions. If allowed to grow, these sets may bolt and form flower stalks. Sets smaller than a dime in diameter produce the best bulbs for large, dry onions; and they usually do not bolt in hot weather.

When you shop, try to match varieties to their location. Long-day onions are bred for best performance in the North and short-day varieties perform best in southern locations, though short-day varieties may perform okay in the North if you plant them very early in the season.

You can plant onions as soon as the garden can be tilled in the spring, usually late March or early April in prime onion producing areas. Good fertility, adequate soil moisture, and cool temperatures aid development.

Plant the larger sets 1 inch deep and close enough to touch one another. Then harvest small young green onions before crowding becomes a prob-lem. To produce dry onions, plant smaller sets 1 inch deep, with 2 to 4 inches between sets. Allow 12 to 18 inches between rows. If sets are 2 inches apart, harvest every other plant as green onions so that remaining onions continue to grow larger.

With transplants, space seedlings 4 to 5 inches apart in the row to pro-duce large-sized bulbs or space 2 to 2 1/2 inches apart and harvest every other plant as a green onion. Allow 12 to 18 inches between rows or space onions 6 to 8 inches apart in all directions in beds. When planting transplants apply 1 cup per plant of a starter-fertilizer solution.

Harvest small green onions anytime after the tops are 6 inches tall. Remember, green onions become stronger in flavor with age and increased size. If too strong, use them for cooking. For larger type onions, pull them in the morning and allow bulbs to air dry in the garden until late afternoon. On especially hot, bright, sunny days, move onions to a shaded location and allow them to dry thoroughly. Then, before evening dew falls, place them under dry shelter on elevated slats or screens or hang them in small bunches. You may wish to braid or tie stems in bunches with string before hanging. Full air circulation for 2 to 3 weeks is necessary for complete drying and curing. Keep dry wrapper scales intact as long as possible on the bulbs because they help to preserve the onions.

# Cooking Tips and Recipes

Onions may be eaten raw, broiled, boiled, baked, creamed, steamed, fried, French fried, or pickled. They are used in soups and stews and in combination with vegetables and meats. Veteran chefs often say that onions are the single most important ingredient a cook can have on hand. If you wish to further explore the onion family you can take advantage of relatives such as chives, scallions, leeks, shallots, and garlic.

As you prepare onions a standard question arises: Why do onions make you cry? When you cut into an onion, you damage its cell walls, which releases a sulfur compound called propanethial-S-oxide into the air. This compound is converted to sulfuric acid when it comes in contact with water, which is why it stings your eyes. Chilling inactivates the propanethial-S-oxide so it does not float into the air. Thus, no tears. Therefore, to keep eyes dry when chopping onions, try chilling peeled onions in the refrigerator first. To get the onion smell off your hands, rub with lemon juice or vinegar. To freshen onion breath, chew a little parsley.

## ONION AND CELERY SEED RELISH

*Try this recipe and others from favorite cookbooks to discover the range of flavors that onions can offer.*

*Makes 3 cups.*

- 1 cup white wine vinegar or distilled white vinegar

2 tablespoons confectioners'
(powdered) sugar
2 tablespoons celery seeds
2 cups thinly sliced small onions,
no green tops
1 cup finely chopped celery
1/2 teaspoon red pepper flakes

▶ In a salad bowl, stir together
vinegar and sugar until sugar dissolves. Add celery seeds, onions,
and celery and mix well until
combined. Cover and chill several
hours or overnight. Serve very cold.
Use on sandwiches, as a side for

any meal, or mix with your favorite
lettuce salad.

## GRILLED GREEN ONIONS

Wash and trim 6 to 8 green
onions. Place on a sheet of aluminum foil. Squeeze the juice of
half a lime over onions. Sprinkle
with 1/2 teaspoon of dried thyme,
salt and pepper to taste. Seal foil
around onions. Place on the grill,
on the side away from direct heat
or over low coals. Grill for 30
minutes.

# Wheat

Wheat is well represented in the
Scriptures and was certainly used
in making the bread that Jesus and
His Disciples ate. Wheat is the
common name for cereal grasses
of a genus *triticum* of the family
*Gramineae*, cultivated for food
since prehistoric times. It is a tall,
annual plant reaching an average
height of 3 to 4 feet. Its leaves
resemble those of other grasses,
followed by slender stalks that ter-
minate in spikes, also called ears,
which contain the grain. It is the
world's most important human
food grain, primarily used to make
flour for leavened, flat, and other
breads, as well as a variety of other
nutritious food products.

# Focus on Scripture

## Wheat

Genesis 30:14—"And Reuben went in the days of wheat harvest, and found mandrakes in the field, and brought them unto his mother Leah. Then Rachel said to Leah, Give me, I pray thee, of thy son's mandrakes."

Exodus 9:32—"But the wheat and the rie were not smitten: for they were not grown up."

Exodus 34:22—"And thou shalt observe the feast of weeks, of the first fruits of wheat harvest, and the feast of ingathering at the year's end."

Numbers 18:12—"All the best of the oil, and all the best of the wine, and of the wheat, the first fruits of them which they shall offer unto the Lord, them have I given thee."

Deuteronomy 8:8—"A land of wheat, and barley, and vines, and fig trees, and pomegranates; a land of oil olive, and honey."

Deuteronomy 32:14—"Butter of kine, and milk of sheep, with fat of lambs, and rams of the breed of Bashan, and goats, with the fat of kidneys of wheat; and thou didst drink the pure blood of the grape."

Judges 6:11—"And there came an angel of the Lord, and sat under an oak which was in Ophrah, that pertained unto Joash the Abiezrite: and his son Gideon threshed wheat by the winepress, to hide it from the Midianites."

Judges 15:1—"But it came to pass within a while after, in the time of wheat harvest, that Samson visited his wife with a kid; and he said, I will go in to my wife into the chamber. But her father would not suffer him to go in."

Ruth 2:23—"So she kept fast by the maidens of Boaz to glean unto the end of barley harvest and of wheat harvest; and dwelt with her mother in law."

1 Samuel 6:13—"And they of Bethshemesh were reaping their wheat harvest in the valley: and they lifted up their eyes, and saw the ark, and rejoiced to see it."

1 Samuel 12:17—"Is it not wheat harvest to day? I will call unto the Lord, and he shall send thunder and rain; that ye may perceive and see that your wickedness is great, which ye have done in the sight of the Lord, in asking you a king."

2 Samuel 4:6—"And they came thither into the midst of the house, as though they would have fetched wheat; and they smote him under the fifth rib: and Rechab and Baanah his brother escaped."

2 Samuel 17:28—"Brought beds, and basons, and earthen vessels, and wheat, and barley, and flour, and parched corn, and beans, and lentiles, and parched pulse ..."

1 Kings 5:11—"And Solomon gave Hiram twenty thousand measures of wheat for food to his household, and twenty measures of pure oil: thus gave Solomon to Hiram year by year."

1 Chronicles 21:20—"And Ornan turned back, and saw the angel; and his four sons with him hid themselves. Now Ornan was threshing wheat."

1 Chronicles 21:23—"And Ornan said unto David, Take it to thee, and let my lord the king do that which is good in his eyes: lo, I give thee the oxen also for burnt offerings, and the threshing instruments for wood, and the wheat for the meat offering; I give it all."

2 Chronicles 2:10—"And, behold, I will give to thy servants, the hewers that cut timber, twenty thousand measures of beaten wheat, and twenty thousand measures of barley, and twenty thousand baths of wine, and twenty thousand baths of oil."

2 Chronicles 2:15—"Now therefore the wheat, and the barley, the oil, and the wine, which my lord hath spoken of, let him send unto his servants ..."

2 Chronicles 27:5—"He fought also with the king of the Ammonites, and prevailed against them. And the children of Ammon gave him the same year an hundred talents of silver, and ten thousand measures of

wheat, and ten thousand of barley. So much did the children of Ammon pay unto him, both the second year, and the third."

Ezra 6:9—"And that which they have need of, both young bullocks, and rams, and lambs, for the burnt offerings of the God of heaven, wheat, salt, wine, and oil, according to the appointment of the priests which are at Jerusalem, let it be given them day by day without fail . . ."

Ezra 7:22—"Unto an hundred talents of silver, and to an hundred measures of wheat, and to an hundred baths of wine, and to an hundred baths of oil, and salt without prescribing how much."

Job 31:40—"Let thistles grow instead of wheat, and cockle instead of barley. The words of Job are ended."

Psalm 81:16—"He should have fed them also with the finest of the wheat: and with honey out of the rock should I have satisfied thee."

Psalm 147:14—"He maketh peace in thy borders, and filleth thee with the finest of the wheat."

Proverbs 27:22—"Though thou shouldest bray a fool in a mortar among wheat with a pestle, yet will not his foolishness depart from him."

Song of Solomon 7:2—"Thy navel is like a round goblet, which wanteth not liquor: thy belly is like an heap of wheat set about with lilies."

Isaiah 28:25—"When he hath made plain the face thereof, doth he not cast abroad the fitches, and scatter the cummin, and cast in the principal wheat and the appointed barley and the rie in their place?"

Jeremiah 12:13—"They have sown wheat, but shall reap thorns: they have put themselves to pain, but shall not profit: and they shall be ashamed of your revenues because of the fierce anger of the Lord."

Jeremiah 23:28—"The prophet that hath a dream, let him tell a dream; and he that hath my word, let him speak my word faithfully. What is the chaff to the wheat? saith the Lord."

Jeremiah 31:12—"Therefore they shall come and sing in the height of Zion, and shall flow together to the goodness of the Lord, for wheat, and for wine, and for oil, and for the young of the flock and of the herd: and their soul shall be as a watered garden; and they shall not sorrow any more at all."

Jeremiah 41:8—"But ten men were found among them that said unto Ishmael, Slay us not: for we have treasures in the field, of wheat, and of barley, and of oil, and of honey. So he forbare, and slew them not among their brethren."

Ezekiel 4:9—"Take thou also unto thee wheat, and barley, and beans, and lentiles, and millet, and fitches, and put them in one vessel, and make thee bread thereof, according to the number of the days that thou shalt lie upon thy side, three hundred and ninety days shalt thou eat thereof."

Ezekiel 27:17—"Judah, and the land of Israel, they were thy merchants: they traded in thy market wheat of Minnith, and Pannag, and honey, and oil, and balm."

Ezekiel 45:13—"This is the oblation that ye shall offer; the sixth part of an ephah of an homer of wheat, and ye shall give the sixth part of an ephah of an homer of barley . . ."

Joel 1:11—"Be ye ashamed, O ye husbandmen; howl, O ye vinedressers, for the wheat and for the barley; because the harvest of the field is perished."

Joel 2:24—"And the floors shall be full of wheat, and the fats shall overflow with wine and oil."

Amos 5:11—"Forasmuch therefore as your treading is upon the poor, and ye take from him burdens of wheat: ye have built houses of hewn stone, but ye shall not dwell in them; ye have planted pleasant vineyards, but ye shall not drink wine of them."

Amos 8:5—"Saying, When will the new moon be gone, that we may sell corn and the sabbath, that we may set forth wheat, making the ephah small, and the shekel great, and falsifying the balances by deceit?"

Amos 8:6—"That we may buy the poor for silver, and the needy for a pair of shoes; yea, and sell the refuse of the wheat?"

Matthew 3:12—"Whose fan is in his hand, and he will thoroughly purge his floor, and gather his wheat into the garner; but he will burn up the chaff with unquenchable fire."

Matthew 13:25—"But while men slept, his enemy came and sowed tares among the wheat, and went his way."

Matthew 13:29—"But he said, Nay; lest while ye gather up the tares, ye root up also the wheat with them."

Matthew 13:30—"Of harvest I will say to the reapers, Gather ye together first the tares, and bind them in bundles to burn them: but gather the wheat into my barn."

Luke 3:17—"Whose fan is in his hand, and he will thoroughly purge his floor, and will gather the wheat into his garner; but the chaff he will burn with fire unquenchable."

Luke 16:7—"Then said he to another, And how much owest thou? And he said, An hundred measures of wheat. And he said unto him, Take thy bill, and write fourscore."

Luke 22:31—"And the Lord said, Simon, Simon, behold, Satan hath desired to have you, that he may sift you as wheat . . ."

John 12:24—"Verily, verily, I say unto you, Except a corn of wheat fall into the ground and die, it abideth alone: but if it die, it bringeth forth much fruit."

Acts 27:38—"And when they had eaten enough, they lightened the ship, and cast out the wheat into the sea."

1 Corinthians 15:37—"And that which thou sowest, thou sowest not that body that shall be, but bare grain, it may chance of wheat, or of some other grain . . ."

Revelation 6:6—"And I heard a voice in the midst of the four beasts say, A measure of wheat for a penny, and three measures of barley for a penny; and see thou hurt not the oil and the wine."

Revelation 18:13—"And cinnamon, and odours, and ointments, and frankincense, and wine, and oil, and fine flour, and wheat, and beasts, and sheep, and horses, and chariots, and slaves, and souls of men."

Judith 2:27—"Then he went down into the plain of Damascus in the time of wheat harvest, and burnt up all their fields, and destroyed their flocks and herds, also he spoiled their cities, and utterly wasted their countries, and smote all their young men with the edge of the sword."

Judith 3:3—"Behold, our houses, and all our places, and all our fields of wheat, and flocks, and herds, and all the lodges of our tents lie before thy face; use them as it pleaseth thee."

Sirach 39:26—"The principal things for the whole use of man's life are water, fire, iron, and salt, flour of wheat, honey, milk, and the blood of the grape, and oil, and clothing."

1 Esdras 8:20—"To the sum of an hundred talents of silver, likewise also of wheat even to an hundred cors, and an hundred pieces of wine, and other things in abundance."

# History and Nutrition Highlights

Wheat originated in southwest Asia in the Fertile Crescent, also known as ancient Babylon and Mesopotamia, which is now Iraq. No doubt wheat arrived early in the Holy Land, considering the many references to this grain in the scriptures.

Wheat and barley were the first cereals known to have been domesticated. The earliest archaeological evidence for wheat cultivation comes from the Levant and Turkey. Plant scientists believe that about 10,000 years ago wild wheat was domesticated in the Fertile Crescent. Primitive relatives of present day wheat were found in Iraq dating back 9,000 years and in the Nile Valley, circa 5,000 B.C. Wheat gained fame and spread widely, reaching into Africa and India, to Europe, and eventually to China. Wheat was first grown in the United States in 1602 on an island off the Massachusetts coast. By the year 2000 world wheat production was approximately 21 billion bushels a year.

Wheat first reached North America with Spanish missions in the sixteenth century, but North America's role as a major exporter of grain dates from the colonization of the prairies in the 1870s. As grain exports from Russia ceased in the First World War, grain production in Kansas doubled. Worldwide, bread wheat has proved well adapted to modern industrial baking, and has displaced many of the other wheat, barley, and rye species that were once commonly used for bread making. The per capita consumption of wheat in the United States exceeds that of any other single food staple. Besides being a high carbohydrate food, wheat contains valuable protein, minerals, and vitamins.

Wheat is well documented in scriptural passages. Today, wheat has become one of our most popular food products. Wheat is the major ingredient in most breads, rolls, crackers, cookies, biscuits, cakes, doughnuts, muffins, pancakes, waffles, noodles, piecrusts, ice cream cones, macaroni, spaghetti, desserts, pizza, and many prepared hot and cold breakfast foods. From biblical times to our modern era, wheat is indeed a basic human food.

# Growing and Harvesting Tips

To grow wheat on cultivated garden ground is easy. Just rototill or dig the soil with a shovel and smooth it with a rake. If you are turning sod, your best bet is to till in the fall so you can plant in early spring. First lightly till the soil to prepare a granular surface. The easiest way to sow is to hand scatter or broadcast the wheat seed, throwing it out in a fan pattern. Spread a few handfuls and try to scatter seeds a few inches apart for your first planting effort. If seed you obtain from farm supply stores has been treated with chemicals to prevent diseases, wear gloves when seeding. For your first sowing, figure 1 to 2 pounds of seed for a 10 x 10 foot area. After spreading seed, rake it into the ground or do a light "tickle" with a small Mantis type tiller. As with all grains, birds will eat the seeds you don't cover with earth, but most seeds will survive to sprout and grow.

Once you seed, let nature take its course. Add water after planting and several times during summer, especially if you live in a dry area. Wheat looks like grass as it first sprouts and grows taller until it begins to develop the seed heads. Plants turn an appealing yellow gold color as seeds ripen for harvest.

Pick kernels when they have fully dried. You can use a cycle or scythe to cut your wheat or just large pruning shears. The four wild species of wheat, along with the domesticated varieties einkorn, emmer, and spelt, have hulls that enclose the grains. When threshed, the hulls are removed and grains released. Then it is ground into flour to make basic bread, an early and vital food during Jesus' time. To thresh wheat after it is cut, grasp bunches and beat it on a clean sheet to release the grains from the heads. You can also use a flail of willow or similar tree branches to beat the wheat and loosen the grains. Store dried grains in glass jars until you wish to use them.

A new fad sprouting across America is to use wheat grass in juices, smoothies, or baked goods. All you need to grow this healthy treat is a container, soil, and wheat seeds. Fill it up with good potting mix and moisten the soil. Add wheat seed, found at natural food stores. Spread seeds rather thickly. Cover the seed with about 1/4 inch of soil, water it and keep moist with a damp towel.

Put your container in a well-lighted area and leave the damp towel on for several days to encourage germination, then remove it. When wheat grass is about 4 to 7 inches tall, it's ready to be harvested. To make juice just cut the grass at the base and put it in a wheat grass juicer. Check with your local health food store for more information about this neat project. The juice has been shown to strengthen the immune system and boost metabolism, among other health benefits.

# Cooking Tips and Recipes

## TASTY AND EASY WHEAT BISCUITS

*These biscuits are perfect for breakfast or as an accompaniment to soup or stew.*

*Makes about 12 biscuits.*

■  1 cup whole wheat flour
1/3 cup shortening
1 cup all-purpose flour
1 egg, beaten
1 tablespoon baking powder
3/4 cup 1% milk
1/2 teaspoon salt

▶  Preheat oven to 450°F. In a medium bowl, combine whole-wheat flour, all-purpose flour, baking powder, and salt. Then, use a pastry blender or fork to mix in shortening to a consistency of coarse meal. Combine egg and milk and stir into dry ingredients, mixing gently until a soft dough forms which should be slightly sticky. Next, turn dough onto a lightly floured surface and knead gently 4 to 5 times. Roll dough to 1/2-inch thickness and cut into 2 1/2 pieces. Place biscuits 1 inch apart on increased baking sheet and bake 12 minutes or until golden brown. Serve while hot.

## BASIC BREAD BOWLS

*Thanks to friends at the Kansas Wheat Commission, here's a neat idea for when the weather gets chilly. Make bread bowls, fill with hearty soup or chili, and banish winter blahs.*

*Makes 12 servings.*

- 2 1/2 cups warm water (105 to 115°F)
2 packages active dry yeast
1 tablespoon salt
1 tablespoon sugar
2 tablespoon oil
6 1/2–7 1/2 cups bread flour
1 egg, beaten
1 tablespoon milk

▶ Measure warm water into large bowl. Sprinkle in yeast; stir until dissolved. Add salt, sugar, oil, and 3 cups flour and beat until smooth. Add enough additional flour to make a stiff dough. Turn out onto lightly floured board. Knead until smooth and elastic, about 10 to 12 minutes. Place dough in bowl that has been lightly coated with nonstick spray, turning to grease top. Cover and let rise in warm place until doubled, about 1 hour. Grease outside of 12 10-ounce custard cups or oven-proof bowls of similar size. Punch dough down and divide into 12 pieces. Cover and let rest 10 minutes. Spread each piece into a circle about 6 inches in diameter. Place over outside of bowl, working dough with hands until it fits. Then, set bowls dough-side up on a baking sheet coated with nonstick spray. Cover with plastic wrap. Let rise in warm place until doubled, about 30 minutes.

Combine egg and milk and gently brush mixture on dough. Bake at 400°F for 15 minutes, until golden brown. Use potholders to remove the bowls. Set bread bowls open side up on baking pan; bake 5 minutes.

If you prefer larger bowls, use oven-proof bowls that are approximately 6 inches in diameter. Divide dough into 6 portions. A 1-pound loaf will make 2 large or 4 small bowls.

## HONEY BREAD

*This slightly sweet whole-some bread is delicious toasted with butter and makes great sandwiches.*

*Makes two loaves.*

- 1/2 cup warm water 1 (10 to 115°F)
4 1/2 teaspoons yeast (2 packages)
2 cups fat-free milk
1/4 cup margarine
1/3 cup honey
1/4 cup brown sugar
2 1/2 teaspoons salt
1/2 cup wheat germ, optional
3 cups whole wheat flour, divided
4 to 4 1/2 cups bread flour, divided

▶ Preheat oven to 375°F. In a large mixing bowl, dissolve yeast in warm water and let stand 10 minutes. Warm milk to 110 to 115°F. Stir in margarine, honey, brown sugar and salt and cool to lukewarm. Add milk mixture to yeast; add wheat germ, wheat gluten, 2 cups whole-wheat flour, and 3 cups bread flour. Beat with an electric mixer about 3 minutes. Stir in remaining cup whole-wheat flour and additional bread flour as needed to make a stiff dough. Place dough on a floured board and knead for 10 minutes or until dough is slightly sticky to the touch. Place dough in bowl coated with non-stick spray, turning once to coat the top. Cover and let rise in warm place, free from draft, until doubled in size, about 75 minutes.

Punch down and let dough rest for 10 minutes. Divide into 2 portions. Shape each portion into a loaf. With a rolling pin, roll each portion into a 9 × 14-inch rectangle. Starting at short end, roll dough tightly; pinch dough to seal ends. Place loaf in a 9 × 5-inch pan coated with non-stick spray. Cover and let rise in warm place until doubled, about 1 hour. Bake for 35 minutes or until loaf sounds hollow when tapped with fingers. To prevent a dark crust cover loaf the last 15 minutes. Remove from pans and brush with butter. Cool thoroughly before storing.

## WHOLE WHEAT MUFFINS

*Here's a time honored basic recipe.*

*Makes about 12 medium-size muffins.*

- 1/2 cup margarine or butter
1/2 cup granulated sugar
1/2 cup light brown sugar
1 teaspoon baking soda
1 egg
1/4 teaspoon vanilla
1 cup milk, 2%
2 cups whole wheat flour

▶ Preheat oven to 400°F. Have ingredients at room temperature. Line the muffin tin using paper baking cups or use cooking spray to coat the bottom of the muffin tin. With electric mixer, cream margarine, granulated sugar, brown sugar, and baking soda together, scraping bowl with spatula. In small bowl, beat together the egg and vanilla with a fork and add to creamed mixture. Beat until light and fluffy. Add the milk to the creamed mixture. Gradually add the whole-wheat flour and lightly stir the ingredients together so dry ingredients are barely moistened. Over-mixing will make muffins tough with tunnels. Fill muffin tins 2/3 full and bake 15 to 17 minutes or until browned and done. Remove from muffin tin and cool on wire rack.

# Chapter 4

# Fruits and Nuts of the Holy Land

## Almonds

**A** large, nut-bearing tree, the almond is celebrated as the first tree to bloom in the spring with its appealing white or pink blossoms. Jacob sent almonds as one of the best fruits of the land to satisfy the Egyptian ruler, as noted in Genesis 43:11. The bowls for the tabernacle had almond-shaped decorations according to Exodus 25:33–34.

Almonds trace their roots back to western Asia, where written records reveal the tree was valued for its nuts well before Jesus' time. Almonds were a prized ingredient in breads served to Egypt's pharaohs. Explorers ate almonds while traveling the Silk Road between Asia and the Mediterranean and transplanted the trees around the Mediterranean, especially in Spain and Italy. Almonds are the most widely-grown and eaten tree nut in the world today. Not only are they tasty, but they are also very nutritious.

# Focus on Scripture

## Almonds

Genesis 43:11—"And their father Israel said unto them, If it must be so now, do this; take of the best fruits in the land in your vessels, and carry down the man a present, a little balm, and a little honey, spices, and myrrh, nuts, and almonds."

Exodus 25:33—"Three bowls made like unto almonds, with a knop and a flower in one branch; and three bowls made like almonds in the other branch, with a knop and a flower: so in the six branches that come out of the candlestick."

Exodus 25:34—"And in the candlestick shall be four bowls made like unto almonds, with their knops and their flowers."

Exodus 37:19—"Three bowls made after the fashion of almonds in one branch, a knop and a flower; and three bowls made like almonds in another branch, a knop and a flower: so throughout the six branches going out of the candlestick."

Exodus 37:20—"And in the candlestick were four bowls made like almonds, his knops, and his flowers . . ."

Numbers 17:8—"And it came to pass, that on the morrow Moses went into the tabernacle of witness; and, behold, the rod of Aaron for the house of Levi was budded, and brought forth buds, and bloomed blossoms, and yielded almonds."

## History and Nutrition Highlights

Some botanists believe that almonds were one of the earliest domesticated fruit trees, perhaps because it is so easy to raise attractive almonds from seed, i.e., the nuts. Because this plant does not lend itself to propagation from suckers or from cuttings, horticulturists say it could have been domesticated even before the introduction of grafting. Historic records reveal that domesticated almonds appeared in the Near East during the Early Bronze Age, 3000 to 2000 B.C and an archaeological example of an almond was found in Tutankhamun's tomb in Egypt, circa 1325 B.C.

Part of the plum family, the almond tree today is native to North Africa, West Asia, and the Mediterranean. The English word "almond" is derived from the French *amande*, which in turn is a derivative of the old Latin word for almond, *amygdalus*, literally meaning "tonsil plum." Ancient Romans also referred to almonds as "Greek nuts," since they were first cultivated in Greece. Almonds date back in print to the Bible. In addition, a recipe dating back to 1390 uses blanched, ground almonds in a gravy for oysters.

Almond is the common name for a small tree of the rose family as well as for the fruit kernel itself, the nut. The appealing trees mature about 30 feet tall and provide blooming display in spring and fruit crop come fall. It is cultivated in the southern parts of the United States and hardier varieties are gaining popularity elsewhere.

The name of the tree and nut means "early rising" and it has been a symbol of the beginning of spring. Some botanists believe that it originated in the Holy Land in a wild form and was ultimately cultivated there, for domestic use and export. We know that another name for the almond was "luz", as used in Gen. 28:19 and later in the Jerusalem Talmud, perhaps because it is 21 days between blossoming and the forming of the fruit, exactly the same time between the breaching of Jerusalem's walls and the destruction of the Second Temple. It then became available in the sweet variety and thrived during the Second Temple period.

Almonds are referred to in the Bible under the name of Shaqued, which can mean "hasten". Other historians say the original name may mean, "Awakening One," which is appropriate considering the almond tree is one of the first to flower at the close of winter, around late January to early February in the Holy Land. Biblical historians note that the almond has been a symbol of watchfulness and promise due to its early flowering which scholars

believe symbolizes God's sudden and rapid redemption of His people after a period when he seems to have abandoned them, as in Jeremiah 1:11–12.

You'll find the almond mentioned in the Bible beginning with Genesis 43:11, where it is described as "among the best of fruits." In Numbers 17 Levi is chosen from the other tribes of Israel by Aaron's rod, which brought forth almond flowers. According to tradition, the rod of Aaron bore sweet almonds on one side and bitter on the other. Seemingly the message was that if the Israelites followed the Lord, the sweet almonds would be ripe and edible, but if they were to forsake the path of the Lord, the bitter almonds would predominate.

Christian symbolism often uses almond branches as a symbol of the virgin birth of Jesus. Early religious paintings often included almonds encircling the baby Jesus and as a symbol of Mary. Almond wood is hard and reddish in color and favored by cabinetmakers. However, these biblical trees are valued mainly for the nuts.

Sweet almonds contain practically no carbohydrates and therefore may be made into flour for cakes and biscuits for low carbohydrate diets. Sweet almonds are used in marzipan, nougat, and macaroons as well as other desserts. Almonds are a rich source of Vitamin E and are also rich in monounsaturated fat, supposedly responsible for lowering LDL cholesterol.

# Growing Tips

You can elect to try full size almonds, but the dwarf almond tree is a low shrub that takes less space and is similar to the common almond but with smaller fruit. It is common in the plains of Central Asia and is frequently planted as an ornamental shrub in England. Flowering almonds, both the shrub types and smaller trees, are cultivated extensively in the United States for their profusion of showy, white to rose blossoms. You get both beautiful blooming displays in spring and your tasty nut crop by fall.

Follow basic directions for planting a tree to get almonds off to a good start (see apples, page 111). As necessary, apply fertilizer in the amounts recommended for the type plant nutrients you prefer and buy, whether spikes, granular, or liquid in sprays.

# Cooking Tips and Recipes

Most people think of almonds eaten on their own, raw, toasted, or roasted. Along with other nuts it is often sprinkled over desserts, particularly ice cream sundaes. Traditionally it is also used in making baklava and nougat. Almond butter is a spread similar to peanut butter that is popular with peanut allergy sufferers and for its less salty taste.

## ALMOND MUNCHKIN MIX

■ 2 cups whole natural almonds, toasted
1 cup shelled sunflower seeds
2 tablespoons soy sauce
1/4 teaspoon ground ginger
2 cups raisins
4 oz (about 1 cup) beef jerky, cut into 1/2-inch pieces

▶ In large bowl, combine toasted almonds and sunflower seeds. Sprinkle with soy sauce and ginger. Toss to coat evenly; spread on baking sheet. Bake in over at 300°F., 15 minutes, stirring once or twice. Cool completely. Add raisins and beef jerky; toss. Store in airtight container.

## TOASTED ALMONDS

To toast almonds, place them in a single layer in a dry skillet, and turn heat to medium. Toast, stirring occasionally, until almonds are fragrant, about 2–5 minutes depending on the form of almonds you are toasting. If almonds are blanched, let them turn golden brown; if they have skins, let their skins just begin to crackle.

To toast in a microwave oven, spread almonds in a single layer in shallow glass baking dish. Microwave on high power 3 minutes, stirring halfway through. Cool on counter.

## ALMOND SHRIMP SALAD

■ 1 6.6 oz. pkg. Near East Toasted Almond Pilaf Mix
8 oz. shrimp
1 cup seedless red or green grapes, halved
1/2 cup chopped celery
3 tablespoons chopped fresh dill
3 tablespoons lemon juice
2 tablespoons olive oil
2 cloves garlic, minced
1 teaspoon honey
Romaine lettuce leaves
Lemon wedges

▶ Prepare pilaf mix as package directs; cool slightly. Stir shrimp, grapes, celery, dill, lemon juice, oil, garlic, and honey into pilaf. Cover; chill two hours before serving. Line serving bowl with lettuce leaves; top with rice mixture. Serve with lemon.

## ROASTED ALMONDS

Spread almonds in an ungreased baking pan. Place in 350°F oven and bake 10 minutes or until golden brown and fragrant. Stir once or twice to ensure even browning. Note that almonds will continue to roast slightly after removing from oven.

# Apples

The apple tree is known in the Old Testament for its fruit, shade, beauty, and fragrance. However, we must pause here to resolve a problem that has been debated for centuries. Is the apple really a plant of the Holy Land?

Some biblical scholars doubt that the Hebrew text is referring to the apple tree. They think the common apple tree was only recently introduced to the Holy Land, and that the wild variety hardly matches the description given to the tree and its fruit in the Bible. In addition, the climate and environment of the Holy Land don't meet the needs of apple trees. They require several cold winter months to produce fruit properly.

According to botanical and biblical scholars, the apricot seems to be most appropriate as the tree mentioned in Scriptures. The apricot was apparently introduced from China prior to the time of Abraham and today is widespread in the Holy Land.

Whether the apple or apricot is the true fruit tree of scriptures, there is no doubt that the apple tree has been long heralded and acclaimed. Therefore, it seems proper to include it here. As a highly popular tree that has provided its tasty fruits to millions of people, apples will lead our list of fruits in this chapter.

# Focus on Scripture

## Apples

You can read scriptural references in their contexts and decide whether an apple or an apricot was the tree of the Bible. It's hard to deny that some references focus on apples, especially when there are phrases such as "apple of the eye." "Apple of the eye" is a figurative expression for something very valuable. In Scripture it portrays God's care:

"He kept him as the Apple of his eye," and in Proverbs 7:2 "Keep my commands and live, and my law as the Apple of your eye."

Deuteronomy 32:10—"He found him in a desert land, and in the waste howling wilderness; he led him about, he instructed him, he kept him as the apple of his eye."

Psalm 17:8—"Keep me as the apple of the eye, hide me under the shadow of thy wings . . ."

Proverbs 7:2—"Keep my commandments, and live; and my law as the apple of thine eye."

Song of Solomon 2:3—"As the apple tree among the trees of the wood, so is my beloved among the sons. I sat down under his shadow with great delight, and his fruit was sweet to my taste."

Song of Solomon 8:5—"Who is this that cometh up from the wilderness, leaning upon her beloved? I raised thee up under the apple tree: there thy mother brought thee forth: there she brought thee forth that bare thee."

Lamentations 2:18—"Their heart cried unto the Lord, O wall of the daughter of Zion, let tears run down like a river day and night: give thyself no rest; let not the apple of thine eye cease."

Joel 1:12—"The vine is dried up, and the fig tree languisheth; the pomegranate tree, the palm tree also, and the apple tree, even all the trees of the field, are withered: because joy is withered away from the sons of men."

Zechariah 2:8—"For thus saith the Lord of hosts, After the glory hath he sent me unto the nations which spoiled you: for he that toucheth you toucheth the apple of his eye."

Sirach 17:22—"The alms of a man is as a signet with him, and he will keep the good deeds of man as the apple of the eye, and give repentance to his sons and daughters . . ."

Proverbs 25:11—"A word fitly spoken is like apples of gold in pictures of silver."

Song of Solomon 2:5—"Stay me with flagons, comfort me with apples: for I am sick of love."

Song of Solomon 7:8—"I said, I will go up to the palm tree, I will take hold of the boughs thereof: now also thy breasts shall be as clusters of the vine, and the smell of thy nose like apples . . ."

# History and Nutritional Highlights

Apples probably originated somewhere between the Caspian and the Black seas. Charred apple remains have been found in prehistoric lake dwellings of Switzerland. We also know that apples were a favorite fruit of the ancient Greeks and Romans.

Wild apple trees were widespread, from the Himalayas to Asia Minor to Europe. According to botanists, by 4000 to 3000 B.C. a more cultivated apple had been developed for food and juice. By the Greek period, apples were the most populous of fruits. Pliny the Elder described many varieties.

From Joshua 12:17 onwards we hear specifically of the apple, and we believe that it was cultivated in the Holy Land from 2000 B.C. Perhaps no biblical food has gotten a worse reputation than the apple. However, digging into botanical facts, it is probably true that Adam and Eve didn't even see an apple, much less eat one. The Bible never says exactly what fruit the serpent uses to tempt Eve in the Garden of Eden.

The word "apple" comes from the Old English word *æppel* and the scientific name *malus* comes from the Latin word for apple, and ultimately from the archaic Greek *mālon*. Linnaeus assigned the apple to the genus Pyrus but later, Philip Miller separated the apple into its own genus. Botanists believe that a single species still growing in northwest China and Kazakhstan is the progenitor of the apples we eat today.

Pioneers brought apple seeds to the New World; the Massachusetts Bay Company records show that apples were grown in New England as early as 1630. American history tells us that one man alone, John Chapman, dubbed Johnny Appleseed, was responsible for extensive plantings of apples throughout the midwestern United States.

Apples certainly have grown in popularity through the centuries. There are more than 7,500 known cultivars of apples for temperate and subtropical climates. Reputedly, the world's biggest collection of apple cultivars is housed at the National Fruit Collection in England.

The apple tree is a deciduous plant that grows mainly in temperate areas of the world. The fruit is a firm, fleshy structure derived from the receptacle of the flower. Blooming apple trees in spring are beautiful—some blossoms are all white, but the majority have stripes or tints of rose. Apple wood is hard, durable, and very fine-grained. Fruit color may range from green to a deep, blackish red. Shapes range from oblong fruits that are hardly larger than a cherry up to fruits as big as a medium-sized grapefruit.

Today, many apple varieties are developed by controlled crossing of desirable parents. Apple trees are best adapted to areas in which the average temperature approaches or reaches freezing during at least two months. Exact chilling requirement varies somewhat with each variety and many trees withstand temperatures down to −40°F.

Nothing compares to sun-ripened, juicy fruit, picked at its flavorful peak from a tree in your backyard. Supermarkets seldom sell the tastiest apple varieties because they don't ship well or because growers prefer to produce only the trees that promise the greatest fruit yield. You can experiment with growing the most delicious varieties right where you live.

Fruit trees are versatile and fit well into outdoor landscapes. They provide shade and appealing shapes and forms to grace your yard. Today you have a choice of dwarf, semi-dwarf, or standard apple trees. The smaller trees fit nicely into limited space and really do bear full-size fruit. Find out more about specific varieties of each type of fruit in mail order catalogs.

It's nice to know that trees also have a proved monetary value. Real-estate agents know that beautiful trees add to the dollar resale value of a home; attractive landscaping can boost property value by 10 to 15%. It pays to make trees one of your first investments as you begin landscaping. Fruitful "plantscaping" makes sense and tastes good, too!

Apples are relatively indifferent to soil conditions and will grow in a wide range of pH values and fertility levels. They do require some protection from the wind and should not be planted in low areas that are subject to late spring frosts. They prefer good drainage, so avoid soggy, clay soils. Pick a sunny spot so trees receive eight hours of sun each day to thrive and produce the sweetest natural sugars in the fruit. To enjoy tastier living all summer and into fall, carefully select varieties that ripen early, mid, and late season. Local nurseries can advise you which are best for your locality. Plant breeders have also developed varieties that resist diseases and reduce the need for chemical sprays. Mail order nurseries like Starks Brothers, Miller Nurseries, and others provide a wide choice of excellent varieties.

For early eating, Lodi is marvelous fresh and for pies. Summer Rambo, dating to sixteenth century France, has appeal for its distinctive taste. Honeycrisp and Honeygold are two newer apples that were developed in Minnesota. Honeycrisp is an excellent dessert apple with large size and crisp flesh. It produces reliably, ripening in September and surviving cold northern areas. Honeygold has sumptuous flavor as a dessert apple, similar to Golden Delicious but with an added honeysweet taste. It also is hardy in northern areas, bearing golden to yellowish-green fruit, and keeps well. Both these varieties cross-pollinate with Jonared and Jonafree, two reliable disease-resistant apples.

Redfree is bright red, resistant to apple scab and other problems, and ripens in early August. Sweet for fresh use, it stores well in refrigerators. Jonafree is an improved, bright red apple that also resists diseases. Especially hardy, it ripens in mid-September. Empire also resists disease. It has the sweetness of Delicious apples combined with McIntosh flavor and ripens in mid-September. Liberty is another extra disease-resistant McIntosh-type apple that produces big crops in late September. Granny Smith is a tart, green-colored apple that resists cedar rust and diseases and ripens in early November.

As we know from time-honored advice, "an apple a day keeps the doctor away," Fresh apples are indeed a healthy refreshing snack. They quench thirst and their acid content makes them a natural mouth freshener. Researchers at Michigan State University call the apple "the all-around health food." They point out these potent healing powers of apples:

- They lower bad cholesterol and high blood pressure.
- The juices in apples are highly effective virus fighters.
- They help suppress the appetite without robbing the body of necessary nutrients, so they're great for dieters.
- They help stabilize blood sugar, an important factor in controlling diabetes.
- They prevent constipation and help treat diarrhea.
- They contain chemicals that scientists believe are vital in stopping cancer.
- Apples prevent tooth decay.

In addition, the apple's ability to keep our hearts healthy and pumping has been confirmed by U.S., French, and Italian researchers.

## Growing and Harvesting Tips

Now that your appetite for fruitful landscaping has been whetted a bit and the appeal of extraordinarily delicious apples has boosted your enthusiasm, it is time to focus on some of the simple basics for planting your home orchard or selected trees. First, walk around your home grounds. Look at the sun each area receives. Examine the soil to determine how you may improve it. Fruit trees do best when they receive full sun, have a well-drained, loamy soil, and are sheltered from prevailing winds. Your fruit trees, as all trees, are permanent parts of your home landscape so it pays to prepare soil well for proper planting. If you have poor soil that is too sandy or has excess clay content, add well-rotted manure, peat moss, or composted humus to improve growing conditions. See Chapter 6 for more helpful hints on soil improvement. Some locally-purchased trees may be balled and burlapped or in containers. Mailorder trees usually arrive bare rooted and wrapped in moist moss. It is important to plant them immediately. Be ready when they arrive. Mix a bucket of compost or composted manure with each bucket of soil to make a fertile mixture that will give trees the best possible start.

Dig a hole twice as large as the root ball. Make a small mound of soil mix in the center of the hole. Place the root ball of container or burlap-wrapped trees carefully in the hole and fill half way with soil mixture. Spread bare roots well. Then, pour a bucket of water into the hole. When it drains away, add more soil mix, tamp down to eliminate air pockets, and add another half bucket of water around the newly planted tree.

Leave a saucer-shaped depression around each tree to catch rain. Next, mulch around each tree with leaves, compost, peat moss, or grass clipping. Mulching is my favorite garden practice. It smothers weeds and helps soil hold moisture.

Next, prune off any broken tree seedling branches. Water weekly with at least an inch of water, so your tree will begin growing new feeding roots and become secure in its new home. Take time to plant well to give your trees the strong, sturdy start they need. Once established, they'll reward you fruitfully, year after tasty year.

Here are spacing guides for apples and apricots.

| | | |
|---|---|---|
| Apples (s/d) 12 × 12 feet | 12 to 15 feet | 2 years |
| Apples (S) 35 × 35 feet | 20 to 25 feet | 3 to 10 years |
| Apricots (d) 10 × 10 feet | 8 to 10 feet | 2 years |
| Apricots (S) 20 × 20 feet | 15 feet | 3 years |

# Cooking Tips and Recipes

## GRANDMA'S APPLE PIE

*My grandma's apple pie was a family tradition that deserves to be shared with all readers. I hope you enjoy it.*

■ Pastry for two-crust 9-inch pie
6 Golden Delicious apples, peeled, cored, and thinly sliced
1/4 cup sugar
2 tablespoons flour
1 teaspoon vanilla extract
1/2 teaspoon cinnamon
1/4 teaspoon ground ginger
1/8 teaspoon ground mace
2 tablespoons butter or margarine
Cream or whole milk

▶ Heat oven to 425°F. Line a 9-inch pie pan with half the pastry. In large bowl, combine apples, sugar, flour, vanilla, cinnamon, ginger, and mace; toss well to blend. Transfer apple mixture to pastry-lined pie pan and dot with butter. Cover apple filling with remaining pastry; pinch together edges of bottom and top crust to seal. Brush top crust with cream or milk; cut several slits to vent steam. Bake 20 minutes. Reduce oven heat to 375°F and bake 30 to 35 minutes or until apples are tender.

## APPLE AND WILTED LETTUCE SALAD

*Apple salad is a refreshing treat. This recipe includes several foods from the Bible to enjoy.*

*Makes about 6 servings.*

■ 6 cups torn romaine lettuce
4 cups torn green or red leaf lettuce
2 Red or Golden Delicious apples, cored and sliced
1/2 cup sliced celery
6 slices bacon
1/3 cup cider vinegar
1/4 cup water
1 package (.6-ounce) Italian salad dressing mix
2 teaspoons sugar
1/4 cup sliced green onion
Ground black pepper

▶ In large serving bowl, combine romaine, leaf lettuce, apples, and celery; set aside. In skillet, fry bacon until crisp; reserve drippings. Drain and crumble bacon into salad. In same skillet, combine reserved bacon drippings, the vinegar, water, salad dressing mix, and sugar; heat to boiling. Pour over salad. Top with green onion and black pepper; toss salad gently. Serve immediately.

## APPLE RHUBARB CRUNCH

*Next to rhubarb-strawberry pie, this is probably my favorite dessert. Makes about 6 good servings but you can stretch it out.*

■ 3 cups (about 3 medium-sized) pared and sliced apples
2 cups diced rhubarb
1/2 cup flour
1/2 cup packed brown sugar
1/3 cup quick-cooking rolled oats
1/2 teaspoon ground cinnamon
1/4 teaspoon salt
1/4 cup butter or margarine
Whipped cream or ice cream

▶ Place apples and rhubarb in shallow 2-quart baking dish. Combine flour, sugar, oats, cinnamon, and salt. Cut in butter until crumbly. Spoon over fruit. Bake at 375°F 25 to 30 minutes or until fruit is tender. Serve with whipped cream or ice cream.

# Apricots

The apricot is the common name for a small tree of the rose family and its fruit. The fruit resembles a peach and is round with yellow flesh. Apricots are thought to have originated in northeastern China near the Russian border. The tree and its fruit have been established in Armenia since ancient times and most likely spread to Europe through Armenia. The tree is small to medium-sized with a dense, spreading canopy.

# Focus on Scripture

## Apricots

Apricots are not mentioned by name in the Scriptures. However, since there is much debate about whether or not the apple actually grew in the Holy Land, many biblical scholars and botanists believe the fruit mentioned in the Bible could be the apricot. Here are some scriptural quotations that could be referring to either the apple or apricot tree.

Song of Solomon 2:3—"Like an apple tree among the trees of the woods, so is my beloved among the sons. I sat down in his shade with great delight, and his fruit was sweet to my taste."

Song of Solomon 8:5—"Who is this coming up from the wilderness, Leaning upon her beloved? I awakened you under the apple tree. There your mother brought you forth; there she who bore you brought you forth."

Joel 1:12—"The vine has dried up, and the fig tree has withered; the pomegranate tree, the palm tree also, and the apple tree—all the trees of the field are withered; surely joy has withered away from the sons of men."

# History

The apricot was apparently discovered 4,000 years ago on the mountain slopes of China, where the fruit was first cultivated. The trees then traveled across the Persian Empire to the Mediterranean. Alexander the Great is said to have brought apricots from China to Greece in the fourth century B.C., and Arabs introduced the tree to Italy, where it continues to flourish. You may have heard the term "nectar of the gods." It was nectar made of the juice and pulp of the apricot, which was reputedly the drink of choice of the Greek and Roman gods. The ancient Persians referred to the apricot as "egg of the sun."

Apricots have also been cultivated in Egypt from ancient times and are popular there today. Historians say that Roman general Lucullus, circa 106 to 57 B.C., exported apricot trees to Armenia and Europe. English settlers reportedly brought apricots to their colonies in the New World, though other records reveal that most apricots came to America from seedlings brought to the West Coast by Spanish missionaries and explorers.

Today, the United States produces 90 percent of the world's apricot crop, mostly grown in California. Apricot trees are perfect for home gardens because they are easy to maintain, take up relatively little space, and the sweet-smelling flowers perfume the air in the spring.

Moorpark apricots are of English origin and have a large, round, orange-red freestone that ripens in mid-season. Newcastle is a freestone with medium-size, round, orange-yellow fruit, and Royal is an early ripening French type with a large, yellow-red freestone fruit.

# Growing and Harvesting Tips

Happily, the apricot is native to regions with cold winters. Trees are slightly more cold-hardy than the peach, tolerating winter temperatures as cold as −30°C. Be aware that the key limiting factor in apricot culture is spring frosts. Apricots tend to flower very early, often during the vernal equinox even in northern locations like the Great Lakes area. That means late spring frosts can kill the blooms. Curiously, trees do need some winter cold to bear and grow properly.

Like the almond, the apricot is a member of the rose family, which is native to eastern Asia. It is popular today in landscaping both for decoration and for its fruit. Apricot trees are smallish with heart-shaped leaves on long stalks. Solitary white flowers appear before leaves in mid-spring. Fruit resembles the peach: roundish, downy, yellow, and sometimes ruddy on one side with typically yellow flesh. For those who dislike the "furry" feel of peaches, apricots offer a smooth alternative.

Apricots are stone fruit, a.k.a. drupes, and are so called because the lone seed is often called a "stone". The name derives from "apricock" and "abre-cox," through the French *abricot* and the Spanish *albaricoque*, which was an adaptation of the Arabic *al-burquk*. Botanists say the Arabic is a rendering of the Greek adapted from the Latin *praecox* or *praecoquus*, possibly referring to the fruit maturing much earlier in the summer than plums.

Most apricot varieties are self-fertile. Full-size trees generally grow between 20 and 30 feet tall and live about 75 years. Most will start bearing in their third or fourth year. Expect 3 to 4 bushels of fruit from a standard-size tree and about 1 to 2 from a dwarf variety. It is hard to find dwarf apricot trees, but you can try a genetic dwarf such as 'Stark Golden Glo.' These trees are naturally small, so they don't need to be grafted onto dwarfing stock. Buy dormant, bare-root, 1-year-old apricot trees if possible and plant them in early spring in the North and East. In California and other mild-winter areas you can plant apricots in the fall.

When planting apricots, choose a site in full sun. In cold climates, set trees on the north side of a building so that trees will warm up later in the spring and blossoms will be delayed until the danger of frost has passed. Apricots are not very particular about soil type as long as it is well drained; you can improve most soils following directions in the soils chapter.

Plant standard-size trees about 25 feet apart and space genetic dwarfs 8 to 12 feet apart. Place your tree in the hole and spread the roots carefully. Water apricot trees slowly and deeply, out past the root zone. If you irrigate, be sure the water penetrates about 3 feet deep and as wide as the tree's canopy. Deep watering helps trees survive drought and promotes bigger, sweeter fruit. To retain water and thwart weeds, mulch around the trees.

# Cooking Tips and Recipes

You'll thank our friends at the Apricot Producers of California for these tasty recipes to try and share with your family and friends. Access their website to find even more delicious recipes (www.apricotproducers.com).

## APRICOT-OATMEAL BREAKFAST CAKE

*Here's another tasty treat to start your day.*

*Makes about 6 servings.*

- 2 cups all-purpose flour
1/2 cup oats, quick or old-fashioned, uncooked
1 teaspoon baking powder
1 teaspoon baking soda
1 teaspoon cinnamon
1/4 teaspoon salt
8 ounces (2 sticks) unsalted butter, softened

1 cup sugar
1/2 cup brown sugar
2 large eggs
1 cup buttermilk
2 (15.25-ounce) cans apricots drained well, or 2 cups chopped fresh apricots
Confectioners' sugar for sprinkling

▶ Preheat oven to 350°F. Butter a 9 × 13-inch cake pan or coat with cooking spray. Set aside. In a medium-sized bowl, mix flour, oatmeal, baking powder, baking soda, cinnamon, and salt and set aside. In a large bowl, beat the butter with an electric mixer at medium speed until creamy. Slowly add the white sugar and brown sugar. Beat until light and fluffy. Add eggs one at a time and beat until smooth. Add dry ingredients alternately with the buttermilk, beginning and ending with the dry ingredients. Stir in apricots. Do not over-mix. Pour cake batter into prepared pan. Bake cake about 35 to 45 minutes, until golden brown on top. When cool, sprinkle the top of the cake with confectioners' sugar.

## CRISP & FLAKY ORCHARD APRICOT POCKETS

*These make elegant desserts or a unique breakfast treat.*

*Makes 16 pockets.*

■ 1 package frozen puff pastry sheets
3 cups fresh apricot halves or 2 jars (26 ounces) apricots, drained
1/2 cup sugar

▶ Preheat oven to 375°F. Thaw puff pastry for 30 minutes or according to directions on box. Drain apricots and slice each half into thirds; set aside.

When pastry is thawed, put each sheet on a lightly floured surface and roll out to extend each side by approximately 1/2 inch. Cut each sheet into eight rectangles to make 16 total. Fill bottom portion of each rectangle with 4 to 5 pieces of fruit; moisten sides with a bit of water and pinch closed to form a square. Place pocket on a baking sheet and sprinkle generously with sugar. Cut 3 slits in the top of each for the steam to escape while baking.

Bake at 375°F for 25 minutes or until the pockets are golden brown.

## APRICOT NUT BREAD

*If you like banana bread you should try this delicious recipe for yourself and as a treat for guests.*

■ Makes 1 loaf of about 16 slices.
1/2 cup coarsely chopped hazelnuts or walnuts
1 1/2 cups coarsely chopped dried apricots
1/4 cup apricot nectar or apple juice
2 1/2 cups all-purpose white flour
1 tablespoon baking powder
1 teaspoon baking soda
1/2 teaspoon salt
1 large egg
2 large egg whites
1/2 cup sugar
2/3 cup nonfat plain yogurt
3 tablespoons hazelnut oil or canola oil

1 tablespoon grated lemon zest
1 teaspoon pure vanilla extract
3/4 cup golden raisins

▶ Preheat oven to 350°F. Lightly oil a 9" × 5" loaf pan or coat it with nonstick cooking spray; set aside. In a shallow pan, toast hazelnuts or walnuts in the oven for 3 to 5 minutes, or until golden brown and fragrant. Set aside to cool. In a small saucepan, combine 1/2 cup of the apricots and nectar or juice. Bring to a simmer, remove from heat, and let stand for 10 minutes. Transfer the apricots and their liquid to a food processor and process until a chunky puree forms; set aside. You should have about 1/2 cup puree.

In a large bowl, whisk flour, baking powder, baking soda and salt. In another large bowl, whisk egg, egg whites, sugar, yogurt, oil, lemon zest, vanilla, and the apricot puree. Stir the apricot mixture into the dry ingredients until just combined. Fold in raisins, hazelnuts, and the remaining 1 cup of chopped apricots for a thick batter. Turn the batter into the prepared pan, smoothing the top. Bake for 50 to 60 minutes, or until the top is golden brown and a skewer inserted in the center comes out clean. Let cool in the pan for 10 minutes. Loosen the edges and invert the loaf onto a wire rack to cool.

# Brambles/Berries

By definition among botanists and gardeners, bramble is the common name for any genus of plants or shrubs with many species. Bramble fruit is the fruit of any plant of the Genus Rubus, such as the blackberry or raspberry. The word comes from the Germanic *bram-bezi*, also German *brombeere* and French *framboise*.

Bramble bushes have a distinctive growth form. They send up long, arching canes that do not flower or set fruit until the second year of growth. Many types of brambles bear edible fruit, and many have re-curved thorns that dig into clothing and flesh when the victim tries to pull away from them. Some types also have hair-like thorns. Brambles usually have trifoliate or palmately-compound leaves.

Brambles are aggregate fruits. Each small unit is called a druplet. In some, such as the blackberry, the flower receptacle is elongate fruit.

# Focus on Scripture

## Brambles

Isaiah 34:13—"And thorns shall come up in her palaces, nettles and brambles in the fortresses thereof: and it shall be an habitation of dragons, and a court for owls."

# Growing Tips

As we read about brambles, perhaps we should think tastier thoughts, such as the sweet treats bramble bushes provide for us. Nothing beats berry treasures you can pick sun-kissed ripe from your own yard: the bright blackberries, rosy red raspberries, and the luscious black and flavorful purple raspberries. Most of the tastiest berry varieties aren't suitable for commercial production because they don't ship well or hold up in stores. Good news for you is that the sweetest are available for growing in your garden.

Even just a few berry bushes will yield many quarts of fruit. Plant three or four bushes this year and you'll have bountiful berries for many years to come. First, prepare the soil deeply; dig or till 10 to 12 inches deep. Add your own compost or composted manure from garden supply stores. Add peat moss if you have heavy, clay, or sandy soils. Peat moss works wonders to open heavy soils and helps hold moisture in sandy soils.

Prepare planting holes twice as large as the bare root ball or size of the container-grown plants you buy locally or from reputable mail order firms. Most mail order firms ship bare root berry plants wrapped in sphagnum moss or similar material. Plant carefully to help them develop a strong, permanent roothold.

Next, pour a half-gallon of water into each hole. Carefully position plants in the holes to avoid disturbing their roots, especially bare root plants. Then, fill the hole half way with soil, tamp down to eliminate air pockets, and water again. After the water soaks in, add the remaining soil to fill the hole, press down until firm, and water. Always leave a saucer-shaped depression around each berry plant to catch rain and direct it to the new plant. Finally, mulch with compost, grass clippings, rotted leaves, or peat moss.

Water weekly so plants establish a good foundation. Most berry bushes won't develop fruit the first year. That's nature's way. But as they do set fruit in future years, be sure to plan for weekly watering to produce the lushest, sweetest fruit crops.

For bountiful harvests you must nourish your berry plans. Many excellent balanced fertilizers especially formulated for berry bushes are now available. Follow directions for amounts to use on the package of the fertilizer you buy. Don't be heavy handed. Too much plant food can be as bad as too little.

---

Be patient as you create your berry treasure gardens. Most berry plants will set only a few berries the first year, but many more the next. By the third and future years, you'll be amazed how prolific they are.

---

Wondering which are the best bramble berries to grow? Blackberries are often overlooked as a backyard berry crop, perhaps because they are thought of as particularly thorny. However, you now have a wider choice of tastier berries thanks to plant breeders, many of which are hardly thorny at all. Here are some of the marvelous new varieties that deserve a test plot in your garden.

Darrow used to be one of the most favored and productive varieties, but is very thorny. Arapaho is the earliest thornless blackberry with very small seeds that ripens in mid-June. Apache is another thornless variety developed by the University of Arkansas. Chester Thornless rates as the hardiest and most productive for the upper mid-western part of the United States with firm berries, ripening in July. Illini, developed in Illinois, also is good for northern areas with vigorous growth and abundant crops of shiny black berries. It ripens in later July. Two Green Thumb Award winners are noteworthy. These are revolutionary new blackberry plants that bear on both old and newer canes. They produce quality berries in a wider range of climates since winter damage to canes no longer means a poor crop the following summer. New first year canes bear berries which begin ripening mid-July and continue to frost. Second year canes bear the heaviest crops in mid-June and all on the same plant. Consider Prime Jim and Prime Jan blackberries; they cost a bit more but certainly offer major advantages.

Blackberries prefer full sun but can tolerate partial shade. Pick a site that is well drained because blackberries are sensitive to wet soils. Blackberries do best in a fertile, loam soil with moderate water holding capacity. Most varieties tend to expand via underground suckers and may need to be trimmed back to control their spread. They ripen from June in mid-summer, when most raspberries are done producing fruit, so you can have tasty berries for your family all through the season.

It is best to plant berries in early spring as soon as you can work the ground. If your soil has low fertility, add one pound of 5-10-5 per one hundred square feet as you till the area.

Dig shallow holes large enough to accommodate each plant's roots. Space plants 4 to 5 feet apart and rows 8 to 10 feet apart if doing several rows. The plants' underground suckers will fill in the row and you'll still have room to weed and harvest from each side.

Next, water the plants to settle the soil. Then cut cane on the plants to 6 inches. Water weekly so your blackberries get a good roothold. Blackberries respond well to fertilizer. Apply fertilizer in early spring when new growth begins. Spread granular type fertilizer along each side of the row in the amount recommended for the type you use.

Mulch is a good bet to thwart weeds. Use rotted bark material, straw, or composted leaves 2 to 3 inches along rows to control weeds and retain soil moisture. If you cultivate do it lightly to avoid damaging shallow plant roots. Cultivate no deeper than 1 to 2 inches to prevent root damage. Blackberries plump up to sweetest taste with ample water. Give them about one inch of water per week from mid-June and especially through harvest. Be watchful for harvest time. Pick berries every few days with a breaking motion rather than by pulling.

# Raspberries

Raspberry is the common name for certain plants of the rose family and for their cap-shaped fruits that separate from the floral stalk when picked. Raspberries are native to the North Temperate Zone. The European red raspberry was one of the first European plants to be introduced into America. The native black raspberry of the United States is hardy and productive. Many raspberry varieties have been developed from these three species. Fruits range from black to purple and red to yellow. Raspberries belong to the genus *Rubus* of the family *Rosaceae*. The European red raspberry is classified as *Rubus idaeus*, the American red raspberry as *Rubus idaeus* variety *strigosus*, and the black raspberry as *Rubus occidentalis*.

Allen is a virus-free black raspberry that ripens in a concentrated period so all fruit can be picked at once. Blackhawk was introduced in Iowa and is one of the hardiest varieties available. Bristol is widely planted. Jewel is noted as a virus-free type with upright growth and is very productive. Munger is an extremely disease resistant black variety with small seeds, noted for large, sweet fruit. It also is tops for preserving and freezing. It ripens in mid to late season.

Purple raspberries are hybrids of red raspberries and blackcaps. They have the same growth characteristics as blackcaps. Some raspberries have yellow fruit and are variations of red raspberries. Except for fruit color they have all the characteristics of red raspberries but are grown chiefly by homeowners in northern states.

Purple Royalty is a virus-free gourmet type purple raspberry with large, high sugar content fruit. It bears late, avoiding spring frost damage and is worth trying for something different. For those looking for unique tastes, there is also Kiwigold, bearing large gold berries that ripen in August. It is disease resistant and reportedly more flavorful than earlier gold rasps. Another treat is Fall Gold, an ever-bearing type that yields from July to late October. It is especially hardy for cold climates.

Red raspberries are perhaps the best known and most popular. Heritage is the most widely planted worldwide. It is virus-free and a truly outstanding everbearing raspberry. It has vigorous upright canes that don't require staking or a trellis. Fruit is superior, berries large, bright red, and firm. It matures in early July and a fall crop begins in early September until the first frost. The late crop often is better than the first. Killarney is another virus-free, subtly sweet berry that came from Canada, so it handles cold winter well. Everbearing Fall Red is a New Hampshire development, ripening first early in July and then with a fall crop by August until the first frost.

---

All rasps prefer full sun for peak performance. You can grow them in beds, along property lines, or in clusters among other landscaping if you wish. To plant them well, dig holes, spread their roots, and tamp down soil over them. Space red varieties 3 to 4 feet apart in rows 6 to 8 feet apart. After planting, remove old, dead canes. Top back tall ones each year to force new side branches that bear the berries that are born on second year canes.

---

Red rasps will tend to form hedgerows that you can cultivate and pick from both sides. Suckers from the roots will fill in the rows. Blacks and purples will remain as bushy specimens and you can propagate new plants by bending canes to insert the tips into the ground, covering with soil, and letting them root. When they have, cut away from the parent plant and dig up to transplant.

To plant rasps, dig holes 12 inches deep and mix in compost and peat since you are preparing permanent beds or growing spots that your plants will occupy for many years. For potted or root balled plants, set them to a depth of about 3 inches. Plant bare root plants 5 to 6 inches deep, which should be about 1 inch deeper than they were grown in the nursery. Water well and weekly so plants get a strong start and set roots deeply. Mulch around black and purple bushes to preserve soil moisture and smother weeds.

For your red raspberries, use the hedgerow system, with rows about 15 inches wide. Let root suckers develop in this hedgerow, but remove all suckers that sprout outside it. Bearing floricanes should be cut back during winter to 4 to 5 feet, which is a good height for picking, and not so tall that canes bend over with the crop weight.

# Date Palms

The date palm is extensively cultivated as a decorative plant and for its edible fruit in many parts of the world that favor its growth. The exact origin is unknown, but dates were probably first cultivated in the desert oases of northern Africa and perhaps also southwest Asia. It is a medium-sized tree, 40 to 70 feet tall, often clumped with several trunks from a single root system, but more commonly growing singly.

Some botanists believe date palms originated around the Persian Gulf, and point out they have been cultivated since ancient times from Mesopotamia to prehistoric Egypt, possibly as early as 6000 B.C. There is archaeological evidence of date cultivation in eastern Arabia in 4000 B.C.

Date palms have flourished in the Holy Land near the site of ancient Jericho since the Neolithic period. The name date probably comes from the Greek *daktulos*, which is derived from a cluster of dark-brown finger digits. No one knows the origin of the cultivated date; it could be anywhere from India to the mountains of northeastern Africa. Originally date palms were grown for the dates themselves, for date honey, and because its leaves were useful for general thatching, fibers for ropes, and baskets, brooms, and its wood for building. The date palm is a symbol of immortality and fertility.

# Focus on Scripture

## Dates Palms

2 Samuel 6:19—"Then he gave a loaf of bread, a cake of dates and a cake of raisins to each person in the whole crowd of Israelites, both men and women. And all the people went to their homes."

1 Chronicles 16:3—"Then he gave a loaf of bread, a cake of dates and a cake of raisins to each Israelite man and woman."

Psalm 92:13—"The righteous shall flourish like the date palm tree . . ."

Revelation 7:9—"After this I beheld, and, lo, a great multitude, which no man could number, throne, and before the Lamb, clothed with white robes, and palms in their hands . . ."

Exodus 15:27—"And they came to Elim, where were twelve wells of water, and threescore and ten palm trees: and they encamped there by the waters."

Leviticus 23:40—"And ye shall take you on the first day the boughs of goodly trees, branches of palm trees, and the boughs of thick trees, and willows of the brook; and ye shall rejoice before the Lord your God seven days."

Deuteronomy 34:3—"And the south, and the plain of the valley of Jericho, the city of palm trees, unto Zoar."

1 Kings 6:29—"And he carved all the walls of the house round about with carved figures of cherubims and palm trees and open flowers, within and without."

1 Kings 6:32—"The two doors also were of olive tree; and he carved upon them carvings of cherubims and palm trees and open flowers, and

overlaid them with gold, and spread gold upon the cherubims, and upon the palm trees."

2 Chronicles 28:15—"And the men which were expressed by name rose up, and took the captives, and with the spoil clothed all that were naked among them, and arrayed them, and shod them, and gave them to eat and to drink, and anointed them, and carried all the feeble of them upon asses, and brought them to Jericho, the city of palm trees, to their brethren: then they returned to Samaria."

Nehemiah 8:15—"And that they should publish and proclaim in all their cities, and in Jerusalem, saying, Go forth unto the mount, and fetch olive branches, and pine branches, and myrtle branches, and palm branches, and branches of thick trees, to make booths, as it is written."

John 12:13—"Took branches of palm trees, and went forth to met him, and cried, Hosanna: Blessed is the King of Israel that cometh in the name of the Lord.

## History and Nutrition Highlights

Wild date palm seeds dating back 50,000 years have been found in the Shanidar Cave of northern Iraq which tells us dates were part of the early cave dwellers' diet. The Sumerians were cultivating the palm by about 5000 B.C. Earliest written records reveal that the date palm was providing the Sumerians with food and shade, building materials, animal feed, tools, and rope. The date palm, symbolizing peace, justice, and supply, was pictured in the earliest sculptures deemed sacred to the Sumerians, the Babylonians, Assyrians, and the Egyptians. Later the date palm was important to three of the world's major religious groups, the Jews, the Muslims, and the Christians.

In the Jewish tradition, palm fronds are used to build the "soukkot," or harvest festival shelter. They are also one of the five sacred plants displayed during the harvest festival. Dates were deeply rooted in the traditions of the Holy Land during Jesus time. They were of great economic importance because of the food, fiber, and oil they provided, and because of their ornamental value.

Dates reach far back into antiquity and provide unique scientific study opportunities. Israeli scientists have germinated a sapling from a date palm seed that is nearly 2,000 years old! "We are interested in preserving very valuable species in the Middle East," says Dr. Sarah Sallon, who heads the project. "Some of them are extinct but may be able to be resurrected." He believes that particular date palm seed is the oldest seed ever brought back to life. It was found at the historic fortress of Masada near the Dead Sea, where 960 Jewish zealots chose suicide over capture by the Romans in 73 A.D. "We managed to get a few of these seeds, and we planted them, and some six or seven weeks later a bud appeared," said Sallon.

The sapling is now about 14 inches tall. If it survives, the team hopes to revive the Judean date palm praised in the Bible. "In antiquity, there was a very famous date of ancient Israel," Sallon said. "It was one of the most important exports of ancient Israel, it was on the coins, it was of extraordinary importance for the economy, for ceremonial reasons and also for medicinal reasons." There are still plenty of lush date palms in Israel today, but they are not the same as the original tree from biblical times. Scientists believe the Judean date might have had very different properties than the modern variety. Over the years, plant breeders have improved the growing rate, amount of yield, and even taste.

The awe and reverence in which ancient peoples held this tree can be appreciated from Scriptures. "And he shall be like a tree planted by the rivers of waters, that bringeth forth his fruit in his season, his leaf also shall not wither, and whatsoever he doeth shall prosper" (Psalms 1:3). Psalms 92:12–14 reads: "The righteous shall flourish like the palm tree; he shall grow like a cedar in Lebanon. Those that be planted in the house of the Lord shall flourish in the courts of our God. They shall still bring forth fruit in old age; they shall be fat and flourishing."

Palms of many varieties were important to the people of Jesus' time. From St. John 12:12–13 we read, "On the next day much people that were come to the feast when they heard that Jesus was coming to Jerusalem, took branches of palm trees, and went forth to meet him, and cried, Hosanna: Blessed is the King of Israel that cometh in the name of the Lord." In those early biblical days, palm leaves carried with them religious meanings. Medieval Christians revered palm fronds, as indicated in the stories of St. Christopher, St. Clare, and St. Francis of Assisi, in which palm fronds figure predominantly. Still today palms maintain their religious significance, being distributed to the devout on Palm Sunday as a reminder of Jesus' triumphal entry into Jerusalem.

# Growing Tips

Date palms grow rapidly, as much as one foot per year, and as high as 80 to 100 feet. They like to have their feet in the water and heads in the sun, like ducks do. Naturally, dates prefer oases, which are typically dry, warm places of little rainfall but with an adequate underground water supply. Palms are different than other types of fruit trees. They are monocots: the growing tip of the trunk is built up into a large mass in the seedling stage and maintains that broad width as the trunk matures. Palm leaves, often large, are formed a few at a time at the stem tips and leave semicircular scars on the stems when they fall off.

The date palm is obviously too tall for most home gardens and is not widely used as a landscape plant outside of larger southern estates and public gardens. Fortunately there are many close relatives that will thrive around your home and grounds. For home or office, palms are reliable container plants because they have no deep taproots. Growing palms in containers also helps restrict their growth to manageable size. They are surprisingly hardy and will thrive for years.

Most representative of the date palm is the pigmy date palm, *Phoenix roebelenii*. It is a compact plant with graceful, arching fronds and does exceptionally well in homes if kept warm and moist. For larger indoor decorating, the Christmas palm and the Solitaire palm are alternate choices. They provide the impression of a full sized palm on a small scale for use outdoors in southern climates or as potted specimens indoors. You also can select other close relatives, such as the Arabian date palm, *Phoenix dactylifrer*, or the general date palm, *Phoenix reclinata*. For most homes and indoor culture, the pigmy or miniature date palm, *P. roebelenii*, will work wonders as a replica closest to the true, tall date palms of the Holy Land.

Check mail order sources and try to get specimens pre-potted or well balled for planting in your own container. Obtain suitable growing mix at your garden center or local supplier and repot the trees you buy. Use a rich loam type mix to which you add generous amounts of composted humus in order to improve water-holding capacity.

The native date palm of the Middle East was mentioned in the Bible as the "tree of life." In the Holy Land today dates often grow in large bunches which can weigh as much as 40 pounds. Some large trees will yield more than 1,000 dates each year.

# Cooking Tips and Recipes

Dry or soft dates are eaten out-of-hand or may be seeded and stuffed with fillings such as almonds, candied orange and lemon peel, or marzipan. Dates can also be chopped and used in a range of sweet and savory dishes, or added to puddings, bread, cakes, and other desserts. Dates are also processed into cubes, paste, date syrup, or "honey" called "dibs," vinegar, or alcohol. Chocolate-covered dates are a newer delicious treat. In some Middle Eastern countries you might also find sparkling date juice, used as a non-alcoholic version of champagne, for special occasions and religious times such as Ramadan. Because dates are so widely grown, they also are fed to camels, horses, and dogs.

Although in many countries dates are added to salads, couscous dishes, and curries, generally in America they're used more often in baked desserts and confections. Here are some tasty samples to try.

## DATE MUFFINS

*Makes 8 to 10 muffins, depending on size.*

■ 1 cup milk
1 egg, beaten
2 cups all-purpose flour (stir before measuring)
1 teaspoon salt
1 tablespoon baking powder
1/4 cup sugar
1/2 cup chopped walnuts
1/2 cup chopped dates
1/4 cup melted butter

▶ Mix milk and egg together in a mixing bowl. Sift together dry ingredients, including sugar. Add to milk and egg mixture and mix well. Stir in walnuts, dates, then butter, mixing just enough to blend. Bake at 400°F for 20 minutes, or until date muffins are browned.

# AUNT MARTHA'S DATE BALLS OR COOKIES

*My Aunt Martha saved this tasty recipe and we still enjoy these treats during the holidays.*

*Makes 30 date balls.*

■ 2 cups corn flakes
3/4 cups dates, chilled
1/2 cup pecans
2 tablespoons honey
1 tablespoon butter
2 teaspoons orange juice
Sifted confectioners' sugar
Pecan halves

▶ Put first three ingredients through meat grinder to mix. Add honey, butter, and orange juice and knead with hands until thoroughly blended. Shape date mixture into one-inch ball size; roll in confectioners' sugar and top each with a pecan half. Or, you can shape as flat cookies.

# DATE BARS

**Crust**
■ 1 3/4 cups oatmeal

1 1/2 cups flour
1/2 teaspoon baking powder
1 teaspoon baking soda
3/4 cup butter, melted
1 cup brown sugar
1/2 teaspoon salt
**Date Filling**
1 pound chopped dates
3/4 cup sugar
1 cup water
1 tablespoon butter
1 teaspoon vanilla
1 cup chopped walnut

▶ Make the filling by boiling dates, sugar, and water until thick, about 5 to 10 minutes. Add butter, vanilla, and walnuts. Set aside to cool a bit. Next, prepare the crust: Combine all dry ingredients with the melted butter. Firmly press half of the mixture into a lightly greased 13" × 9" pan. Cover with filling mixture and top with remaining half of crust mixture. Press lightly. Bake at 350°F for 25 minutes, but no longer. Cut into squares when cool.

# Figs

Fig is the common name for plants of a genus of the mulberry family and the fruits of those plants. The common commercial fig, native to southwest Asia, is widely cultivated in tropical and subtropical countries. It is

a low, deciduous tree, about 15 to 25 feet tall, with deeply lobed, alternate leaves that are rough above and smooth beneath. Branches are covered with downy, greenish bark. Trees bear small flowers and the fruit forms at the end of the receptacle.

Figs can be eaten fresh or dried, in pressed cakes, or from a string or beehive as they still are sold in the Mid East. Figs are popular in the Holy Land and Mediterranean for cooking and as a shade-tree and remain a symbol of peace. According to friends in the Holy Land, the sap of unripe figs or "milk" of ripe figs make a strong drink on a par with barley or mulberry beer. In ancient times fig tree timber was used on the Temple altar for sacrifices because it did not produce smoke.

# Focus on Scripture

## Figs

Genesis 3:6—"And when the woman saw that the tree was good for food, and that it was pleasant to the eyes, and a tree to be desired to make one wise, she took of the fruit thereof, and did eat, and gave also unto her husband with her; and he did eat."

Genesis 3:7—"And the eyes of them both were opened, and they knew that they were naked; and they sewed fig leaves together, and made themselves aprons."

Deuteronomy 8:8—"A land of wheat, and barley, and vines, and fig trees, and pomegranates; a land of oil olive, and honey . . ."

1 Kings 4:25—"And Judah and Israel dwelt safely, every man under his vine and under his fig tree, from Dan even to Beersheba, all the days of Solomon."

> Proverbs 27:18—"Whoso keepeth the fig tree shall eat the fruit thereof: so he that waiteth on his master shall be honored."

# History

Figs were probably cultivated as early as 3000 B.C. from wild varieties that originated in the Arabian Peninsula or the Mediterranean Basin. They can be traced back from archeological digs to the Neolithic Age. Figs constitute the genus Ficus of the family Moraceae.

> To the Egyptians the fig tree represented the Tree of Life; one of their goddesses was said to present figs to mortals thought worthy of eternal happiness. Bethphage, or "house of unripe figs," is a town on the Mount of Olives, famous in ancient days for its figs.

Commercial fig production is widespread throughout the Mediterranean region and most of the fruit is dried before marketing. In the United States, the major commercial growing centers are California and Texas. Popular Californian varieties are packed fresh or dried while most Texas figs are canned.

There is another species of fig, the sycamore fig, which is a taller tree that also bears edible fruit. The figs are pear-shaped, sweet, and slightly aromatic but inferior in taste to the common fig. This tree is the true sycamore, mentioned several times in the Old Testament, and is a favorite shade tree in the Middle East. The pipal, or sacred fig, is a taller type mainly grown in Southeast Asia. It is venerated by Buddhists and Brahmins, to whom it is known as the bo tree. Curiously, the common rubber plant, which is familiar in United States homes and conservatories, is a species of fig. In warm Southeast Asia, fig tree growth is much greater than under temperate conditions, and in this form it is known as the India rubber tree. The banyan tree, or Indian fig, produces edible fruits.

# Growing and Harvesting Tips

If your soil pH is low, adjust it to 5.5 to 6.5 with limestone and spread evenly over the entire area where figs will be planted. Then deep till the soil, at least a 6-foot by 6-foot area, where each bush will be planted at least 8 inches deep. Figs grown in bush form may be set as close as 10 feet apart in the row, but those grown in tree form should be set 15 to 20 feet apart.

Fig trees from nurseries may be grown in the field and sold bare-rooted or grown and sold in the container. Because confusion exists about fig variety names, order fig plants only from reputable nurseries. Never purchase or attempt to grow the kinds of figs grown in California if you live anywhere else. They require pollination by a tiny wasp that cannot survive under other climatic conditions.

Best bet for growing figs is to buy pre-started plants in containers. Carefully remove all packaging material and prune back any broken stems. Water if necessary but remember that fig trees prefer dry conditions, so don't over water. Purchased plants may have some twisted leaves but this will be corrected as the plant adapts to its new home. In warm southern areas you can plant any time of year in Zones 9–10. In colder areas, it's best to plant in spring. Look up details at mail order nurseries for tips on growing figs as part of your indoor plantscaping.

Acclimate your new fig tree for a few days in your garden before planting and protect it from full sun during this time. Keep the trunk and leaves moist, but the soil on the dry side. Usually, a fig tree has been planted in a soil mixture to which perlite has been added, so aeration in the pot should be excellent. If you are potting your fig in a larger container, adding perlite will benefit the plant. As with all container grown plants, be sure there is adequate drainage at the bottom of the pot. You can use rocks, broken pottery, Styrofoam, peanuts, or gravel to assist with drainage.

Pick a well-drained location in full sun. Hardy figs will grow in a variety of soil types, from neutral to acid, clay to sandy, but they prefer a loose soil. Plant an inch lower than the pot soil level to help protect the surface roots.

Figs benefit from fertilizing. They are rapid growers, but go easy on fertilizer because excess will promote overgrowth. High nitrogen levels can inhibit flowering and fruiting. Too much fertilizer and water in late summer will make trees less winter-hardy, so reduce both beginning in August if you live in a cooler region.

Fig trees benefit from pruning so remove any crossing branches during the growing season. Prune to an open vase shape in spring. Protect young trees from temperatures below 32°F with mulch and windbreaks. As fig trees mature, they usually can survive temperatures below 20°F if well rooted in the ground. Check mail order catalogs to be sure you order hardy type figs for northern areas.

> The Hebrew name for fig means "to spread out." Although the fig tree is not very large, some may grow to 25 feet, creating wonderful shade. To sit under one's fig tree was the idea of peace and prosperity to the Jews as indicated in 1 Kings 4:25.

Figs are eaten fresh in the Holy Land, but also are dried and put on strings to be taken as food for journeys, much as they were in biblical times (you'll find "cakes of figs" mentioned in 1 Samuel 25:18). Even now fig leaves are sewn together in the Middle East and natives use them to wrap fresh fruit sent to market. It is best to pick figs as soon as they're ripe (when it's drooping from the tree), before the birds get a chance to feast on them.

# Cooking Tips and Recipes

## STUFFED FRESH FIGS

Fill stemmed fresh figs with cultured sour cream and grated orange peel or with ham salad and serve as appetizers.

## FIG PUDDING

*Makes 6 to 8 servings.*

- 1/4 cup butter
1/2 cup sugar
1 egg
1 1/2 cups sifted flour
2 cups chopped dried figs
2 teaspoons baking powder
1/4 teaspoon salt
1/2 cup milk
1/2 teaspoon vanilla

▶ Cream the butter, add the sugar and the well-beaten egg. Take out about 2 tablespoons of the flour and mix with the figs. Sift together the remaining flour, baking powder, and salt and add alternately with the milk to the butter and egg mixture. Stir in the flour-coated figs and add the vanilla. Bake in a greased baking dish for about one hour at 350°F. Serve hot with lemon sauce or hard sauce to which a little lemon juice has been added.

## FIG RAISIN CAKE

*Makes 6 servings.*

- 1 cups chopped figs
1 cups raisins
1 cup boiling water
1/2 cup shortening

1 cup brown sugar
2 teaspoons baking powder
2 teaspoons cinnamon
1/4 teaspoons salt
2 eggs, well beaten
2 cups flour

▶ Pour boiling water over raisins and figs and allow to stand while

preparing other ingredients. Cream shortening and sugar. Add eggs. Sift flour, measure, and sift with baking powder, cinnamon, and salt. Add alternately with fruit mixture to creamed sugar and shortening. Beat thoroughly. Pour into well-oiled loaf pan. Bake at 375°F about 40 minutes.

# Grapes

Grapes are one of the world's favorite fruits. You can find historic records of grapes, along with the wine and raisins that are made from them, throughout the Bible, from Genesis to Revelation. Along with the olive tree and fig tree, grape vines were often used as symbols of the fertility of the Promised Land of Israel.

You'll also find that Noah is the first human recorded to have grown grapes (Genesis 9:20). We learn that existing vineyards awaited the Israelites when they crossed the Jordan into the Promised Land. Scouts or spies sent out by Moses returned from the Valley of Eshcol with huge clusters of grapes according to Numbers 13:23.

There are many biblical references to raisins (dried grapes), which were often stored or carried as pressed cakes as presented in 1 Samuel 25:18 and 30:12, 2 Samuel 16:1, and 1 Chronicles 12:40. Naturally, water was often not fit to drink, so people of Jesus' time relied on wine made from grapes. A drink offering of wine was presented with the daily sacrifice, per Exodus 29:40–41 and with the offering of the first fruits per Leviticus 23:13.

Wine was used at the Passover and Jesus used it with unleavened bread at the Last Supper as symbols of His body and blood (Matthew 26:26–29). He then said that, "I shall not drink again of this fruit of the vine until that day when I drink it new with you in my Father's kingdom" (Matthew 26:29 RSV). Actually, the first recorded miracle of Jesus Christ was the turning of water into wine at a wedding in Cana in Galilee. He also used the grape vine in His teachings about the church.

"I am the true vine, and My Father is the vinedresser. Every branch of mine that bears no fruit, He takes away, and every branch that does bear fruit He prunes, that it may bear more fruit. You are already made clean by the word which I have spoken to you. Abide in Me, and I in you. As the branch cannot bear fruit by itself, unless it abides in the vine, neither can you, unless you abide in Me. I am the vine, you are the branches. He who abides in Me, and I in him, he it is that bears much fruit, for apart from Me you can do nothing. If a man does not abide in Me, he is cast forth as a branch and withers; and the branches are gathered, thrown into the fire and burned. If you abide in Me, and My words abide in you, ask whatever you will, and it shall be done for you. By this My Father is glorified, that you bear much fruit, and so prove to be My disciples."

# Focus on Scripture

## Grapes

You'll find many scriptural references to grapes and many more when you search for "wine". There isn't room to include all quotations with each food in this book. Here are some.

Genesis 40:10—"And in the vine were three branches: and it was as though it budded, and her blossoms shot forth; and the clusters thereof brought forth ripe grapes."

Genesis 40:11—"And Pharaoh's cup was in my hand: and I took the grapes, and pressed them into Pharaoh's cup, and I gave the cup into Pharaoh's hand."

Leviticus 25:11—"A jubilee shall that fiftieth year be unto you: ye shall not sow, neither reap that which groweth of itself in it, nor gather the grapes in it of thy vine undressed."

Numbers 13:20—"And what the land is, whether it be fat or lean, whether there be wood therein, or not. And be ye of good courage, and bring of the fruit of the land. Now the time was the time of the first ripe grapes."

Numbers 13:23—"And they came unto the brook of Eshcol, and cut down from thence a branch with one cluster of grapes, and they bare it between two upon a staff; and they brought of the pomegranates, and of the figs."

Deuteronomy 24:21—"When thou gatherest the grapes of thy vineyard, thou shalt not glean it afterward: it shall be for the stranger, for the fatherless, and for the widow . . ."

Judges 9:27—"And they went out into the fields, and gathered their vineyards, and trode the grapes, and made merry, and went into the house of their god, and did eat and drink, and cursed Abimelech . . ."

Isaiah 5:2—"And he fenced it, and gathered out the stones thereof, and planted it with the choicest vine, and built a tower in the midst of it, and also made a winepress therein: and he looked that it should bring forth grapes, and it brought forth wild grapes."

# History and Nutritional Highlights

The European grape has been used as food since prehistoric times. Grape seeds have been found in remains of lake dwellings of the Bronze Age in Switzerland and Italy and in tombs of ancient Egypt. Today, grapes are commercially cultivated in warmer regions all over the world, particularly in Western Europe, the Balkans, and in America, especially in California and New York state. Grapes belong to the family *Vitaceae*.

Grape is the common name of an edible fruit in the buckthorn family, and of the vines that produce the fruit. Botanists believe that the Caspian Sea region was the original home of the European grape. Distribution of seeds by birds, wind, and water carried the plant westward to the Asian shores of the Mediterranean. Grape culture, practiced when Jesus lived, was introduced to the Mediterranean region by seagoing Phoenicians. The ancient Greeks cultivated grapes and the Romans later adapted the fruit to their empire as well. Grapes are indeed deeply rooted in France, which is still famous for its fine wines.

The European grape was introduced to eastern North America during colonial times, but in those days grape cultivation failed due to the attacks of diseases and pests. Successful grape varieties of the eastern United States, such as Concord and Delaware, are strains developed from hybrids between the European grape and several native species. Today, Eastern U.S. grapes are characterized by a juicy layer between the skin and pulp of the fruit, which permits easy removal of the skin.

Grape varieties are classified according to their ultimate use. Consider these facts as you think about growing grapes in your biblical garden. European varieties are considered superior to Eastern U.S. varieties for use as table wines, table grapes, dessert wines, and raisins. In contrast, Eastern U.S. grapes are preferred for juices and jellies.

Grapes used to make table wine must have relatively high acidity and moderate sugar content. Those used for dessert wines and other sweet wines must have high sugar content and moderate acidity. Table grapes must be low in both acidity and sugar content and must conform to definite standards of size, color, and shape. Grapes used to make juices and jellies must have a pronounced flavor combined with high acidity and moderate sugar content. Finally, raisin grapes are preferably seedless, with high sugar content and low acidity.

As you think about different varieties of colorful grapes and the joys they provide for eating fresh and making great grape jam, jelly, juice, and perhaps wine, it is good to know how valuable grapes are to health. Grapes (especially red grapes) are now recognized as being very beneficial for preventing heart problems. A cup of raw grapes contains only 58 calories; a minuscule 0.3 grams of fat; zero cholesterol; and vitamins A, B and C. Grapes fight tooth decay, stop viruses in their tracks, and are rich in other ingredients that many researchers believe can help to prevent cancer.

Researchers are now rediscovering what the physicians of the Bible knew centuries ago: that wine, in moderation, may have a profound impact on out health and healing. One of the earliest recommendations about wine comes from St. Paul who wrote: "Stop drinking water only, but use a little wine for the sake of your stomach and for your frequent cases of sickness" (1 Timothy 5:3). We also read in Psalm 104:15, "And wine that makes the heart of mortal man rejoice." It is obvious from Scriptures that in the Holy land, wine was used for both celebrations and medicinal purposes.

Glancing back to biblical times we realize that grapes were central to life. In Numbers 12:23 we read, "When they came to the torrent valley of Eshcol, they then proceeded to cut down from there a shoot with one cluster of grapes. And they went carrying it with a bar on two of the men." That must have been some gigantic cluster of grapes! But such abundance was not unusual in the vineyards that were so important to the people of the Bible. Grapes were eaten fresh or dried and eaten as raisins, just as they are today. Most grapes were made into juice, wine, and vinegar, although some were also pressed into cakes. Since those ancient times, grapes remained a major food and beverage source to the time of Jesus. In fact, grapes still are one of the world's more popular foods and the source of many wines made around the world today.

## Growing and Harvesting Tips

Grape cultivars may be of the American, European, or French hybrid types. American and French hybrids are best suited for northern growing conditions because they tend to be more winter-hardy. Recommended American cultivars include Niagara, Delaware, and Canadice.

Consider these white seedless grapes: Neptune, Lakemont, and Marquis. You might also try a blue Concord seedless. Glenora is another very hardy Concord type seedless grape. Jupiter is a reddish blue seedless and Flame is a reddish one. The prized Concord grape, a classic since 1843, is the standard of flavor for prize-winning jams and jellies. It ripens in late September and is the most widely planted grape east of the Rockies. It is hardy in most northern areas except truly cold winter states. For cold areas, consider Bluebell, Fredonia, Van Buren, and Worden.

Several French-American hybrids, such as Seyval Blanc and Vidal Blanc are recommended for their wine making qualities and good winter hardiness. If wine making has appeal, here are several more cultivars to consider: Golden Muscat, Marechal Foch, Chardonel, and Frontnac.

You have a colorful choice with grapes, too, as you thumb through mail order catalogs. Depending on the cultivar, grapes may be red, blue, white (which is really greenish-yellow), purple, or black. You can choose either seeded or seedless types. Grapes don't store well, so a longer harvest period is useful. Earliest cultivars ripen beginning about mid-August, while the latest cultivars ripen fruit from late September to early October. As with other fruits, check out ripening times so you'll have a longer season for enjoying fresh grapes. For example, Ontario, Seneca, Fredonia, and Hardy Worden are early ripeners. Mid-seasons include Delaware, Niagara, and Steuben. Late ones include Sheridan and Golden Muscat.

Growing grapes well requires long-term dedication. Vines tale several years from planting to first harvest. Normally they don't reach full production until the fifth or sixth year. The good news is that grape plants can survive for 50 to 100 years if you and your family tend them well. Considering these facts, it is important to carefully select both the vine site and devote time to soil preparation.

Avoiding frosty areas is vital. Grape growing sites should be located on sloping land that faces south so any cold air drains away to the bottom of the slope. The first step toward producing high-quality fruit is a sunny location. Sheltered home surroundings usually are warmer. A sloping area, especially a south or southwest slope, usually has higher temperatures and is less likely to get frost. Plant rows north to south so that fruit and leaves will be better exposed to sunlight than in east to west rows.

Grapes can grow in a wide variety of soil types but drainage is important. Your grapes won't prosper if you have heavy clay soils with poor drainage. You can improve most soils, but if you can pick deep, well-drained, loamy soils for your arbor, that's an advantage. Also consider that grapes need full sunlight and high temperatures to ripen. Shielding vines from prevailing winds is worthwhile. Avoid sites with standing water, especially in spring.

Veteran grape growers suggest spring planting, as soon as the soil can be worked. Space plants 6 to 8 feet apart. Before planting vines remove all except the most vigorous cane. Trim off any broken or overly long roots. Next, dig a hole large enough so you can spread the root system out without bending roots. Plant vines at the same depth as in the nursery.

Spread roots evenly and cover them completely with soil. After planting, shorten the remaining cane to two strong buds. Each bud will develop into a cane.

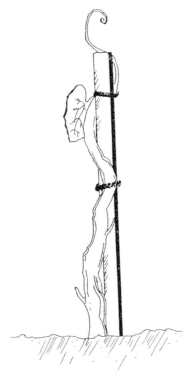

*A new grape vine needs support as it begins to set its permanent roots.*

Pack soil well around roots to remove air pockets and water thoroughly. Leave a slight depression around the base of the plant to catch rain. Young grapevines can't compete with weeds or lawn grass for water and nutrients. Keep the planting free of all weeds. Mulching a foot or more around newly planted vines is useful. If you cultivate the ground, do it no deeper than 1 to 3 inches to avoid injuring roots.

Grapes require some type of support. Space vines for training on a trellis 8 feet apart and have it in place before planting or at least before vine growth begins the second year.

Feed grape vines well and they'll feed you with abundant harvests. Your grapes will do best where soil pH is between 5.0 and 6.0. Apply lime only if soil analysis indicates a need. To properly feed new vines, apply 8 ounces of 10-10-10 fertilizer per plant 7 days after planting. You should then increase the amount to 1 pound of 10-10-10 in the second year and 1 1/2 pounds per vine in the third and later years. Apply fertilizer about 30 days before new spring growth begins, spreading it evenly 6 to 12 inches from the trunk of the vine.

Grapes benefit from a evenly balanced fertilizer of nutrients. Water plants after planting and during dry periods. An inch per week the first year is advisable. Mature vines seem to thrive with rainwater, except in droughts or dry climates when you should irrigate vines, especially as they set fruit and it matures.

Grape vines need careful attention to pruning, more than most gardeners believe or are willing to do. You must achieve a balance between vegetative growth and fruiting. It is best to prune vines when they are dormant during winter using either cane or spur pruning. Frankly, the most common care problem with grape growing is that gardeners don't prune hard enough. For grapes, you must remove the majority of wood produced the previous season, which will be about 90 percent. That's right! Read this again. In proper pruning very little wood is left to produce the following year's crop. Shoots that develop from the remaining buds are more prolific and bear grapes of high quality.

Now for the good part, picking and enjoying your grape crops. The trick is to pick at proper maturity. Fruit color isn't a sure indication of ripeness. In table grapes, maturity usually is determined by taste. All grapes become sweeter and usually less acidic as they approach maturity. To determine when to pick, consider that the average temperature must be greater than 50°F for grapes to continue to mature on the vine. Fruit does not ripen further once picked. Sample some grapes as they appear to be mature. When you like what you taste, it is harvest time. Write down the date. Watch the calendar the next year and you'll be able to focus on the best grape picking period for your crops.

# Cooking Tips and Recipes

## PERFECT PASSOVER PIE

**Crust**
- 3 containers chocolate macaroons

1 bottle Concord grape wine

**Filling**

1 lb. sweet chocolate or semi sweet chocolate

1/2 cup sugar

6 tablespoons Concord grape wine

8 eggs, separated

1 teaspoon vanilla

▶ Mash the chocolate macaroons with enough Concord grape wine to make a moist consistency. Press into 10" pie pan. Crust should be approximately 1/4" thick throughout. Melt the chocolate, adding sugar and wine, in the top of a double boiler until smooth. Cool. Separate eggs. Add egg yolks, one at a time, to the cooled chocolate mixture, beating well after each egg is added. Add vanilla to the chocolate/egg yolk mixture. Next, beat egg whites until a soft peak forms. Fold egg whites into chocolate/egg yolk mixture. Pour into prepared pie shell. Refrigerate for at least 4 hours. When ready to serve, top with whipped cream.

## BOSTON LETTUCE SALAD WITH GRAPES AND WALNUTS

■ 12 cups lettuce, washed and in bite size pieces.
2/3 cup walnut pieces
1/2 cup feta cheese, crumbled, about 4 oz.

1 cup grapes, sliced in halves, red, green, or white
5 tablespoons walnut oil
3 tablespoons vegetable oil
2 tablespoons white wine vinegar
Salt and pepper

▶ In a large salad bowl, toss together lettuce, walnuts, crumbled cheese, and grapes. In a small screw top jar, combine oils, vinegar, and freshly ground black pepper to taste. Shake until dressing appears creamy. Drizzle dressing over salad and toss just before serving.

# Melons

Melons have captivated people since time began, and rightfully. Their sweet taste, delightful and distinctive flavors, and even their aromas captivate home gardeners. It is appropriate that they are mentioned in the Bible. In fact, melons remain one of the favorite and most widely grown foods in Egypt and other parts of the Middle East. Melons were typically eaten fresh and as salads in ancient times. In addition to common melons such as watermelon and muskmelons there were other types of flavorful melons grown. Today we can enjoy many of these same varieties as well as the improved melons that plant breeders have perfected from the ancient types.

"O fleur de tous les fruits. O ravissant melon!" ("Oh, flower of all the fruits. Oh, ravishing melon!") was the way a 16th-century French monk praised the Charantais melon. Now, five centuries later, there still is nothing quite as delightful as the sweet scent of ripe melons wafting on the breeze on a summer's day. Their appeal lead the National Garden Bureau to celebrate the myriad luscious, delectable large fruits we call melons with a Year of the Melon recently.

According to Webster's *Dictionary*, melons are "the large round fruit of various plants of the gourd family, with sweet pulpy flesh and many seeds which include popular honeydew, cantaloupe, muskmelon." They are vining, warm-season fruits that grow best in regions with long summers. Bees are necessary for pollination and fruiting. Today, plant breeders have perfected delicious, productive hybrid varieties that produce abundantly in northern short growing season areas.

Melons range in size from slightly larger than a softball to hefty 15-pound varieties. Skin color varies from pale grayish-white to very dark green and the flesh can be any color from the palest yellow to the brightest orange and green. Their seeds fill the hollow center of the fruit.

> Melons are a summertime delight, sweet and juicy, freshly picked or cooled in the refrigerator. They're versatile, too. You can use them as an ingredient in salads, salsas, side dishes, entrees, or drinks.

Melon is a common name for any one of numerous varieties of sweet fruits of the gourd family that grow on two species of trailing vines. One vine bears muskmelons, winter melons, and the European cantaloupe. The other type bears watermelons.

Muskmelons have a soft, ribbed rind with distinct netting, salmon-colored pulp, and a musky aroma. They are the most perishable of the melons and are particularly popular in America, where they are also called cantaloupes, a misnomer taken from the quite distinct European cantaloupe.

You can also grow winter melons, of which the honeydew, Persian, casaba, and Crenshaw are best known. These are less aromatic than musk-melons, take more time to mature, and have harder rinds that preserve them well after the growing season. The honeydew has a smooth rind with green pulp. Persian melons have dark rinds with orange pulp. Casabas have a

yellow, wrinkled rind with green or white pulp, and the Crenshaws have a dark green, wrinkled rind with pink pulp.

True cantaloupes are grown mostly in Europe and have hard, warty, scaly rinds with deep grooves and do not have the characteristic netting of muskmelons. For best results, stick with muskmelons!

Watermelons vary in shape, size, and markings and range from round to oblong, from 2 1/2 to 50 pounds, and from dark green to striped light green. The flesh is usually red, quite sweet, extremely watery, and distinctly crisp.

# Focus on Scripture

## Melons

Numbers 11:5—"We remember the fish, which we did eat in Egypt freely; the cucumbers, and the melons, and the leeks, and the onions, and the garlick . . ."

# History

Melons belong to the family *Cucurbitaceae*. Muskmelons are derived from *Cucumis melo* variety 'Reticulatus.' The true cantaloupe is classified as *Cucumis melo* variety 'Cantalupensis.'

Muskmelons, winter melons, and European cantaloupes are believed to have originated in Iran and the Transcaucasia before being cultivated by the Egyptians and the Greeks and Romans. Watermelons originated in tropical Africa, and early Egyptian records indicate that they have been cultivated for more than 4,000 years.

The first documented use of the word "melon" was about 1395. Today, there are numerous types of melons available; most popular in North America are the cantaloupe, muskmelon, and honeydew types. Unusual types of melons are available primarily from seed. Look for them in mail order catalogs or seed packets sold in retail stores. For fun and easy reference, here are some other melons that trace their roots to the Holy Land area. Most melons trace their roots to the are of the Mediterranean.

Ananas melons, a.k.a. Middle Eastern melons, are oval shaped with medium-fine netting over pale green to orange rind. They have very sweet, aromatic white flesh. One variety has orange-pink flesh. Average weight is three to four pounds.

Athena cantaloupes are Eastern U.S. cantaloupes; they are early maturing, oval-shaped, yellow-orange summer melons with firm, thick, yellow-orange flesh, and the skin is slightly sutured with coarse netting. Average weight is 5 to 6 pounds. Left on the vine or harvested, the flesh remains firm.

Canary melons, a.k.a. Spanish, Juan Canary, Jaune des Canaries, and San Juan canary melons, have bright yellow rinds and an oblong shape. Inside, the pale, cream-colored flesh is juicy, and the flavor is very mild.

Casaba melons have an oval shape with a pointy end, which, coupled with wrinkled yellow skin, sets casabas off from other melons. They weigh 4 to 7 pounds. The pale, almost white flesh is extremely sweet.

Charentais melons, a.k.a. French Charentais, are French melons identifiable by their smooth, gray, or gray-blue rinds with sutures and orange flesh. Small, cut in half they serve two for breakfast.

Christmas melons, a.k.a. Piel de Sapo and Rochet, have a football shape, weighing upwards of 5 to 8 pounds. Cut through the yellow to green mottled rinds to reveal palest orange or light green sweet flesh depending upon the variety.

Crenshaw are a Casaba cross with a slightly more oblong shape, weighing at least 5 pounds. The slightly wrinkled green rind ripens to yellow. Inside, the flesh is pale peachy orange. It has a strong, spicy aroma.

Galia melons are Israeli melons you'll find easily on a trip to the Holy Land. These have netted rinds similar to cantaloupes but paler in color. The sweet pale green to almost white flesh has the consistency of a honeydew, with a spicy-sweet or banana-like aroma. When ripe, they slip from the vine.

Honeydew melons are second in popularity only to "cantaloupes," by which most people mean muskmelon in America. Honeydews have smooth, white to greenish-white or slightly yellow rinds and open to reveal refreshingly sweet flesh that may be green, white, or orange. Its texture is similar to a cantaloupe, but the flavor more subtle and sweet.

Muskmelons, of course, are our familiar American cantaloupes with orange flesh and netted skin.

Oriental melons are small, weighing a little more than a pound. These are elongated yellow melons with white sutures, and sweet, pale peach to white flesh. Because the seeds are so small and the rind is so thin, the entire melon can be eaten.

Persian melons are bigger than cantaloupes and have a dark green rind with light brown netting. As it ripens, the rind turns to light green. Bright pink-orange flesh has a delicate flavor. Unlike most melons in the Reticulatus group, Persian melons do not slip from the vine when mature.

> The true Cantaloupe is named for the town of Cantalupo near Rome, Italy and has rough-warty, not netted skin. This is the European cantaloupe, rarely grown in America.

Finally, the winter melon is the catchall name for the long-season, long-keeping (up to a month or more at room temperature) melons, including crenshaw, casaba, canary, and Christmas melons.

# Growing and Harvesting Tips

Most melons ripen in late summer or early- to mid-fall. If you are in a northern state, you should always start melon seeds indoors to gain growing time, if possible 6 to 8 weeks before soil and temperature is right and while frost still threatens planting seedlings outdoors. You can also select new hybrid varieties that ripen in shorter time.

As warm-season fruits, which thrive in temperatures of 70° to 80°F, melons prefer slightly acid soil with a pH between 6.0 and 6.5. Melons are thirsty and hungry plants, so be prepared to provide ample soil moisture and plant nutrients for them, especially as fruit ripens, to boost sweetness.

Like other cucurbits, melons can easily crossbreed, so allow plenty of space between different types or cultivars. To be completely safe from possible cross-pollination, keep them away from other family members including cucumbers, squash, and pumpkins.

In mild-winter areas, sow seeds directly in the garden at the same time as you plant tomatoes, after all danger of frost is past and the ground is warm and has dried from winter wetness. Make a small hill of rich, amended, well-drained soil and plant 3 to 5 seeds two inches apart and about one inch deep. Water well. Once vines have two sets of true leaves, thin out the smaller or weaker vines, leaving the two strongest to grow on.

To boost growth, especially in cold-winter climates, plant melons through black plastic mulch. The dark plastic absorbs heat, warms the soil early, conserves moisture, controls weeds, keeps some pests and diseases away, and makes harvesting a whole lot easier and cleaner. We always do this and get about a 2-week growing advantage that gives us more melons before fall frosts in Maine.

Lay plastic over the future melon garden in late winter to start warming the soil. Weigh down edges with soil or old boards. When the soil is above 60°F you can start planting. Make 5-inch x-line cuts at least 4 feet apart on 6-foot centers if you grow in rows. Then, plant seeds, or transplant melons that you started indoors.

Melons need a minimum of 1-inch of water a week—2 inches is better. Water in the morning, ideally at soil level, using drip irrigation so the leaves can dry before evening, preventing fungal diseases. Watering is critical when the fruit starts setting and when the fruit is maturing.

Fertilize every 2 to 3 weeks, using an all-purpose fertilizer, such as 5-5-5. Add several inches of compost to all root areas monthly. Some gardeners use an organic or inorganic mulch. The soil should be lightly moist, up to a foot deep.

The best and sweetest melons ripen when weather is hot and dry. If you have humid summers, give melons a boost by planting them in soil that is very well drained and with ample space for good air circulation around the entire vine.

Be aware that melons need heat to ripen properly. Most summer melons are fragrant when ripe. Sniff the skin and if you smell the flavor of the melon it is ripe for the picking. Another indicator for ripeness is when the stem separates or slips easily where the vine attaches to the fruit. After a few tries you'll get the 'feel' of when to pick for best flavor. The sweetest and most flavorful melons are those picked ripe from the vine and eaten right away.

If you have a small, sunny space, you can grow melons in containers. The secrets are size and soil. Select a large container and a dwarf melon variety, which refers to size of the vine. The melons themselves will be full-size. Fill a half whiskey barrel that has drainage holes with rich soil. Pop in a dwarf melon that grows only 3- to 4-feet long, producing a 4-inch fruit, and water. Grow up a trellis if you wish. Support the fruit with nets made of old pantyhose or onion bags.

# Wonderful Watermelons

Because the watermelon requires somewhat different treatment than the other melons (and because it is so popular and delicious), it deserves its own little section. It too is a tender, warm-season vegetable. Watermelon is truly one of summertime's sweetest treats. It is fun to eat and good for you. First brought to this country by African slaves, today there are more than 100 different varieties of watermelons. The flesh may be red, pink, orange, or yellow. There are seedless varieties and super-sweet round ones that fit nicely into the refrigerator.

Watermelons are low in calories and very nutritious. They are high in lycopene (second only to tomatoes), a powerful antioxidant that research suggests is effective in preventing some forms of cancer and cardiovascular disease. According to a study conducted at the University of North Carolina at Chapel Hill, men who consumed a lycopene-rich diet were half as likely to suffer a heart attack as those who had little or no lycopene in their diets.

Watermelon is also high in vitamin C and vitamin A in the form of disease fighting beta-carotene. Lycopene and beta-carotene work in conjunction with other plant chemicals not found in vitamin/mineral supplements. Watermelons also have potassium, which is believed to help control blood pressure and possibly prevent strokes.

Watermelons can be grown in all parts of the country, but the warmer temperatures and longer growing season of southern areas favor these melons. If you live in northern areas choose early varieties, start seedlings indoors, and use transplants

when danger of frost has passed. Mulching with black plastic film also promotes early growth by warming the soil under the plastic.

> Seedless watermelons are self-sterile hybrids that develop normal-looking fruits but no fully developed seeds. Because germination of these types is often more difficult, it is best to start them in peat pots and use as transplants for your outdoor garden.

Among regular garden watermelons, here are some recommended varieties, with typical ripening dates to guide northern gardeners especially. Check mail order catalogs for specific varieties by description. Early season varieties mature in 70 to 75 days and main season varieties mature in 80 to 85 days. Good varieties include Sugar Baby, with red flesh, 6 to 10 pounds; Yellow Baby with hybrid-yellow flesh, 6 to 10 pounds; old time favorite Charleston Gray with red flesh, reaching 20 to 25 pounds and will thrive in southern states; and Queen of Hearts, red, 12 to 16 pounds.

Plant watermelons after the soil is warm and when all danger of frost is past. They grow best on a sandy loam soil, although yields on clay soils can be increased significantly by mulching raised planting rows with black plastic film. Watermelon vines require considerable space. Plant seeds 1 inch deep in hills spaced 6 feet apart and allow 7 to 10 feet between rows. After seedlings are established, thin to the best 3 plants per hill. Plant single transplants 2 to 3 feet apart or double transplants 4 to 5 feet apart in the rows.

To get a jump on spring and gain more growing and ripening time, start the seeds inside 3 to 4 weeks before they are to be set out in the garden. Plant 2 or 3 seeds in peat pellets, peat pots or cell packs and thin to the best one or two plants. Don't start too early because large watermelon seedlings transplant poorly. Growing transplants inside requires a warm temperature, ideally between 80°F and 85°F. Place black plastic film over the row before planting and use a starter fertilizer. Keep watermelons free from weeds by shallow hoeing and cultivation or mulching. These plants have moderately deep roots and watering is seldom necessary unless weather turns dry for a long period.

Sometimes it is difficult to know when to pick because watermelons, unlike muskmelons, don't give easy indicator signs. Use a combination of the following indicators: First, wait for light green, curly tendrils on the stem near the point of attachment of the melon to turn brown and dry. Second, check the surface color of the fruit as it turns dull. When ripe, the skin becomes resistant to penetration by the thumbnail and is rough to the touch. Also, the bottom of the melon, where it lies on the soil, turns from light green to a yellowish color. These indicators for choosing a ripe watermelon aren't perfect but are much more reliable than "thumping" the melon with a knuckle.

## Preparation Tips and Recipes

No matter which of the melons you grow, add them to your culinary repertoire and you'll be sure to impress family and guests. All melons are flavorful enough on their own, but you can enhance them with a sprinkle of ginger or salt. A squirt of lemon or lime juice will bring out the melon's sweetness.

Serve individual portions of chilled soup, such as cucumber, melon, or Vichyssoise in hollowed out melon halves. Replace bowls with melon halves for serving dips, salads of all kinds, and punch, depending on the size of the melon. Get creative and cut the melons with scalloped or jagged edges.

Garnish food with slices of melon or melon balls. They enhance the look and flavor of almost any dish from ice cream to cakes, salads to soups. They add verve to punches or drinks. In fact, Midori is a liqueur made from melons.

Our thanks to the National Garden Bureau and a long time friend, Cathy Wilkinson Barash, for the good growing advice about melons. I also thank melon experts Robyn Coffey of Willhite Seed, Inc., Tracy Lee of Park Seed Co., Inc., and Dan Croker of Seminis Vegetable Seeds who tuned me into melon culture.

The National Watermelon Promotion Board suggests washing whole watermelons with clean water before slicing to remove potential bacteria. The flavor of watermelon is best enjoyed raw. To make melon balls, cut the watermelon in half lengthwise and then into quarters. Watermelon balls can be scooped right out of rind. Create perfect balls using a melon baller and a twist of the wrist. Then, the watermelon shell can be used to hold the melon balls as well as other fruit. Watermelon punch is also served from the hollow rind. By sitting the round end inside a ring or bowl, the shell remains stable during serving.

## WATERMELON GRANITA

*Here's one way to dress up watermelons for a special treat.*

*Makes 4 servings.*

■ 5 cups seeded watermelon pulp
1 cup sugar syrup (recipe below)
2 tablespoons fresh lemon juice

▶ Slice a few thin watermelon wedges and cut into strips for a garnish. Puree the remainder of the watermelon in a food processor. Pour into a 9" × 13" inch baking dish. Stir in the syrup and lemon juice. Freeze for about 4 hours or until frozen solid. To serve, scrape up granita with a large spoon and place in goblets, tulip shaped wine glasses, or ice cream dishes. Garnish with a narrow wedge of watermelon.

To make sugar syrup: Combine 1/2 cup water and 1 cup sugar in a saucepan. Bring to a boil over medium-high heat. Boil for one minute, stirring constantly until all of the sugar has dissolved. Cool in the refrigerator.

## WATERMELON SMOOTHIE

*Here's a special cooling drink you can offer as a summer surprise.*

*Makes 4 servings.*

■ 1 8-ounce lemon flavored fat-free yogurt
3 cups cubed, seeded watermelon

1 pint fresh strawberries, cleaned and hulled
1 tablespoon honey or strawberry jam
3 ice cubes

In a blender or food processor combine yogurt, watermelon, strawberries, honey or jam, and ice cubes. Process until smooth and frothy. Serve in tall glasses with a straw.

# Olives

One of the most uplifting mentions of olive trees in Scripture is Hosea 14:6, in which the olive tree is used as a symbol for what is good: "His branches shall spread, and his beauty shall be as the olive tree."

As you reflect on the passages that refer to olive trees, remember that in biblical days gardens were not as we know them today. Often gardens consisted mostly of olive trees, perhaps with fig and nut trees scattered among them or in corners. The Garden of Gethsemane was, in reality, an olive orchard at the foot of the Mount of Olives. In fact, Garden of Gethsemane translated means "garden with the olive press." No doubt oil presses were located there to press the precious oil from the fruits of those magnificently productive trees.

The olive is a species of small tree native to coastal areas of the eastern Mediterranean region, from Lebanon and the maritime parts of Asia Minor and northern Iran at the south end of the Caspian Sea. It is an evergreen tree or shrub, typically short and squat, and rarely exceeding 20 to 40 feet in height. Olives are now widely cultivated all over the world in areas with Mediterranean-type climates. The olives yield an edible oil which is made from fresh, ripe fruits that contain about 20 percent oil, and today is favored as for use in cooking and for salad dressings. A full size olive tree yields an impressive half-ton of oil yearly.

Unripe olives are green and remain so

during pickling. Ripe olives are dark bluish when fresh and turn blackish during pickling. The wood of the cultivated olive, being hard and variegated, is valued for making furniture.

From Jesus' time to the present, olive trees have been the most important tree cultivated in the Holy Land. The olive oil is often used instead of butter and unripened green fruit eaten with a brown bread. In the past, olive oil was prepared for burning in the lamps of the temple. In Exodus 27:20 we read, "And thou shalt command the children of Israel, that they bring thee pure olive oil beaten for the light, to cause the lamp to burn always."

# Focus on Scripture
## Olives

Judges. 15:5—"And when he had set the brands on fire, he let them go into the standing corn of the Philistines, and burnt up both the shocks, and also the standing corn, with the vineyards and olives."

Micah. 6:15—"Thou shalt sow, but thou shalt not reap; thou shalt tread the olives, but thou shalt not anoint thee with oil; and sweet wine, but shalt not drink wine. with a loud voice for all the mighty works that they had seen . . ."

2 Esdras. 16:29—"As in an orchard of olives upon every tree there are left three or four olives . . ."

# History

Olive is the common name for a plant family and for the fruit of the olive tree. Originally a wild tree, botanists believe as early as the Palaeolithic period the Jews used olives to produce olive oil, though not to eat fresh. According to earliest written records, the cultivation of edible olives was a Second Temple period accomplishment. From the Holy Land and Syria, cultivated olives made their throughout the Mediterranean area.

The olive is one of the earliest plants cited in recorded literature. In Homer's Odyssey, Odysseus crawls beneath two shoots of olive that grow from a single stock. Horace mentions olives in reference to his own diet, which he describes as very simple: "As for me, olives, endives, and smooth mallows provide sustenance." Pliny the Elder told of a sacred Greek olive tree that was 1,600 years old. The olive tree is one of the symbols of Athena, the Greek goddess, and is frequently mentioned in both the Bible and the Quran.

> Some Italian olive trees are believed to date back to Roman times. An olive tree in Crete, claimed to be over 2,000 years old, has been verified on the basis of tree ring analysis. Another, on the island of Croatia, has been calculated to be about 1,600 years old and reportedly still gives fruit, about sixty-five pounds per year, which is made into top quality olive oil.

One olive tree at Neot Kedumim has roots going back perhaps 1,000 years or more. A brief story by Beth Uval about that tree is worth sharing. Opposite the olive press in the Seven Species area of Neot Kedumim in the Holy Land stands her favorite olive tree. It is not the biggest, or the most beautiful, or the oldest but is one that embodies an idea very close to her heart. The ancient trunk seems completely lifeless, but next to the base of this dead trunk are fresh, new shoots. Some are mere infants, some already teenagers. All are bursting with the vitality of the young. Though the cells of the ancient tree trunk are inert, the roots are still producing life in the form of these green-leafed shoots.

As Beth Uval explains, "These offshoots are the babies of the olive tree. We can take one of these shoots, together with a piece of the root that nourishes it, and keep it for several months. When we put the shoot in the ground, it will send down new roots and grow, and in four or five years start producing fruit. Psalm 128 says, "Your children are like olive shoots around your table."

"Our progeny sit around our table like the next generation of the olive tree around its trunk. And the last verse of the Psalm says, "May you see children of your children, and peace in Israel." The continuity that is inseparable from peace. These shoots, the olive tree's children, have a special name in Hebrew, which is netzer, from the Hebrew root meaning "to guard or preserve."

"The farmer doesn't leave all the shoots, which sap the strength of the parent tree, but only a few, the most promising, to produce new trees," Beth Uval explains. She quotes the prophet Isaiah: "A branch will grow from the trunk of Jesse, (father of King David)), and a shoot will sprout from its roots." In his historical context, in the 8th century B.C., Isaiah was prophesying the destruction that threatened Jerusalem. But, as always in Isaiah, destruction is never final. Assyria would conquer a large part of the Kingdom of Judah. But afterwards, Judah would be ruled by a new king, from the House of David who would be wise and righteous: "The spirit of the Lord shall rest upon him, the spirit of wisdom and understanding, the spirit of counsel and valor, the spirit of devotion and reverence for the Lord." Destruction would be followed by an era of peace and justice. This idea of rebirth following death and destruction is still very much alive for us.

"In the spring, after Passover, we have two modern days in the Jewish calendar," she explains: "Yom Hashoah, the Holocaust Memorial Day, then exactly one week later, Yom Hazikaron, the memorial day for fallen soldiers and terror victims, followed immediately by Yom Ha'atzma'ut, Israel Independence Day. It is during this week especially, when we relive the miraculous emergence, in our time, of new life from tragedy, that we show visitors this particular olive tree.

"We show them that destruction is never final. There is always hope for renewal. It happens in nature, and it happens in human life and human history, in the times of the Bible and in ours. May this spring bring the new life and hope that always lies possible in crisis and disaster, as the tree lies waiting in the seed," Beth Uval concludes.

Today there are thousands of cultivars of the olive but only a few are grown extensively. Since many cultivars are self sterile or nearly so, they are generally planted in pairs with a single primary cultivar and a secondary cultivar selected for its ability to fertilize the primary. If you plan to try growing olives in suitable areas in America, be sure to check your sources for proper pollinating varieties. In recent times, efforts have been directed at producing hybrid cultivars with qualities such as resistance to disease, quick growth, and larger or more consistent crops.

# Growing Tips

Olive trees prefer limestone bearing soils and favor coastal climate conditions. They tolerate drought well, thanks to their sturdy, extensive root system once they get established. Olive trees can be exceptionally long-lived, up to several centuries, and can remain productive for as long, provided they are pruned correctly and regularly.

Olive trees grow very slowly, but over many years the trunk can attain a considerable diameter. Although they can reach great ages, trees rarely exceed 45 feet in height. Follow planting directions as you would for all fruit trees (see apple trees, page 111).

You can grow olive trees outdoors if you live in a climate that favors their growth, such as the southwestern United States, southern California, Texas, and Florida. These trees will survive even in poor soils if given proper care, adequate water, and applications of fertilizer with nitrogen beneath their branches.

Be warned that you may not see the fruits of your labors in the form of tasty olives, since these trees require special climatic conditions similar to their native Middle East. However, if they like their home, you can expect some fruit in 7 or 8 years. In southern states they are worth a try. You also can try growing them as specimens in containers in your home regardless of where you live. Best bet is to order started plants from nurseries that offer these trees.

# Cooking Tips and Recipes

The only real difference between green olives and black olives is ripeness. Unripe olives are green. Fully ripe olives are black. Olives are cured or pickled before consumption, using various methods that include oil-curing, water-curing, brine-curing, dry-curing, and lye-curing. Green olives must be soaked in a lye solution before brining, whereas ripe black olives can proceed straight to brining. Authorities explain that the longer the olive is permitted to ferment in its own brine, the less bitter and more intricate its flavor will become. Green olives are usually pitted, and often stuffed with various fillings, including pimientos, almonds, anchovies, jalapeños, onions, or capers.

## MEDITERRANEAN SALAD

*As you may know, Mediterranean diets are favored for their nutritional value. You can add this salad to your own family favored food plan.*

*Makes 4 to 6 servings.*

■ Olive oil
1/4 cup wine vinegar
1 bay leaf
1 clove garlic, peeled
1 teaspoon oregano
1/4 cup chopped parsley
1 bunch romaine lettuce, torn into pieces
1/2 head lettuce, torn into pieces
4 endive lettuce leaves, torn into pieces
2 red onions, thinly sliced
2 ripe tomatoes, cut into chunks
1 cucumber, scored and sliced
1/2 green pepper, cut in strips
12 Kalamata olives, pitted
1/4 to 1/2 pound crumbled feta cheese

**Dressing**
▶ Combine reserved anchovy oil and olive oil to equal 1/2 cup. In a jar, combine oils, vinegar, bay leaf, garlic and oregano. Shake well and chill several hours.

**Salad**
▶ In a large salad bowl, combine anchovy fillets, parsley, lettuce, onions, tomatoes, cucumber, green pepper, olives, and feta cheese. Remove bay leaf from the jar of dressing, shake dressing well, and pour over salad.

## AMERICAN CREOLE OLIVE SALAD

■ 1 cup pitted brine-cured black olives, sliced
1 cup large pimiento-stuffed olives, sliced
1/2 cup extra-virgin olive oil
2 tablespoons minced shallots
2 tablespoons finely chopped celery
2 tablespoons minced fresh flat-leaf parsley
2 teaspoons minced garlic
1-1/2 teaspoon freshly ground black pepper

▶ Combine all the ingredients in a medium mixing bowl and mix well. Cover and refrigerate until ready to use. Use your favorite salad dressing.

# Pomegranates

The pomegranate tree, *punica granatum*, is a small tree reaching a height of about 20 to 30 feet. Ancient artwork reveals that the fruit adorned the sash of high priests and was carved into the walls and pillars of Solomon's temple. According to biblical scholars, the pointed lobes of the fruit probably served as the inspiration for Solomon's crown and for many crowns since then. The Hebrew word in the Old Testament passages is "rimmôn."

During ancient times the pomegranate was a sacred plant and, curiously, a symbol of fertility or fruitfulness due to the large number of seeds. Early Christians believed that the pomegranate tree was the "tree of life" in the Garden of Eden. As time progressed it became the symbol of eternal life in early Christian art. This unique fruit was used as an ornament on the walls of the Jewish temple at Capernaum in which Jesus preached. Even today, we see pomegranate adornments in Christian churches as a symbol of the eternal life given to us through Jesus Christ.

The pomegranate tree grows mostly as a shrub or small tree about 10 to 15 ft. high with fresh green, oval leaves that fall in winter. It has brilliant scarlet blossoms (the beauty of an orchard of pomegranates is referred to in Song 4:13). The apple-shaped, reddish fruit ripens around September. Under the hard rind you'll find hundreds of seeds. The juice squeezed from seeds is made into a kind of syrup for flavoring drinks. During Jesus' time it was made into wine as we learn in Song of Solomon 8:2: "I would cause thee to drink of spiced wine, of the juice of my pomegranate."

Today, pomegranates are becoming more popular because of their reputed antioxidental powers.

# Focus on Scripture

## Pomegranates

Exodus 28:34—"A golden bell and a pomegranate, a golden bell and a pomegranate, upon the hem of the robe round about."

Exodus 39:26—"A bell and a pomegrante, a bell and a pomegrante, round about the hem of the robe to minister in; as the Lord commanded Moses."

1 Samuel 14:2—"And Saul tarried in the uttermost part of Gibeah under a pomegranate tree which is in Migron: and the people that were with him were about six hundred men . . ."

Song of Solomon 4:3—"Thy lips are like a thread of scarlet, and thy speech is comely: thy temples are like a piece of a pomegrante within thy locks."

Song of Solomon 6:7—"As a piece of a pomegranate are thy temples within thy locks."

Song of Solomon 8:2—"I would lead thee, and bring thee into my mother's house, who would instruct me: I would cause thee to drink of spiced wine of the juice of my pomegranate."

Joel 1:12—"The vine is dried up, and the fig tree languisheth; the pomegranate tree, the palm tree also, and the apple tree, even all the trees of the field, are withered: because joy is withered away from the sons of men."

Haggai 2:19—"Is the seed yet in the barn? yea, as yet the vine, and the fig tree, and the pomegranate, and the olive tree, hath not brought forth: from this day will I bless you."

# History

Botanical experts believe that this attractive fruit tree of Syria was probably indigenous to Persia, Afghanistan, and the neighborhood of the Caucasus, and was introduced to the Holy Land in very ancient times. The spies who reported to Moses upon first entering the Promised Land brought specimens of figs and pomegranates, along with grapes from the Vale of Eshcol Vines (Numbers 12:23). Figs and pomegranates are mentioned again in Numbers 20:5 as fruits the Israelites missed in the wilderness. We also recall that the Promised Land was to be one "of wheat and barley, and vines and fig trees and pomegranates."

Over centuries the pomegranate has been used in ornamentation by both Egyptian and Hebrew artists. For example, it was embroidered in many colors on the skirts of Aaron's garments, together with golden bells. Hiram of Tyre introduced the pomegranate into his brass work ornamentation in the temple as we note from this Scripture in 1 Kings 7:20: "And the pomegranates were two hundred, in rows round about upon the other capital."

Further research tells us that the pomegranate was cultivated as early as 3000 B.C. It is native to Iran and to the Himalayas in northern India and today is still widely cultivated throughout the Middle East and even into tropical Africa. Supposedly, early Spanish settlers brought this tree to the United States where it is grown commercially today for its fruit in California and Arizona.

## Growing and Harvesting Tips

Pomegranates should be placed in the sunniest, warmest part of the yard, although they will grow and flower in shade. The attractive foliage, flowers, and fruits of the pomegranate make it an excellent landscaping plant. Pomegranates do best in well-drained ordinary soil, but also thrive on acidic loam or rocky gravel. Once established, they can take considerable drought, though for adequate fruit production they should be irrigated every 2 to 4 weeks during the dry season. Pomegranate lovers say that trees should be given 2 to 4-ounce applications of ammonium sulfate or other nitrogen fertilizer the first two springs. After that, very little fertilizer is needed, although the plants respond to an annual mulch of rotted manure or other compost.

Pruning helps to keep plants within bounds. Cut back when they are about 2 feet tall. Then, allow 4 or 5 shoots to develop evenly distributed around the stem to keep the plant well balanced. These should start about 1 foot from the ground, to show a short but well-defined trunk. Remove shoots above or below and any suckers. Fruits are borne only at the tips of new growth, so the first few years prune branches annually to encourage the maximum number of new shoots on all sides. After the third year, remove just suckers and dead branches.

Fruits are ripe when they have developed a distinctive color and make a metallic sound when tapped. If left on the tree too long fruit tends to crack open. Pomegranates rival apples for a long storage life. They can keep at a temperature of 32°F to 40°F up to 6 months. Stored fruits improve, becoming juicier and more flavorful. Pomegranates tend to be messy to eat. For eating out of hand, deeply score several times vertically and then break the fruit apart and lift out clusters of juice sacs. These also make an attractive garnish for beef or duck dishes, and are delicious sprinkled over vanilla ice cream.

Pomegranate fruits are most often consumed as juice. Simply remove the sacs and put through an ordinary orange juice squeezer. Or you can roll a fruit between your hands to soften the interior, then cut a hole in the stem end, place on a glass, and let the juice run out, squeezing from time to time to get all the liquid. You can drink it or use it to make jellies, to flavor cakes or baked apples, or to make into wine.

As you think about growing pomegranates, consult mail order firms for the best varieties. If you don't have appropriate outdoor growing conditions, consider container culture with dwarf varieties that provide nice flowers and some fruit, though not much to eat. Recommended outdoor varieties include Cloud from the University of California pomegranate collection, a medium-sized fruit with a green-red color with sweet juice. Or try Early Wonderful, a large, deep-red, thin-skinned, delicious fruit on a medium-sized bush with large, orange-red fertile flowers that is very productive. Granada, King, Utah Sweet, and Wonderful, a Florida introduction, also do well.

Pomegranate trees are common in the tropics, subtropics, and subtemperate regions and is well adapted to areas with hot, dry summers. It is considerably more cold hardy than citrus and some varieties can tolerate temperatures as low as 10°F. For best results, pomegranates should be grown in full sun.

Basically, pomegranates are well-adapted to practically any soil that has good internal drainage and favors a slightly acidic pH range. For most home gardeners in much of America, pomegranate plants will most likely be container-grown in soil-less media. To start, wash an inch or so of the potting medium from the root ball to expose the peripheral roots to the soil mix. The plant should begin growth soon after planting, in contrast to those that are simply planted intact from the nursery container.

Water thoroughly at planting and again every few days for the first couple of weeks. Then water every 7 to 10 days. Outdoors, construct a ring of soil several inches high and a couple of feet in diameter around the newly planted tree. Then just fill the ring with water as necessary to direct the moisture to plant roots. Growers suggest you fertilize lightly after growth begins: about 1 to 2 cups of ammonium sulfate in the first year should be sufficient, split into three to four applications. Use about twice as much fertilizer in the second year and three times as much in the third year and do applications in February, May, and September. Mulch to eliminate weed competition and conserve soil moisture.

A warning: as seedlings, a pomegranate may undergo severe fruit drop during its first couple of years of production, but this will change as the plant matures. Fruit drop lessens with vegetatively propagated pomegranates. In temperate climates, fruit maturity should begin in summer and extend for several weeks in the fall.

## Cooking Tips and Recipes

The sweet, juicy taste of the pomegranate has made it a favorite fruit in Mediterranean and Middle Eastern cooking. Pomegranate arils make a striking garnish on everything from salads to desserts. And the juice, whether straight or boiled down into an intense, syrupy molasses, adds an exotic twist to the most basic foods. Pick or buy a few pomegranates and tap into them for the arils and juice. Use juice as flavoring or to drink, and arils as garnish on salads for eye appeal and flavor.

# CHICKEN SALAD WITH ALMONDS

■ 1 cup arils from 1 large fruit
1/2 cup golden raisins
1 pound cooked chicken breast meat, cut into 1-inch chunks
1/3 cup toasted sliced almonds
1 chopped apple
1/2 cup chopped or thinly sliced celery
1 tablespoon chopped Italian parsley
1/4 cup chopped green onion
1/4 to 1/2 teaspoon curry powder (optional)
1/3 cup extra-virgin oil
3 tablespoons balsamic vinegar
Salt and pepper to taste

▶ Score 1 fresh pomegranate and place in a bowl of water. Break open the pomegranate underwater to free the arils (seed sacs). The arils will sink to the bottom of the bowl and the membrane will float to the top. Sieve and put the arils in a separate bowl. Reserve 1 cup of arils from fruit and set aside. (Refrigerate or freeze remaining arils for later use.) In a large mixing bowl combine the pomegranate arils, raisins, chicken, almonds, apple, celery, parsley, green onion, and curry powder. In a small bowl whisk together the olive oil and vinegar. Pour in chicken mixture, mix well. Add salt and pepper to taste. Refrigerate until ready to serve.

# ZESTY POMEGRANATE LEG OF LAMB

■ Medium semi-boneless leg of lamb (2 to 3 lbs.)
3 cups pomegranate juice
1/4 cup Dijon mustard
4 cloves of garlic, minced
1 tablespoon of rosemary, minced

▶ Combine juice, mustard, garlic, and rosemary in a large bowl or dish. Mix well. Place lamb in mixture and cover tightly. Marinate for 2 days. After lamb has marinated, place in a roasting pan or glass baking dish in an oven pre-heated at 350°F. Roast for 1 to 1 1/2 hours depending on oven and your own preference. Once lamb is in the oven, strain the marinade through a mesh sieve. Simmer liquid in a saucepan for one hour, or until reduced to a thick glaze. Serve glaze over lamb.

# Chapter 5

# Site and Soil for Abundant Growth

To grow abundantly you must provide your plants with what they need. Give them the right place to grow, improve their environment, feed them properly, and they in turn will prosper and feed you.

The first key step for gardening success is to pick the right location. Sounds easy, but your land may be limited by poor exposure to the sun, or have problems with nearby trees, buildings, or other growing situations. Soil may be too sandy or have excess clay. You can solve those problems in time. First, focus on the site.

Examine your garden areas at different times of day. See how the sun shines on your proposed biblical food growing areas. Try to pick a sunny, well-drained location with at least 6 to 8 hours of direct sun each day. Southern exposures are best because they provide maximum sun for peak plant growth. If you don't have a southern exposure, next best in order of desirability are eastern, then western, and finally northern exposure plots because they provide less good sunlight.

Look for problems before you start gardening. Avoid areas where shadows from trees or buildings block the sun too long each day. Shy away from paved area runoff, or arrange to direct excess water and street pollution wastes away from the garden areas. Also avoid areas near hedges or trees with shallow roots that draw water and nutrients from the soil.

As you plan your garden, arrange for beds running north and south when possible so that each row has an equal amount of sunlight. On slopes consider contour planting as farmers do to avoid erosion.

You'll also find good growing advice in the Bible. For example, in Exodus 23:11 we find the admonition to let the land lie fallow on the seventh year, a practice that keeps the soil from becoming depleted of its nutrients. The better the humus and soil conditions you can build, the better your plants will grow. Healthy soil produces healthy plants. It's a proven fact that insects dislike healthy plants! They actually prefer sickly and weak plants. When you improve the good earth and fertilize plants properly, you'll have strong, healthy growth, few insects, and bumper crops of fine food.

After you've chosen a spot for your garden, examine the existing soil. Don't despair if it isn't rich and fertile. Natural gardeners know that soil improvement is an ongoing project. Your soil may be too sandy or even rocky. It may be muddy from excess clay content. Whatever you have can be improved. It has been well said, "and they made the deserts to bloom, and it was good." This ages old admonition reminds us that as the people in the Holy Land worked hard to grow crops, we too should work to grow our gardens better and our lives too with help from God.

As legions of dedicated gardeners in the Holy Land have demonstrated, you can apply the techniques of accomplished gardeners to improve your own growing ground. The Holy Land has come alive and blooms and bears productively today thanks to attention to soil improvement methods and proper fertilizing to meet plant needs.

Every soil has a profile composed of "horizons," which differ in color, texture, structure, and porosity. In shallow soils, horizons may be only an inch thick. In deeper soils they may be a foot or more. Scientist identify three major horizons as A, B, and C. True soil is the combined A and B horizons which are the direct result of the soil formation process and are the growing area for your plants. Soil is truly alive. Millions of bacteria and fungi, plus plant roots, small animals, and insects are at work in the soil.

Take a spade and dig into your garden soil to reveal its profile. Next get down on your knees and examine your soil. (You'll probably do a fair amount of crawling as you garden, so buy a pair of sturdy kneepads. They're

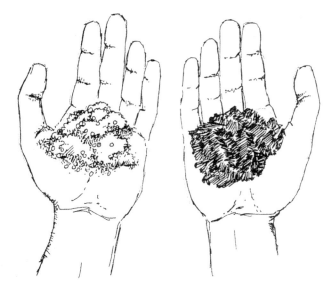

*Soil should feel crumbly as shown in the right hand. Don't dig or till when soil is overly wet.*

especially helpful when you crawl through rocky soil.) Look carefully at the soil texture, meaning the size of the majority of particles that make up the soil, from microscopic clay particles to small gravel. Clay soils can be stony clay, gravelly clay, or sandy clay, depending on what other materials are mixed with the clay. Clay soils tend to hold excess water but can be improved by adding organic material to open them up. Loamy soils include sandy loams, medium loams, to clay loams. Sandy soils can be gravelly sands, coarse sands, or even loamy sands.

What is the ideal garden soil? A loamy garden soil is best for practically all plants. Therefore, your goal must be to focus on producing that ideal. A loamy soil combines all three of the major classifications of soil particles: sand, silt, and clay in about equal parts.

Whether your garden soil is too sandy or has too much clay, the solution lies in addition of organic matter, including peat moss, compost, or animal manure. Today, garden centers provide dried animal manure of various kinds.

Another good way to add organic matter is by growing and turning under cover crops, such as winter rye, hairy vetch, or buckwheat. Organic matter increases the water and nutrient-holding capacity of sand, nd improves drainage and aeration of clay soil. Be patient. Soil improvement is not a quick fix. It is a sound, ongoing gardening program. You goal is to balance structure, texture, and porosity. When you pick up a handful of rich soil in the spring and it crumbles freely in your palm you are approaching the ideal.

# Understand Underground Basics

Plants benefit from balanced diets just as you do, so you must feed them properly. First learn what nutrients already are in your soil. You can get help with soil testing from your local County Extension Agent or local garden center advisors. Testing is the easy part. Interpreting results can be confusing, but you'll learn in this ongoing soil improvement process.

Even if a garden is growing well there are good reasons to test your soil. By knowing what sort of soil is working well, you can learn how to adjust other soils that may not be performing as well. Different plants require different ratios of nutrients to grow their best. For example, fruiting crops like melons have different needs than leafy crops like lettuce or root crops like horseradish. If any of your plants aren't growing as well as you'd like, a soil test is in order.

It's good practice to test soil every 3 to 4 years, in the fall, when fertility is lowest. Use the same kit or source to have consistent comparisons. With experience you can do testing yourself. When you're starting out, the most accurate tests can be conducted by university and private soil laboratories. They've had years of experience testing the soils in your state and giving specific fertilizer recommendations based on the soil types and crops grown. Basic tests usually cost less than $20 but can vary. You may also wish to have your soil evaluated for any toxic materials from construction backfill or previous owners use of various herbicides or chemicals.

Test results will indicate relative levels of each nutrient including the basic elements, nitrogen, phosphorus, and potassium or potash. It is important to test different garden areas because there can be wide variations in soils around your home grounds. That's especially true in suburban developments where soil has been removed, fill added, and changes made to the areas around new homes.

## Understand Soil's pH

Proper pH is another key factor in healthy soil. Some plants prefer neutral soil while others require more acidic conditions. Soil pH is measured on a scale of 1 (acid) to 14 (alkaline). Most garden crops grow well at a pH of 6 to 7, but specific plants such as blueberries and azaleas may need a lower (more acidic) pH. In general, lime is used to raise pH, while sulfur is recommended to lower it.

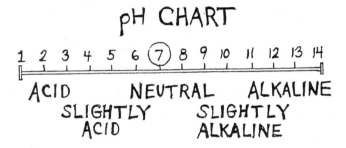

Most plants grow best in slightly acid soils of pH 6.1 to 6.9 because nutrients needed for plant growth are most available in soil water at pH 6.5. Above that level some nutrients become bound to soil particles and therefore are unavailable to plants. Lime sweetens soils that are too acid. However, soil nutrients are most readily dissolved and therefore available to your turf and plants when the soil is slightly acidic. Since plants grow best in slightly acid soil, you should never add lime unless a soil test recommends it.

## Learn ABCs of NPK

It is important to know the ABCs of NPK. These are the Big Three nutrients. By law they must be listed in the same order on all fertilizer containers you buy.

First is N for nitrogen, the key nutrient needed for plant growth. It tends to leach out of the soil easily, which means levels can fluctuate during the growing season. Nitrogen deficiency symptoms include pale yellow leaves and stunted growth.

P stands for phosphorus. Soil may have adequate levels of phosphorus, but it may be "tied up" by soil pH conditions. Often, just raising or lowering the pH to the ideal 6.5 will free up phosphorus for plant use. Excess phosphorus can create problems by running off during rain or garden irrigation causing pollution. Phosphorus deficiency is indicated by purple leaves, brittle roots, skinny stems, and late fruit set and plant maturity.

K is for potassium, which is vital for stem strength, root growth, and disease resistance. Many soils are naturally high in potassium making it readily available to plants. Sandy soils may be deficient. Potassium shortage signs are irregular yellowing of lower leaves and poor root growth.

Other nutrients also are needed for proper plant growth. Each has its own function. Calcium, for example, is important for cell-wall integrity, and root and leaf growth. Symptoms of shortage are deformed new leaves or branches and weak stems and roots. Lime adds calcium.

Another minor element is magnesium, which is needed for chlorophyll and green leaf development. Pale leaves with green veins indicate magnesium deficiency. Most modern fertilizers have trace amounts of calcium and magnesium. Ask your plant test person or fertilizer supplier about best combinations for your area and gardens.

It's also important to know the percentage of organic matter in soil. Organic matter usually has little nutritional value. However, it's essential for nitrogen absorption and release and as a food for microorganisms that help make other nutrients available. A level of 3 to 5 percent organic matter is considered ideal. Organic gardeners believe that soil can't have enough organic matter. It opens clay soils and also helps sandy soils retain moisture for plants. Be aware that soils high in some un-decomposed organic matter, such as wood chips or sawdust, actually tie up nitrogen because it gets used as cellulose materials break down. That means you may need to add extra nitrogen to that soil. Generally, compost is the best soil-improving additive.

Most labs provide recommendations for adding specific nutrients to bring garden soils up to their optimum levels. These nutrient levels are usually given in pounds of that element per 1,000 square feet of garden. Today many new types of plant foods are readily available. There isn't room to provide details for all of them, but some key considerations should be noted. Liquid fertilizers have won popularity for their simplicity. You just mix according to package directions and spray on. Some kinds are for food crops, others for fruits, still others for flowers and trees. Read the labels, asks the advisors in your garden centers, and buy what you need for the types of crops and plants you will grow.

Be sure to apply the right amount of nutrients to meet plant needs, without repeat applications. Pelleted or prilled fertilizers are handy. They are easier to spread and come in slow release formulations. That means the plant food is released over a period of time to nourish your plants over many weeks. I favor these types of fertilizer. They save work and are reliable.

Read and heed instructions for whatever type fertilizer you use. Buy smaller quantities of the types you need for the variety of plants you have for best results for all of them. Avoid using high-nitrogen lawn fertilizers for other purposes because nitrogen promotes foliage growth. You'll get leaf growth at the expense of fruit or veggie production.

> At this point, make a mental note. Too much fertilizer is often as bad as too little. You waste money if you add unneeded fertilizer and it may over-stimulate plants. Excess nitrogen forces excess leaf growth at the expense of fruit and flower production.

# Learn More About Soil

A somewhat deeper understanding of soils is useful for improving growing conditions, wherever you live and garden. Once you know the results of your soil test and know what nutrients it has already, the next step is to focus on improving the organic matter content. This may be overlooked by budding gardeners, but veterans attest to the importance of building soil organic matter.

Soil organic matter is fundamental to soil productivity, especially for food crops. In addition to the chemical nutrients in it, soil actually is alive. Soil changes and improves through continuing decomposition of organic materials in it and especially as you add new raw materials.

Don't let the color of soil fool you. Rich-looking dark or black soil can be low in nutrients. Reddish, sandy soils can be high in them. No matter where you live or what soil you find there, you can improve it, rebuild it, and upgrade your growing conditions.

All soils contain organic matter, water, air, and minerals. The proportion of these elements vary, but the components remain essentially the same. Bacteria and fungi, which also occur in your living soil, are vital contributors to soil formation. They live on animal and plant residues and break down complex compounds into simple forms. Nitrogen-fixing bacteria in the nodules of legumes, for example, actually take nitrogen from the atmosphere and help make it available in the soil for future plants. Planting legumes such as clover and alfalfa as rotation cover crops and then plowing or tilling them under helps add nitrogen to garden soil.

Our initial objective is to aim for a balance in texture and porosity. Texture refers to the size of the majority of particles making up the soil and ranges from microscopic clay particles up to small stones and gravel. Porosity refers to the pores in the soil though which water, nutrients, roots, and air most move. Good growing is a matter of balance. Excesses are what throw gardens off balance, just as they throw us out of balance in life.

Pick up a handful of rich, warm soil in spring. Crumble it in your hands. If it crumbles freely in your palm, you are approaching the ideal texture. The closer your soil is to that granular feel, with clusters of soil that easily shake apart, the better your garden will grow.

Too often, we are tempted to purchase "topsoil" or "loam" as a quick-fix approach to garden building. Rich-looking topsoil may be offered at low prices by some contractors, but be wary. Some obtain this dark soil by dredging silt in rivers or old swamps and mixing it with sand, which creates a soil that looks great but won't do your plants much good at all.

If you really need some garden loam, check with local reputable nurserymen and garden centers owners who are aware of problem soil in your area, such as pesticide or herbicide residue in farm fields from which topsoil is being sold. Ask their recommendations for improving your growing ground. They want your business for seeds, plants, and trees and will answer questions honestly.

The riches within soil must be unlocked in order to produce a productive garden. Compost—the key that turns soil into productive land—is the result of combining organic matter and manure that decays into a valuable soil additive.

# Compost-Making Tips

Soil, like the plants that grow in it, truly is alive! Millions of bacteria, fungi, minute animals, and other microorganisms inhabit it. There is a close relationship between the amount of life in the soil and the soil's basic fertility.

Your objective is to increase the life, and consequently the productivity, of the soil. The better the compost, the better the soil.

Compost production depends upon the decay or decomposition rate of the various materials used. Bins or pits in the ground, above the ground, or piled along garden rows, plus many other variations, have been successful. Any soil can be improved with compost, even the hard, caked subsoil often found around new home developments. The addition of humus, which is generally defined as well-rotted compost, provides the best and least expensive way to improve your soil.

Remember that your soil can never get enough organic matter. Good topsoil contains from 2 to 8 percent organic matter by dry weight, which is the residue of growing plant materials. You should continue to add organic matter every year in order to keep building your soil bank. Each deposit you make will yield dividends.

Compost piles don't have eye appeal and can smell (it's rotting organic material). Select an out of the way location and plan to screen the area from view with a hedge, shrubs, or perhaps a fence around it. We use a berry hedge where possible. The bushes form thick bramble patches, hiding the compost piles and providing tasty berries in the bargain.

Choose a site convenient to water so you can periodically wet down the pile to keep it moist. A shady area is good, but avoid low areas in which rain collects and the ground remains soggy. While the bacteria that help make compost into good humus require ample moisture, they must have air and oxygen, too. That's why turning a compost pile is helpful. It lets bacteria obtain oxygen to do their work better and faster, breaking down organic material.

The next step in preparing compost is construction of the pit or pile. Remember, the more air that circulates through the pile and around it, the faster the decomposition. Turning a compost pile is good exercise, but work! It is worthwhile to have at least two piles of compost. You can use finished compost from one while still making more humus in the other. Finished compost is well-rotted organic material, called humus, and has a crumbly feel. It is a basic soil improvement ingredient for all gardens.

# Compare Compost Piles

Most any organic material can be composted with the simple Indore method. This method was developed and practiced in England by Sir Albert Howard, father of the modern organic movement, and is the method used by small and large gardeners because it is both practical and efficient. Basically, the Indore method is simple layering of various materials to rot down.

Begin with a 6-inch layer of green organic material from grass clippings or dried leaves (which may be brown but are considered "green" matter in the terminology of organic gardening). Next, add a 2-inch layer of manure over this first layer of green material—clippings, leaves, old weeds and vegetation pulled from the garden. The objective is to add nitrogen to hasten the decay process. Cow, horse, sheep, and poultry manure will do the best job if you can obtain them. It is ideal if the manure also includes straw, shavings, or other usual bedding materials used on most farms. If you do not have manure readily available you may substitute other nitrogen sources: blood meal, digested sewage sludge, cottonseed meal, or soybean meal. Your local garden center authorities can provide details about these options. Most garden centers and hardware stores or chain stores with garden centers also have commercially prepared dried manures and compost kits that are excellent to use in compost making.

The next layer should consist of an inch or two of garden soil taken from your garden and evenly spread to insure effective interaction. It will have natural and useful soil bacteria in it to help with the composting process. Following the layer of soil, add a one-inch layer of mixed rock phosphate and limestone, which you can obtain from local garden centers. Top this off with manure or a soil covering a few inches thick.

You can build a small pile, just 4 feet wide, 4 feet long, and 4 feet high, or you can increase the dimensions if more material is available. It is desirable to have several smaller piles so they will be in varying stages of decomposition and some ready for use in your garden.

As you apply the layers, sprinkle them with water. All organic material going into the pile should be moist, especially if dry leaves, grass clippings, and other dry materials are being used. When you have finished building the pile, leave a saucer shaped depression on the top of it so rain water can be caught and allowed to trickle down through the layers. This helps keep them moist. If you are in a drought period, be sure to water the compost pile once or twice a week.

Two types of bacteria will be at work in your compost. These are called aerobic and anaerobic. The first type, aerobic, needs air circulation in order to do its job. The second type, anaerobic, works more slowly and proceeds without much aeration of the pile. Turning the pile by fork or spade or otherwise, providing improved aeration, will quicken the entire process. Spading means work, but only two or three turnings are required before the humus is ready.

To save yourself some work, you might build the pile around several pipes with holes through them. This method lets the air penetrate, helps the heat build up as decomposition occurs, and saves your back from spading chores. Alternately, you can by a home compost tumbler bin.

When you build a pile with the Indore method you can make it as high as is practical. A 4 to 5 foot high pile is probably best as it enables you to have several series of layers; green matter, manure, lime, rock phosphate, soil, in one easily manageable pile. If you turn the pile once a week, you can expect finished compost within 2 to 3 months, depending on weather and other variables. Several factors influence decomposition. The first is the amount of manure and nitrogen sources, and the moisture that was included as the pile was built. Next is the amount of aeration that is provided, either through hand turning or mechanically. A third factor is the addition of earthworms. Their tunneling and digestion of organic material hastens the process, but they should not be added until the first heating-up period has ended. As the first phase of decay proceeds over a few weeks, the internal heat of the pile may reach 150°F or more. The earthworms can be added after this period, when you can reach into the pile and determine that it has cooled down. I find this occurs after I've turned the pile about three times.

Bacteria, of course, are the microscopic helpers in any compost building activity. It can be beneficial to inoculate the pile with them as it is built. Soil bacteria cultures may be purchased from various sources including Plants Alive company, a major natural gardening product firm. Alternately, you can save the remnants of a previous compost pile when it is still not completely decomposed. Add the material to the new pile or to the soil or manure layers. The bacteria will multiply and go right to work with their millions of beneficial bacterial neighbors.

Spring and summer are the best times for making compost. Sun and rain, warm weather, and water speed the process. Very little action takes place from November until April, except in southern areas of the country. When a compost pile is prepared in the fall from old leaves and debris, not much action can be expected until spring sets life in motion again.

# Simple Field Composting

Field composting is easier to do but takes much longer to produce the finished compost. Basically, it is a layering method that needs no pit or special pile. As you gather green matter, apply it in layers to a pile or along garden rows and just let it rot by itself. Keep adding more organic material, raked leaves, grass clippings, and weeds, until you have a satisfactory 4 to 6 inch layer. Then add manure or other nitrogen-containing materials from your garden center. Sprinkle on an inch or so of soil, add lime and rock phosphate, and then just let it stand. Nature will take its course and the material will slowly decompose.

You can add more green matter until there are several sequences of layers. By the following year, providing you take the time to turn the field pile at least once, you will have good humus. Even if you do not turn the pile, you can expect this field composting method to yield good humus in time. Actually, I like this system because all I have to do is spread organic materials along garden rows and let them rot down in place as a natural mulch that also helps stop weed growth.

Whichever compost system you choose, you can always find ways to improve upon it with ingenuity. One thing is certain; good compost makes good gardens. If that's what you are after, start composting right now and stick with it! Compost truly is the golden key to more productive, fruitful gardening.

# Tap Green Manure Values

Green manure is a curious phrase that can be confusing. Green manure is the term for cover crops planted in the spring or fall and then turned under to improve the growing ground. By planting a crop and tilling it under you add organic matter, which loosens clay soil and makes nutrients more available to the roots. It also improves sandy soil by holding things together and prevents minerals and nutrients from leaching away. Veteran veggie gardeners are enthusiastic about planting green manure in an area they will use for crops the next year.

Others plant cover crops every fall and till them under in the spring before tilling and planting their vegetables. Legumes such as clover and vetch can improve nitrogen levels by pulling nitrogen from the air and fixing it on nodules on their roots. Other useful green manure cover crops are cowpeas, soybeans, buckwheat, and winter rye. Except for winter rye, turn under green manure crops when they begin flowering. You can speed decay by mowing the crop before tilling. You should mow winter rye and turn it under as soon as possible in the springtime. It is wise to let the soil rest for two weeks after turning the green manure crop under before planting your vegetables. This gives soil bacteria ample time to break it down into organic matter for your plants.

## Turn on Water Know How

Water behaves in different ways, depending on the soil it falls on. Gravitational water is water that drains out of soil after it rains or when you water your garden. In sandy and sandy loam soils, water may leave too quickly from the pore spaces causing plants to wilt. On the other hand, in heavy soils with lots of silt and clay, water may remain too long, which can rot roots. Both conditions can be corrected with soil amendments. In very soggy spots it may be necessary to install drainage tiles to eliminate overly wet spots.

Peat moss is one of the best materials to quickly improve sandy and clay soil. It comes in small to huge bales, most about 6 cubic feet. Peat opens heavy soils and helps retain moisture in sandy soils. Talk to neighbors. Perhaps you can buy a truckload together and divide it between your gardens.

Once the moisture is in soil it takes one of two forms. Hygroscopic soil water is chemically bound with soil materials and is unavailable to plants. It may be bound more or less closely depending on the chemical composition of your soil. Capillary water is moisture that is available to your plants. It is chemically free to leave the soil to enter plant roots. There it carries the dissolved nutrients to roots, stems, stalks, leaves, blooms, and fruit. The more you improve soil texture and structure the greater will be its capacity to hold and transfer capillary water.

To learn more about soils and soil improvement programs, check out U.S. Department of Agriculture resources. Other good local literature is available from the information office at your own state agricultural college.

county agricultural agents can obtain these and other gardening information that relates to your particular state and area. Many are free. Better yet, state agricultural college garden literature focuses on specific soil and climatic conditions in your own home state.

# The Magic of Mulch

Mulch preserves moisture, prevents weeds, improves soil condition, diminishes erosion, cuts down disease problems, and adds organic matter to the soil. Mulch is an organic gardening bonanza. Next to composting, mulching is the single most vital natural gardening activity. Most mulch materials are free and readily available, wherever you live. Once you try it, you'll agree with millions of gardeners that mulching pays in many ways.

A mulch is any organic material you can find as a protective covering for the soil. Grass clippings leaves, chopped or ground brush and twigs, pine needles, straw, hay, ground corn cobs, peat moss, sawdust, shavings, composted refuse you or neighbors make, and even gravel, sand or stones are all good options. You can also use peanut hulls, ground bark, redwood chips, layers of newspapers covered with grass clippings, or anything else that will decompose to add nutrients to the soil.

The black plastic that you buy for weed control in garden centers and similar available coverings can also be used as mulch. So can other materials that stop weeds, help soil retain moisture, and save you weeding time, such as aluminum foil. However, consider appearance. More importantly, consider your goal, improving the soil and growing ground.

Focus first on organic materials that break down and recycle into the good earth to improve soil tilth. Whatever material you use and apply depends on what you have available and fits into your budget. If you like to see dark, rich-looking soil along garden rows, you can opt for peat moss, ground sphagnum moss, or chipped bark and wood chips. Well-decayed sawdust is darker. Redwood chips and pine bark look nice. There are drawbacks and basic problems with some woody materials, however. Wood chips and cellulose materials draw nitrogen out of soil, so you must compensate for that by adding higher nitrogen fertilizer to your garden ground.

Dry lawn clippings are fluffy when first spread. You can gather them abundantly from baggers on your power mower. After a few rains, they tend to form a compact, thin layer. They decompose so you can add more layers as the season progresses and decomposition improves your garden soil. We should think of mulch as a long-range goal to improve garden soil for garden improvement. By smothering weeds with mulch we also preserve soil nutrients and fertilizer we apply so they feed our desired plants.

Controlling weeds is an annual, tiresome chore. True, you can pull or cultivate or till them away, but some weeds are frustratingly persistent. They also leave seeds in the ground, just waiting for you to till so that the seeds can sprout, grow, and rob your plants of the nutrients and moisture they need. Weeds may be hosts to harmful insects that will cross over to attack your vegetables. Happily, proper mulching stops weed growth by smothering the seedlings, prevents other seeds from sprouting, and encourages those useful underground allies, earthworms, to work their wonders in the soil around your garden plants.

Hard rains can cause erosion on bare ground. The problem is made worse when you cultivate too often with a hoe, weeder, or rototiller. A mulch takes up the shock of pounding rain, letting it seep into the soil below more evenly and then holds that water by preventing evaporation from the sun. Mulch also discourages hardpan, that undesirable baked top layer of soil, from developing on the surface in dry periods.

Some plants prefer warm, sunny weather. Others favor cooler conditions. Mulches, together with proper planting and culture techniques, can help you extend your gardening season by adjusting soil temperatures. You can prove that point to yourself. Place a thermometer an inch or so deep beneath a mulch of grass clippings or leaves. The temperature may register 75 to 85 degrees. Then place the thermometer in the same patch of soil and remove the mulch for three or four feet around it. You'll notice that the temperature may climb 10 to 15 degrees. Next, place the thermometer on a block of wood on top of the soil. The temperature may climb to 100° plus. That high temperature can be stressful to many plants.

In effect, mulch helps you regulate and balance soil temperature to the desires and needs of your plants by controlling the micro-climate around them. Light-colored materials such as pebbles, gravel, straw, and light-colored sawdust, will reflect light. Darker materials including peat moss, pine bark, compost, and humus will absorb light and heat.

Timing is important for mulching. Many natural gardeners prefer permanent mulching. This is basically like composting right in your garden. As mulch materials continue to rot, they give the added advantage of continued humus production. To plant seedlings merely move the mulch to one side and plant what you wish. Then replace the mulch to smother weeds, preserve soil moisture, and let your valuable plants grow better without weed competition for space, water, or nutrients.

When your veggie seedlings are up and growing well, apply mulch around them to thwart weeds. At the end of a garden season, you can elect to leave mulch in place or till it under to further improve soil texture, condition, and fertility. Because mulch materials may not be readily available in large quantities, selective mulch fits into most garden plans better. Either way, mulching pays big growing dividends.

Compost is really your best mulch. As you create compost and humus, this decomposed organic matter provides an attractive and more useful mulch because it already contains some nutrients. In addition, many weed seeds are killed through the composting process that generates high temperatures in compost piles.

Keep one thought in mind with all types of mulch. It is usually necessary to add a nitrogen source to organic mulch, especially when you use wood chips or similar material high in cellulose fiber. It can be added before mulching, of course. But as mulches decay, they tend to take some nitrogen from the soil for this natural process. It is up to you to keep things in balance.

Naturally, you can use conventional commercial fertilizers that provide various percentages of nitrogen in them. Read the labels on fertilizer containers to be certain you are using the proper fertilizer formulas for the type crops you plan to grow. Ask your garden center specialists about the many types of fertilizer available today. They are often your best source for useful information on new garden products that are being introduced to help us grow better.

Remember that too much nitrogen leads to vegetative, leafy growth. Biblical vegetables and fruits need phosphorous and potash, too. Fortunately, the handy new slow-release fertilizers, prilled and pelleted types, give season long feeding to plants. Popular new liquid fertilizers, applied in hose end sprayer units, are another modern blessing for gardeners everywhere.

Peat moss is probably the most readily available and common mulch. However, peat moss has no nutrient value, and most other mulch materials do. For example, lawn clippings provide about one pound of nitrogen and two pounds of potash for every 100 pounds of dry clippings. Researchers also have found that leaf mold or shredded leaves can provide a nitrogen content as high as 5 percent. Alfalfa and clover hay are higher in nitrogen than orchard grass or timothy because these legumes have nitrogen-fixing bacteria in their root nodules. That is why farmers prefer alfalfa or clover hay to provide a high protein value for their livestock.

Don't mulch the soil when it is excessively wet. Molds can start below the surface and the trapped moisture combined with heat can cause hidden mold problems. You may also contribute to damping off diseases on seedlings if you mulch too early before they have true leaves and a strong roothold. As you plan your garden, think mulch.

# Consider Raised Beds

If you have a bad back, or poor garden soil, raised beds may be worth trying. Fill raised beds with high-quality purchased loam. You can use regular garden soil, but digging up enough may leave a large hole in your ground, so buying topsoil is a better idea. Many seniors have returned to gardening in raised beds and containers. They let you tend crops more easily and grow more intensively by fertilizing plants grown closer together. It's also easier to control weeds and harvest crops. Also, with raised beds you can plant, tend, and harvest crops without walking on and compressing soil, which means the air and water can continue to move easily into the soil, allowing you to grow healthier, more vigorous plants.

Raised beds have historic roots. Remember the Hanging Gardens of Babylon? This centuries-old technique increases the soil depth to improve the health and productivity of a garden. If they're properly constructed, raised beds will have better soil structure and drainage. Soil in raised beds also dries out more quickly in spring to give you an earlier start.

To begin, lay out your bed's dimensions with stakes and string. A width of 3 or 4 feet is a comfortable reach from either side. Lengths of 6 to 10 feet seem good for the typical backyard. Cut and remove turf. Dig or till soil to a depth of at least a foot. Incorporate organic material such as compost, peat moss, or chopped leaves into the soil by tilling under with a light tiller like a Mantis to blend soil and organic matter well. Plan your path around each bed. Remove the valuable top few inches of topsoil from the paths and add to the raised bed. Then, use wood chips, old planks, or better yet, gravel in the path area to avoid muddy pathways.

Next, rake and level the surface of the mounded soil in the bed and if you wish add purchased enriched topsoil and you are ready for planting come spring. While it is not necessary for raised bed gardening, boxing each bed with 2 by 10 inch wooden planks prevents erosion especially in heavy rains, makes beds easier to manage, and looks more attractive. Walls also provide a way to attach watering systems, poles, or other devices for growing vertically. Wood, concrete blocks, bricks, or stones can also be used. Old time gardeners report that raised beds provide a way to save space, maintain soil texture better, gain easier cultivation with less bending, and can even have fall plastic or glass frame covers attached to the frames to extend your growing season.

Once you build or have a contractor frame the beds, the most important consideration is the soil mix. Don't economize on this vital growing ground. Raised bed fans recommend a mix of approximately 2/3 topsoil and 1/3 leaf humus. First calculate how much you will need to fill your beds, leaving 3 inches from the top boards so soil doesn't wash out. Calculate the volume of the bed in cubic feet by multiplying the length times the width times the depth in feet. Typical depth for raised beds is 8 inches, which equals 0.67 feet. Although you may wish to start with a smaller raised bed, here's how we did one for our extensive raised bed garden with a raised bed 3 feet wide, 16 feet long, and 8 inches was 32 cubic feet. Now, we divided 32 cubic feet by 27 because there are 27 cubic feet in one cubic yard and that gave us the volume in cubic yards, which is how most topsoil is sold.

To fill that bed you'll need one yard of topsoil and one-half yard of leaf humus or compost. Happily today, garden centers and landscape contractors are offering premixed raised bed soil mixtures. Check around for them.

With soil mixture in place, you're ready to plant. Some gardeners like to set up a drip watering or soaker hose system to provide moisture for plants more easily. With a timer at the tap you can tend your raised bed crops more easily. Try mixing and matching biblical flowers for beauty and biblical veggies and herbs for tastier living.

Even veteran gardeners who have spent years growing in the ground are giving raised beds a try. They have been popular in Europe for decades. Transplanting such good ideas to your home grounds might be worth a try.

# Chapter 6

# Container Gardening Rewards

Even if you have no backyard gardening space, you can still enjoy growing foods that Jesus ate. The answer is in containers.

Your choice of containers is appealingly wide; wooden barrels, decorative ceramic tubs, glazed pots and planters, and good old-fashioned window boxes. I've talked with families in apartment complexes who are busily growing vegetables and flowers in many types of containers. Frankly, anything that holds soil mix and provides proper water drainage will work. Garden centers and chain stores offer a wide range of shapes, sizes, and colors and don't overlook flea markets and yard sales for old baskets, barrels, kettles, and buckets.

Container plants need more water than those in backyard gardens because of their restricted growing habitat. Their roots cannot roam in search of moisture. They also are impacted by sun and heat radiated from building walls. Proper drainage is especially important because plants hate wet roots, so be sure your containers provide adequate drainage of excess water. Place several inches of coarse gravel in the bottom before adding soil mixture.

Before buying containers envision your container garden area. Veteran gardeners explain that wood, plastic, or composition containers are better than terra cotta, common clay pots whose porous sides let water evaporate too fast, thus drying the soil mix, which also is harmful to plant growth.

Another key to container growing success is "soil-less" soil. Today you can easily obtain growing soil mixes at local stores. These container soil mixtures are scientifically prepared to give plants their optimum growing conditions. Many have fertilizer elements included. If not, no problem. You can easily mix time-release fertilizer into the soil mix to help feed plants as they grow. Then, just add granular or liquid feeding during the season as your plants need it.

Next step is planting. You can sow seed directly following directions on the packet. Thin seedlings as specified. Or, buy bedding plants locally to get a faster start on blooming time and veggie harvest. A common question is how many plants to put in each container. If you provide enough soil and water you can space plants somewhat closer together than usual recommendations for backyard gardens. You can create entire gardens in containers using wooden half-barrels or large, 24-inch diameter pots. You can also grow the ingredients for your favorite sauces and vegetable dishes. Among biblical plants, you can grow cucumbers abundantly for salads. Compact vine varieties are excellent for container growing. So are compact melons that yield full size fruits. Don't overlook salad patches that keep on producing greens every time you cut some for meals. Harvest ripe fruits promptly so plants continue to produce new growth.

You can try onions and related veggies such as shallots and scallions, too. Leeks take time but can give you a few pickings for tasty leek soup. Don't overlook some of the biblical herbs in containers that can provide marvelous new flavoring for meals. You'll find a list of free garden catalogs at the end of this book. Browse through catalogs during winter and plan your own container biblical gardens. You'll also find a variety of containers in specialty catalogs that offer excellent growing environments. For even more information, tap the knowledge and talents of gardening experts at some of my favorite garden websites. Gather container growing ideas, tips, and advice and come spring you'll be on your way to growing adventures in containers on porches, balconies, patios, and even city rooftops. Of course, you can also enjoy growing container gardens indoors if you wish, near a southern window for best light.

Here are some other ideas to whet your appetite. For a container salad bowl, plant patio tomato and sweet pepper in the center and one or two cucumber plants near the edge so they can spill over without support. Add red and green leaf lettuce in the middle spaces. Another salad garden might include spring leaf lettuce followed by beans. Sow beans while lettuce is still growing and bean plants will provide lettuce with a bit of shade from the summer sun.

To encourage children, let them have their own container garden to grow. Ask what they would prefer to grow. Cucumbers may not win any votes. Melons may be a better idea. Some kids may surprise you and want a flower garden instead.

Once you have planted your veggies, check your containers daily, especially smaller ones that can dry out faster. Poke a finger into the soil. If it feels dry, water well. Container gardens need deep watering to insure that moisture gets to all parts of the soil mix, which encourages deeper rooting for sturdier plants. Wick and trickle watering systems are available to provide moisture on a regular basis, even when you are away. Some modern containers come equipped with their own bottom or wick watering systems.

One of America's most respected gardening groups, the National Gardening Association based in Vermont, has focused on container gardening. Go to NGA's National Garden Month Web page at: www.nationalgardenmonth. org. The National Gardening Association (www.garden.org) is a nonprofit organization established in 1972 to help people with their gardening. This year, dig into the rewarding world of container gardening, wherever you live. You'll be abundantly pleased with what you can grow and enjoy.

There are other ways and places to garden if you don't have much backyard room or landscape space. Here are ideas collected from around our country that you may transplant to your own home grounds as they apply.

# Grow UP, i.e. Vertically

You can save space by growing vertically in the air space above your plants. Vertical gardening offers several advantages; better air circulation, access to sunlight, fewer problems with moisture causing diseases, and easier harvest of veggies. By combining this idea with raised boxed beds (see page 187) you can boost your growing capacity nicely. You can grow plants vertically more closely together and produce more in the rich, friable soil of a properly managed raised bed. Using air space for certain crops takes up only a few inches of surface soil, so you have lots of bed left to be intensively planted with low-growing vegetables. Orient beds on a north-south axis to insure that plant-laden trellises do not block the sun from lower growing plants as it moves from east to west during the day.

For vertical gardening try hoops of wire and wooden trellises available in garden centers. More advanced systems are featured in mail order garden catalogs. Best bet is to attach supports to the planks that enclose a raised bed using cedar, redwood, or cypress which resist rot. You also can erect teepees for beans, cukes, and flowering vines as decorative accents in your garden.

Whether you grow in containers, raised beds, or vertically, here is a list of vegetables that perform well growing up. Not all are biblical plants but all will give you a chance to enjoy tasty foods as you and your family grow together with God in your garden. Consider beans, both pole snap and pole limas, cucumbers, melons, peas from pod type to snap and snow peas, various squash, and of course all types of tomatoes. Cherry, pear, and plum do very well but so do larger types.

As you grow up, consider combining vining plants, such as beans and cucumbers or peas and gourds on the same support, whether a fence, A-frame trellis, or in a wire hoop to get multiple crops in the same space. Think about the historic so-called "three sisters" method employed by native Americans. They planted beans with corn and pumpkins. The corn stalks provide support for the beans to climb while the pumpkins or other squash sprawl on the ground beneath as a living mulch to control weeds and help retain soil moisture. Space saving cucumbers, in containers or in the ground, produce straighter, cleaner fruit when you grow them vertically. Sow seeds along a cage, netted A-frame. Or flat trellis and guide the plants up onto the netting. Once plant tendrils form, they naturally curl around on their own to climb your supports, but at fist they need a bit of training help.

Melons are one of the favorite crops among gardeners, but often are not grown because earlier varieties took up too much space for vines to crawl around the ground. Today, plant breeders have provided new varieties that love to climb. Melons climb by means of tendrils but their heavier fruit requires some extra support when you grow the plants vertically to prevent their weight from pulling vines down. You can make cloth slings and attach to the uprights of poles or trellis to support melons.

Don't overlook flowers to complement veggies in containers, raised beds, or as part of your vertical garden plots. Here are some good choices. Among vines, consider balloon vine (*Cardiospermum halicacabum*), black-eyed Susan vine (*Thunbergia alata*), cup-and-saucer vine (*Cobaea scandens*), moonflower (*Ipomoea alba*), morning glory (*Ipomoea tricolor*), nasturtium (*Tropaeolum*), and passion flower (*Passiflora caerulea*).

Look around your home today and decide where containers, even on rolling platforms and other types of vertical growing methods, can give you gardening opportunities. Let your imagination soar and you too can enjoy biblical foods wherever you live.

# Chapter 7

# Plant a Row
# for the Hungry

**A**s we think about the foods that Jesus and His Disciples ate and plan to grow a selection of them in our own gardens, we should also remember how Jesus shared foods with others. The epic story of His breaking the five loaves of bread and dividing the fish that the little boy had and sharing with the 5,000 gathered around should prompt us to reflect on how we can share our crops with others. Sharing is a basic commandment of the Scriptures and part of the foundation of all faiths and denominations.

Today, there is a remarkable and worthwhile program that all biblical gardeners can adopt. It began as an inspiration of a former president of the Garden Writers of America (GWA), Jeff Lowenfels, in 1995. Since then it has been growing and gaining ground all across America. It is the marvelous Plant a Row for the Hungry (PAR) program. You can be part of this exceptional opportunity to grow with God in your garden and in many meaningful ways wherever you live.

This remarkable program offers a way for those who love vegetables, fruits, and other foods to have an immediate, direct impact on the stubborn problem of hunger in the United States and Canada. Think how satisfying it will be for you to turn your personal joy of gardening into a useful service by growing extra food and donating it to neighbors who struggle to feed their families. PAR is a simple, logical, and productive idea. There are no bureaucratic hassles, no funding issues; only grass roots efforts by neighbors to help neighbors.

Hunger is an international problem. Hunger in America is less well understood, yet it cuts across geographical and cultural lines. It impacts senior citizens, infants, the unemployed and underemployed, children, and the homeless. Hunger in America is far more extensive than we may believe. Estimates vary, but projections reveal that as many as 35 million people worry every day about where (or if) they will get their next meal.

Periodically we read or hear about hunger in our own communities. Churches and other charitable organizations have led the efforts to resolve this problem with food banks, food pantries, soup kitchens, and other useful programs. Yet the problem still exists. According to the U.S. Conference of Mayors, hunger continues to be a problem in most of the largest metropolitan areas across the country, despite a prolonged period of economic health. Figures released late in 2000 revealed an increase in food assistance requests in 1999 of 17% above the previous year. The largest group suffering from hunger is the working families and their children, especially those in single parent families with one income. Senior citizens are another group that has not benefited from the strong economy. A national food relief agency, Second Harvest, reports that their 200+ food banks serving 50,000 people actually had to turn away more than one million requests for help one year.

One garden writer, Amy Richards, recalled what it was like to be hungry. She explained that when she was a child her father's business closed and her mother also lost her job. They went from being middle class to poor. She reports how her mother went alone to the food bank because she was too ashamed to take the children with her. "When she came home with food, it was like Christmas," she recalls.

The Plant a Row for the Hungry idea Jeff Lowenfels pioneered has taken root, grown, and led to millions of pounds of food being grown by American gardeners and donated to the hungry nationwide. Today this program continues to help less fortunate people in our country. You can become an important partner in the plan. This chapter outlines the program and provides details of how people from every faith and denomination can help.

Jeff's idea began with imagining the amount of food that could be produced if every gardener purposely planted more than he or she needed. It could be vast numbers of pounds, actually tons of nutritious food. If each gardener planted one extra row and donated the harvest to a local food bank, gardeners could make an enormous difference. Other GWA members caught the enthusiasm. Plant a Row sprouted, grew, and thrived.

PAR was conceived at the outset as people-based, not institutional or bureaucratic. The success of PAR depends on the good will, time, and energy of thousands of gardeners and gardening groups. The concept took root and was nourished by hundreds of garden writers who wrote stories for their local and area media and encouraged gardeners to dig in and grow that extra row for the hungry. Thousands of home gardeners volunteered and PAR grew naturally, as it deserved to do.

Backyard gardeners are literally and figuratively the heart of the PAR effort nationwide. Their understanding of the importance of fresh, healthful food and their experience with the uncertainty of the harvest (and therefore uncertainty of food to eat), as well as their long time tradition of sharing generous harvests with friends and neighbors prompted them to embrace PAR with unbridled enthusiasm.

Back in the Victory Garden era during World War II, homeowners dug in and grew millions of pounds of food. The excess produced was graciously shared with friends and neighbors and around their communities. Today, the PAR program has reinterpreted the meaning of the old adage "just grow what you and your neighbors can use." That was a caution against excess production of foods that might be wasted. But PAR gardeners now interpret the adage as a charge to deliberately grow extra and then donate the surplus to local agencies that feed the hungry.

Local food banks, soup kitchens, and similar programs usually have sources of bakery, package, and canned goods, but finding fresh produce with its superior nutrition, has been a challenge. This is the need that local gardeners fill. They deliver their surplus harvest to designated drop-off collection points in their communities or nearby towns. There it is weighed, recorded, and delivered to a nearby food relief agency and often used that day. According to GWA records, sometimes gardeners get involved because they have over grown and want to give the excess away. Virginia Davidson had enough winter squash when she picked her first 20 pounds. What could she do with the other 250 pounds? She called a local food rescue program in Mechanicsburg, PA, learned about PAR, and donated her surplus squash. Now, she and office friends cultivate a rented garden plot where all rows are planted for PAR food.

Joan Jackson, a California garden columnist, pioneered the PAR program among her readership and her community set a fast pace. With the support of her newspaper she devoted many of her columns to describing the program and encouraging gardeners to sign a pledge to grow and contribute fresh produce. By September of the first year, her readers had donated nearly 34,000 pounds of fruit and vegetables to area hunger relief agencies. Since then they have greatly expanded their tonnage.

Gardeners who take part in PAR grow crops that do best in their region so they can harvest large amounts. They sow extra of the crops that are most appreciated and needed by food kitchen organizations. Some agencies prefer certain crops because they are popular with their clients or are especially high in nutritional values. Others request foods they use and need frequently.

Most food agencies appreciate any fruits and veggies that will store on a shelf for a day or two if necessary. They want food that is dense in nutrients. Many also welcome fresh herbs for making soups and stews that are staples of their menus. PAR gardeners often also donate flowers to perk up the lives of those who are in need of food. Collectively, GWA reports that PAR gardeners donated more than one million pounds of fresh food during the year 2000, and the program was just beginning then.

You may wonder what gardeners get in return. Here are some accounts from PAR participants.

"As I opened my car trunk, which was full of plums for the food bank, an old van drove up with a family of six, including four little kids, looking for some groceries. The mother was delighted to take a pailful of plums to make jam. Her little boy looked up at me with such a happy smile and in that moment I had my quiet thanks for the small effort it took us to make a contribution," reports Darlene White of British Columbia.

Every participant has a story to tell. Perhaps Beth Bangert's experience in Calthan, Colorado, when she delivered 6,000 pounds of fresh food to the need sums up the rewards for giving from your garden. "The response from folks getting the food was like someone had opened the door to the toy store and said 'go to it.' I wish I could have bottled all the smiles and hugs. It's the best summer I ever had."

The National Garden Bureau donated funds to continue the program and assisted with an international publicity program. Home & Garden Television contributed nationwide media coverage to its more than 50 million viewers. The

Scotts Company promoted PAR on every box of Miracle-Gro fertilizer sold nationally and Fafard promoted PAR on millions of soil amendment bags.

With growing support, GWA leaders set a major goal as the program began, "A Million for the Millennium," a million pounds of food for the hungry. It was an ambitious goal and it was met with tonnage to spare and to share. Think about it. Picture a million pounds of fresh vegetables grown in home gardens and donated to food pantries to feed the hungry. According to one gardener participant, "Giving from the garden is a simple, deeply satisfying way to meet a growing need." That hits the nail on the head. Ask any of the thousands of gardeners who participate in the Plant a Row for the Hungry program why they give away some of the food they grow and they will likely say the same thing.

You can be part of this worthwhile, meaningful program and perhaps even be an organizer and leader in your area. There may be local programs underway, of course. But because this is only a few years old, it is logical that many more gardeners across the country may not have heard of it yet. You can help. Here's how others did and what it meant.

When William Dunn delivered a load of fresh vegetables to the Women with Infant Children Food Center in Chicago, the people there were so grateful for the fresh produce that they came out and shook his hand. He was amazed because Dunn works in a jail garden. We understand that his experience helped motivate him even more.

Gardeners who participate in PAR are from all regions of the United States and Canada. They are rural, urban, suburban individuals and families and they are everywhere. They include children, teenagers, adults, and seniors. Among the PAR gardeners are teachers, executives, local business people, church members, scouts, garden club members, dentists, mechanics, and students of all ages. Some garden alone or with their families while others are part of a group or PAR network and purposely coordinate their planting to produce certain crops for local food banks. Many people garden in backyards, in community plots, on corporate campuses, in schoolyards, behind churches, in prisons, and on apartment balconies. The key thing that PAR gardeners have in common is a love of gardening and a desire to help out neighbors who are not always sure where their next meal is coming from.

In Rhode Island, Lisa-Marie Ricci discovered a new dimension in her life. She notes that: "The first time I went to meet a woman from a soup kitchen at the market in her town was probably one of the best experiences of my life."

Thanks to veteran garden writer Liz Ball, here are some growing guidelines for all who wish to become involved with PAR:

- Contact local food banks and soup kitchens, nutrition programs or food recovery organizations for information on what they need for their clients.
- Extend the main growing season by planting cool weather crops in both spring and fall.
- Space plantings so that produce ripens over several weeks rather than all at once.
- Grow foods that will stay fresh with minimal care for a few days.
- Pick promptly to stimulate more production on crops that do so.
- Chose foods that travel well and withstand handling.
- Clean off excess soil, but do not wash vegetables.
- Store excess crops properly prior to taking them to a collection place.
- Discard any damaged produce to prevent spoilage.

No matter what size your garden, you can maximize its productivity. Wide beds about 3 feet across are better than rows because you cut down the number of paths you need, especially in small backyards. Vegetables need full sun, so select a site with southern exposure. Plan to put tall vegetables such as tomatoes and trellised vining crops on the north sides of your garden so they don't shade lower growing crops.

In addition to familiar, traditional veggies, try a few newer ones to expand your culinary experiences. Today, people like Tex-Mex food, stir fry meals, and other new flavor treats. So, include bok choy, Japanese eggplant, jalapeno, or other hot peppers. Add Thai basil, cilantro, and other unusual foods and herbs to flavor foods as well. Select easy to grow veggies that you can sow directly in the garden.

According to Plant a Row specialists among garden writers, here are five sure fire vegetables that are most appreciated by many people who need food. They are also easy to grow. These five will perform well sown from seed in the garden soil and with regular watering and fertilizer will produce bumper crops.

**Beans.** You can grow various types and varieties of beans on small bushes or as pole beans that will climb 6 to 8 feet tall on supports. Because they are warm weather vegetables, beans do not germinate well in cold soil, so wait until late spring to plant them. Pole beans produce over a longer period of time than bush beans and occupy no more space because they will grow up poles or trellises or bamboo teepees. Sow pole beans thinly in blocks in a wide bed, along the base of a trellis or around each pole. Sow bush beans in rows or blocks about 2 feet apart. To harvest beans more easily, stick a few twiggy shrub prunings in the bed when you plant to keep slightly vining stems upright. For longer, more abundant harvests, sow bush beans every 3 to 4 weeks until midsummer. For colorful eating, try green, purple, and yellow pod varieties.

**Cucumbers.** Try both slicing and pickling cucumbers as warm weather crops for abundant harvests. To save space, grow cukes on a trellis or in a wire cage instead of letting them sprawl on the ground. You'll find fruit turns out straighter that way. Sow sparingly and thin seedlings to about 1 foot apart. Guide plants into the trellis or cage and they'll grow upright.

Keep cukes well watered and apply some fertilizer during the growing season to keep plants producing prolifically. Follow directions for the type fertilizer you buy. Harvest cucumbers when small for best taste, 4 to 8 inches long, depending on variety. If you plan to pickle, a few plants will be sufficient. Most families enjoy these salad veggies and you can keep harvesting right up to frost.

**Peas.** Peas are a cool weather crop, so it is best to plant an early spring and fall crop, too. Sow this short-fining vegetable in blocks or double rows with a short trellis or pea fencing to make harvesting easier. Among peas, try sweet snap peas, snow peas, or the English type traditional shelling peas. Harvest the pods of the first two when small to eat whole or even raw. Shell the pods of snap and shelling peas. If you grow food for a soup kitchen, stick with snap or snow peas, which makes preparation easier and faster for the cooks.

**Radishes.** Probably the easiest vegetable to grow, radishes mature in 25 to 30 days. Sow seeds sparingly and periodically, 10 days apart. Instead of devoting one row to them, sow between other veggies and pick when ready. Sow in late summer for fall but avoid growing in summertime as that produces hotter radishes.

**Summer squash.** Plant summer squash in hills 3 to 4 feet apart. When seedlings reach 2 to 3 inches high, thin each hill to the two strongest plants. Be aware squash are very productive, especially zucchini varieties, so 4 to 6 plants feed a family of four generously with squash to spare. By midsummer make a new planting if you have space and get a fall harvest before frost.

Yes, you can grow many other vegetables, from ever-popular tomatoes in many different varieties to root crops as well. What you grow will be your decision based on what your family likes and also what you learn from the local food pantry or PAR organization about local tastes.

Here are a few pointers to increase your harvest and have surplus to give. First, let your crops grow and grow! Pick four-inch bean babies for your own table and let a give-away portion of the crop mature to seven and eight inches. Too many tomatoes is what happens when you let the plants sucker. They'll slow the crop a bit but yield lots more later. You'll have loads of extra cucumbers, zucchini, and squash if you allow the plants to mature to 10-inch vegetables instead of harvesting 4 to 5 inchers. Ditto the root vegetables and much else. Don't allow fruit to rot on the ground. Bag it and take it where it will do some good in your community.

Here are some tips for those of you who would like to establish and lead a PAR program in your community. At the end of this chapter you'll find the GWA and PAR contact people and addresses. Call, e-mail, or access their Web sites. Here are some of the easy steps that can lead you into a successful PAR program in your community. everything you need to know is also in the excellent, easy-to-follow kits from GWA.

The first step is to recruit dedicated volunteers. Most successful PAR campaigns are started by one person who develops a network of helpers, including master and community gardeners, garden clubs, garden centers, and nurseries. They usually include these elements:

- A local coordinator, perhaps a dedicated person like yourself with connections in the gardening community to recruit the network and run the campaign.
- A food distribution agency partner to contact organizations who want garden produce and who will give donor receipts. Look for a dynamic staffer from a food bank, soup kitchen, or shelter.
- A publicist to create stories about the local campaign and support it from kickoff through the growing season. Publicity is essential! Often local media people become enthusiastic supporters for PAR programs.

- An events organizer to arrange the PAR "kickoff" day and site and to plan the closing harvest celebration. PAR can provide brochures, posters, row markers, and other supplies for "starter kits" to give away. You or one of your associates should contact local garden center owners, nurserymen, farmers markets, and other businesses for input. Naturally, you should check into and be sure to comply with all municipal laws.
- Finally, a local PAR group should have a collections organizer to arrange for dropoff and collection sites and transport of food if needed.

Actually, it is easier to organize and run a local PAR effort than you realize, and most who do say that it is one of the most rewarding and fulfilling projects they have ever undertaken. It fits into their faith, their love of humanity, and their interest in gardening.

Here's how a typical PAR campaign looks: When planting season opens there is an attention-getting launch for the campaign and give away of starter kits for participants. That is followed by publicity and requests to extension services, community gardens, churches, schools, garden clubs, businesses, even food banks to start PAR gardens. An effort is made to enlist market gardens and truck farmers in donating unsold produce.

As harvest season advances there are gleaning opportunities from home orchards and truck farms. It is important for PAR organizers to give them receipts and get receipts from the recipients. Organizers should call food distribution agency partners weekly to ask for donation reports. Naturally, it is important to publicize the donations to build further support for the program.

In addition to growing vegetable, herb gardeners have become active with PAR. In fact, there is a PAR garden at the National Herb Society's headquarters in Ohio. GWA members Connie White and Joanna Bristol, Director of the Herb Society of America, spearheaded the establishment of this 250-square foot PAR herb and vegetable garden at the Society's headquarters in Kirkland, OH. The Society's head gardener, Joan De Lauro, worked with Master Gardeners, HSA members, and volunteers from the community.

"When they heard what we were doing we had tremendous support from local gardeners," Joanna said. "People took the idea to their own garden clubs and got them producing and making their own donations." The volunteers came every Thursday, Joanna said, in spite of rain and unusual heat. "And we had fun! Some vegetables came out looking like pieces of art. The purple peppers were so beautiful I put one on my desk and just admired the color before sending it to the food bank." The gardeners fell in love with "all-organic, poster beautiful" heirloom tomatoes and peppers donated to the project by Johnny's Selected Seeds of Maine, and local nurseries including Mulberry Creek Herb Farm and Whalecrest Herb Farm. The Lake County Food Bank was thrilled!

"I believe in this," one volunteer said. "We don't have to go to Africa or Afghanistan to make a difference. We can do it in our own back yard!" In my home state of Maine, students planted and tended three PAR gardens at the Good Will-Hinckley Home for Boys & Girls. Visits to food pantries and soup kitchens receiving the 1,500+ pounds they harvested helped the young people to realize the importance of the contribution they were making in their community. According to another Maine report, the most dedicated gardener at a Portland, Maine, shelter for homeless men, the Prebel Street Resource Center, actually is a former resident who now has a home of his own again and completed the Master Gardener course. The quarter-acre plot was created for the center by Master Gardeners.

On the West Coast, Bob Tanem heard about New Beginnings, a Marin County shelter planning to house, train, and hopefully find jobs for the homeless. A retired nurseryman, Bob is a member of GWA. "It struck me that a great way to support PAR would be to teach the homeless to grow food," Bob said. "And it's a marketable skill."

With the blessing of Robert Puett, the shelter program director, Bob directed residents in prepping and planting a garden at the shelter. "They're good workers, but more familiar with canned beans than the real thing. One young man came out to watch and asked me what we were doing. I said, 'putting in an organic vegetable garden'. 'You can grow vegetables?' he asked. It was incomprehensible to me that a person wouldn't know where vegetables come from! But he wound up on the end of the rototiller the day we planted."

Five weeks later, 80 shelter residents were eating their first homegrown onions, lettuce, and squash. Extras went to the Marin County food bank. "Knowing that folks in trouble are being encouraged to garden is a real thrill," PAR National Director Jacqui Heriteau said. "Garden writers know gardening can lift you up, get you going again."

"Food banks say clients are especially pleased when they get fresh produce," Heriteau said, "so they're going after it." An informal survey showed 12 percent of the 700 or so PAR 2001 campaigns are led by food banks and pantries. An outstanding example is the Kenai Peninsula Food Bank in Alaska whose director invited volunteers to transform the weed-eaten yard. Now the yard has raised beds, a lawn for picnic tables, a 40' x 50' vegetable garden and a 30' x 90' potato patch.

To learn more about Plant a Row or GWA you have several options. You can visit the Plant a Row page on the GWA website at www.gwa.org. For general information and to get a kit or brochure call toll free at 1-877-GWAA-PAR or E-mail at PAR@gwaa.org

GWA also offers useful support supplies. You can get a giant row marker for PAR gardeners, small row markers suitable for gardens of publicity giveaways, and even ad slicks to use in local media. PAR marketing brochures with general interest, guidelines for starting your own campaign and a PAR self-help video are also available. In additional there is a workbook and press kit to help enlist local media coverage and a quarterly PAR newsletter.

The GWAA organization also suggests that anyone interested in PAR can call Foodchain, the national food rescue network 1-800-845-3008 for a local contact. Or Second Harvest 1-800-771-2302, Ext. 121, Dan Michel. Other organizations involved include churches, temples diocesan offices, various United Way groups, the Salvation Army, or check your local telephone book for agencies that serve the hungry.

Whether you are a novice or veteran gardener, active or casual member of a congregation, the PAR program offers everyone a unique and worthwhile opportunity. Dig into that idea and cultivate it as you wish. You'll find a wonderful new growing opportunity and be of help to those who need it.

# Chapter 8

# Neot Kedumim— World's Most Extensive Biblical Garden

**D**evoted biblical gardeners have created marvelous collections of biblical plants in glorious displays around America and overseas. In this chapter you'll find the latest information about these gardens.

Undoubtedly the most extensive and dramatic garden is the 625-acre Biblical Landscape Reserve in Israel, Neot Kedumim. It is the most remarkable and magnificent biblical plant garden in the entire world. It is more extensive than any other biblical garden, has a wider range of authentic biblical plants and landmarks, and presents a restored natural environment and plant habitat as gardens once were in ancient times in the Holy Land. Because it is such a biblical plant landmark in the world with such marvelous and meaningful outreach programs of classes, courses and literature, and serves people of all faiths, it is appropriate to make it the focus in this chapter. There are lessons growing there that are eminently transplantable to other gardens, even small backyard plots all around the world.

Neot Kedumim began as a dream shared by Dr. Ephraim and Hannah Hareuveni, two Russian Jewish emigrants to Israel who envisioned these gardens of flora and fauna. Both were trained botanists who dedicated themselves to research of the land and its relationship to the ancient literature of Israel. They conceived the idea of developing a living replica to reflect the interrelated botany, history, and traditions of the land of the Bible, which would create a bond between the past, present, and future. The Biblical Landscape Reserve in Israel thrives today and exists on a far grander scale than they may have envisioned. It stands on 625 formerly barren acres in Israel's Modi'in region as a pastoral network of Biblical and Talmudic landscapes, which attracts more than 100,000 visitors a year.

As Helen Frenkley, the Director Emerita of Neot Kedumim has observed, it conveys messages through accounts of people interacting with a particular land. The language of the scriptures is alive with sights, sounds, fragrance, and graphic visual perspectives of the Holy Land's natural landscapes. It is through such images and landscapes that the Bible conveys its ideas.

The word "Neot" means pastures or places of beauty, as in Psalm 23: "He maketh me to lie down in green pastures." The word "Kedumim" means ancient and simultaneously contains the Hebrew roots of the word that indicates forward movement in time. The name Neot Kedumim, therefore, expresses hope of future growth from past roots. That is a most apt name for this remarkable Biblical Landscape Reserve.

Appropriately, one of Neot Kedumim's themed trails includes the seven varieties of food that Moses mentions in Deuteronomy 8:8 as the most important crops of ancient Israel: wheat, barley, figs, pomegranates, grapes, olives, and dates. Naturally, you'll find all these significant plants in this book with details about them and tips for growing them too.

All plants in the reserve are well marked with appropriate quotes from the scriptures in both Hebrew and English. Walking the sloping hills and paths, visitors see gleaming man-made lakes, old Byzantine cisterns and chapels, ancient Roman olive oil presses, and other relics of two millennia ago. Because it is a reserve, representative animals of the Scriptures reside there. A camel, gazelles, sheep, goats, and cattle wander and ducks paddle on the tranquil Pool of Solomon. Additionally a number of "biblical sojourners" such as the stork and crane, drink from Neot Kedumim's six reservoir pools during their migrations to and from Africa.

You can rest under an elegant, ancient Cedar of Lebanon tree. You can inhale the scents from the flowers, the herbs, the essence of earliest times. Visitors can walk several self-guided trails with the assistance of a trail guide and map and most paths are handicapped accessible. These trails provide ideas for all who wish to explore the outreach potential of biblical gardens at their churches or temples or organizations.

In one walk during the appropriate season, approximately between February and April, you find the fields brimming with flowers, which are an array of the wild and wonderful flowers of the Holy Land. You'll also see several varieties of Iris and an array of cyclamens. Daisies and Sharon tulips grace the pathway. Anemones, a classic flower of the Scriptures and Holy Land, provide their red, purple, and sometimes white delights. As part of this recreated Biblical Reserve visitors may see a Gallein wolf, camel, fallow deer, or even a camel near the water cistern.

Another trail guides visitors to vistas of plants in the Song of Songs. White lilies reflect the passages, "his lips are like lilies, dripping flowing myrrh" (Song of Songs 5:13). Along the way are red buttercups, from Song of Songs 2:12, "The red buttercups appear on the earth." Further along, people see grapevines and striking clusters of white and yellow narcissus that reflect that Biblical image, "I am the narcissus of the valleys" (Song of Songs 2:1).

In the fall, there is an ingathering, a harvesting time for crops and preparing for the coming rainy season at Neot Kedumim. Visitors see figs and grapes being sun dried to preserve them as energy rich food, as was done by the people there thousands of years ago. Fields are plowed and sown with seed grain in anticipation of the coming winter rains. In Hebrew the word for ingathering is *kayitz*, which comes from the same root as two other Hebrew words, *ketz* and *kotz*. *Ketz* means "end," because plants die or go dormant in the brutal heat and dryness of Israel's summer months. Kotz means "thorn," the kind of plants that can dominate Israel fields at this drying time of year. As their posted plant descriptions explain even thorns can be beautiful as the purple thistles that we can grow as replicas in our gardens.

White squill, meadow saffron, which is a type of crocus, and other flowers, herbs, and trees are part of this and other hiking and walking trails, well described in markers about the plants. From these trails, printed flyers in various languages enable visitors to further enjoy and understand the important scriptural, historic, and ecological significance of what they see growing.

Neot Kedumim continues to grow in many worthwhile directions today, a tribute to founder Nogah Hareuveni's vision, dedication, and perseverance dating to 1965. It was his vision and efforts that brought this marvelous reserve into being as a living, growing reflection of the flora and fauna of original scriptures. He was born in Jerusalem in 1924. From childhood he worked with his parents, the founders of the Museum of Biblical Botany at the Hebrew University. For years he traveled afield throughout Israel with them as they collected and recorded the vast flora of the land of the Bible, so important to several of the world's religions.

Neot Kedumim remains dedicated to exploring and demonstrating the ties between the biblical tradition and Israel's nature and agriculture as expressed in prayers, holidays, and symbols. Equally significant, it has deep roots in Judeo-Christian traditions. Today it has a staff of 80 and hosts tens of thousands of visitors of the Jewish and Christian faiths from around the world annually.

Years of devotion to this exceptional, living and growing Biblical landscape project led Nogah to write several distinctive books. His hardcover books include *Nature in Our Biblical Heritage*, the perfect gift for anyone interested in Bible, nature, history, or Judeo-Christian traditions. *Tree and Shrub in Our Biblical Heritage,* an in depth exploration of the biblical plants, and *Desert and Shepherd in Our Biblical Heritage*, which explains Psalm 23 in a new light, are equally worthwhile. Two other books, *Ecology in the Bible*, and *The Emblem of the State of Israel,* both of which take a look at these topics through the lens of the plants native to ancient Israel, are also from American Friends of Neot Kedumim, as in the resource section at the end of this book.

When biblical garden enthusiasts travel to this reserve, in person or via the Internet website, they can wander among groves of palm, fig and olive trees, observing the intertwining of Jewish and Christian traditions. In these extensive gardens, olive trees stand symbolically as they have since ancient times. According to universal tradition, olive branches are a symbol of peace, and they are included in the state emblem of Israel. In Exodus 27:20, God commanded that olive oil was to be used in kindling the light of the menorah because it provided the brightest and steadiest flame.

Also prominent in the gardens is the moriah plant, which is a member of the sage family. This herb, which grows wild throughout Israel today as it did in biblical times, has special significance to the Jewish people. The menorah is first mentioned in the Bible when God instructed Moses in the preparation of the Ark of the Covenant. As described in Exodus 25:31–40 which you can read, the specifications seem almost couched in botanical terms of branches, calyxes, cups, and petals. Ephraim and Hannah Hareuveni were the first to point to a direct relationship between the menorah and the moriah or sage plant as a particular biblical plant. The moriah may not always have seven branches, but it does have an even number growing on each side of a central branch, and its pattern is strikingly similar to the menorah. Because sage plants do have flowers as well as herbal attributes, I have included them in this book with growing advice about them in Chapter 3.

Neot Kedumim is located in an area known in the Bible as the Judean foothills or lowlands. This area lies between the flat coastal plain that composes the western edge of Israel and the Judean hills that rise toward Jerusalem to the southeast. The typical landscape of these hills, without care, is rather dry, barren, and seemingly inhospitable, unless you have a vision and the determination to make this land bloom again as it did more than 2,000 years ago. That is one of the aspects that makes Neot Kedumim so remarkable, that people with vision and historical facts to foresee the potential, could and did make a garden bloom in what had become, over centuries of neglect, a desolate area. Overgrazing, battles, and abuse of the land had eroded it down to bedrock. To create gardens, thousands of tons of soil had to be trucked in to the site.

## Educational Programs and Outreach

The Holy Land is a microcosm of diversity in nature. Neot Kedumim itself is a microcosm of a microcosm. This 625-acre reserve recreates a series of landscapes that are found in Israel and explores the intertwining between the land of the Bible and the texts of the Hebrew Bible and the Christian New Testament. Lectures and programs shed light on this important linkage of biblical Scriptures and natural history. Neot Kedumim is an ongoing educational project based on the tenet that many Jewish and Christian traditions, holidays, and symbols are rooted in the ecology, ancient agriculture, flora and fauna of the Land of Israel, the Holy Land.

This garden network containing plants and animals mentioned in the Bible provides visitors with a living panorama of Judeo-Christian history and an explanation of its roots in the physical land. The original concept continues to grow and expand. On-site educational programs are conducted regularly and outreach programs continue to grow as the gardens do.

More than a decade ago, Neot Kedumim became part of Israel's educational system. More than 60,000 pupils from kindergarten through high school and all parts of the country's religious and social spectrum have been visiting Neot Kedumim annually during the past decade. In addition, Neot Kedumim has reached classrooms via the hundreds of teachers who participated in their teacher enrichment and in-service training programs. Teachers from all parts of the country, religious and secular, young and old, regularly take part in educational programs. The programs have at times transcended religious differences as well. Four Muslim Arab teachers from a village in the Galilee participated in one of the courses. The following year they brought some of their colleagues to the program. Growing together in peace is a worthwhile theme at Neot Kedumim, in the Holy Land, and around the world and is the underlying theme in this book, too.

The innovative and wide-ranging courses at Neot Kedumim provide programs about ecology, conservation, and the environment, which are all important topics in an area where land and water preservation is vital. Other courses deal with parables and symbols in the Bible and with archeology. In addition to formal courses, both students and teachers often come in search of resource materials on the "green archeology" that Neot Kedumim uniquely offers. Courses are open to teachers and students from other countries in English, Hebrew, and Russian.

Many people creating and sustaining biblical gardens also are concerned with funding and with integrating the viewing of flowers with other aspects of biblical and everyday life. The folks at Neot Kedumim do both by serving meals created with foods and decorated by flowers grown in biblical gardens. The meals allow visitors to "taste and see" biblical foods. The proceeds from meals also help to fund operations much like church dinners help support religious programs, groups, and gardens in the United States.

## Foods and Traditional Feasts

Church suppers have been and are a traditional fund raising activity for thousands of churches across America. Perhaps some of the special food and feast projects at Neot Kedumim will provide food for thought as fundraiser projects for churches and temples here in the United States. After all, foods that trace their history to biblical plants can have special meaning for special events. Neot Kedumim folks realized that visitors get hungry. They have come up with a range of biblically inspired, tasty meals to feed the multitudes, or a few visitors at a time, as the case may be.

From Proverbs 15:17 we read, "Better a meal of vegetables where there is love than a fatted ox where there is hatred." In keeping with that passage, Neot Kedumim offers vegetarian menus. You may not wish to become as deeply involved as operating a regular food service at your church or temple requires, but there may be some opportunities for special events, fundraisers or Holy Day suppers that come to mind as you read their menus.

---

Innovative ideas deserve a salute. Here is part of a typical menu from Neot Kedumim.

**Appetizers**

Garbanzo beans with olives in hyssop

Cucumber strips in tehina

Roasted pita with olive oil and garlic

Flavored cheeses: natural, creamed, with olives, walnuts, dill, or onion, plus four kinds of fresh bread, reflective of the grains grown there now and historically. Flavored butters—natural, dill, onion, or garlic—and pickled vegetables including a choice of cucumbers, onions, turnips, mixed veggies.

**Salads**

Pickled quail eggs with herbs, yogurt and cucumber strips with dill and mint

Tabouleh, which is cracked bulgur wheat with herbs, vegetables, and olive oil

Garbanzo beans with capers, chopped olives with parsley, garlic, lemon squares, and olive oil

Spinach leaves with red lentils, garlic, olive oil, and mint

Sliced cucumbers with pickles, dill and purple onion

**Entrees**

Squash and onion casserole with rice and lentils and thick lentil stew

Squash stuffed with rice and raisins or cheese

Herb salad with parsley, coriander, mint, dill, and pine nuts

Strips of squash, lightly cooked with hot and sour sauce

Squash with onions and herbs

White beans with chopped spinach and onion rings in olive oil and lemon

Lettuce salad, cabbage, and sesame in sweet and sour sauce

Raw carrots with walnuts and raisins

Beets with walnuts and herbs

Grape leaves stuffed with rice

**Desserts**

In-season fruit, dough puffs with choice of home-made jams and honey. Beverages are cold lemon and almond drinks and hot herbal tea. Wine is optional.

For those who wish a morning treat, a biblical-style breakfast is offered as a buffet. It includes shepherd cheese, farmer's cheese, garden cucumbers, olives and olive oil, hyssop seasoning, fresh-baked pita bread, along with yogurt, date honey, bee honey, raisins, walnuts, and seasonal herbal teas. As noted in their literature, the menu seems to demand a quotation from Psalm 78:29: "And they ate and were well filled."

This delightful array of menu items offers lots of ideas for biblical meals for fund-raising events at churches and temples with biblical gardens here in North America. In fact, their creative menus invoke ideas for special biblical meals, whether your church has a biblical garden or not. For example, the First Congregational Church in Fair Haven, Vermont, includes one or more biblical food items in a more traditional church supper as a special highlight. As the season allows, biblical flowers are used for table decoration.

## Weddings and Special Events

Weddings along the Wedding Trail at Neot Kedumim have become increasingly popular. The Wedding Trail is a gentle trail through landscapes evoked in the Song of Songs 8:7. Proceeding from a pool reminding participants that "torrents of water cannot quench love, nor rivers drown it," the trail skirts young pomegranate trees, reflecting another scriptural passage, "Your limbs are an orchard of pomegranates, with all choicest fruits."

After walking through the landscapes of the "tulip of Sharon," the "apple among the trees of the forest," and the "narcissus among the thorns," wedding guests arrive under the tall date palms beside the Pool of Solomon. The trail is illuminated at night and provides a truly romantic setting for a wedding. After the ceremony, the Neot Kedumim Wedding Trail takes guests to a reception area, a spot-lit clearing in a pine forest for eating, singing, and dancing. That too has its scriptural reflection from Isaiah 55:12, "For you shall go out with joy, and be led forth with peace; the mountains and the hills shall break forth before you into singing, and all the trees of the field shall clap their hands." Neot Kedumim also offers indoor reception facilities, including Ophira's Winter Garden, the décor of which is evocative of a biblical village courtyard.

Your biblical garden can serve as a site for weddings or other special events. It might also serve as a special site for wedding photos, with flowers and plants selected that may have a special significance to the event or people involved.

Another aspect of Neot Kedumim deserves special focus, again for ideas that may be useful as we see how others have overcome obstacles, creatively planted, and cultivated their gardens. According to Shlomo Teitelbaum, Neot Kedumim's Director, the planners there faced some dilemmas while reconstructing the landscapes of the Song of Songs and had to come up with creative solutions.

"It was King Solomon's words in Ecclesiastes that gave us the inspiration and courage to develop a portion of the bare, rocky tract to the Song of Songs. Two hills hugging a valley of varying width would be ideal for verses from the Song: 'His aspect is like Lebanon, noble as the cedars,' and 'I went down to the walnut garden to see the budding inside the stream banks,' and 'you stand like a date palm.'

"But how could we plant cedars and walnut trees which grow in high cold habitats, next to date palms and the narcissus of the valleys which need warmth and large quantities of water?" Teitelbaum asked rhetorically. "How could we put 'mountains of spices' next to the Sharon tulip, grazing areas for animals next to cultivated gardens of grapevines and pomegranates?

"Solutions to some of the problems were suggested by the words of the Song itself: 'I went down to the walnut garden.' Walnut trees normally grow at high elevations, but as the verb 'went down' suggests, walnuts also can grow in a micro-climate created by a topographical depression surrounded by hills. The cold air sinking into such a pocket provides nights of winter frost, which the walnuts need.

"Red sandy loam was brought from the Sharon plain. The topsoil, with the seeds of wildflowers in it, was taken from an empty field just before apartment towers were built there. Along with the white broom and oaks of the Sharon habitat, we planted bulbs of the Sharon tulip.

"A pond was dug at the edge of the valley to catch runoff rainwater and provide a source for irrigating the walnut trees. Today, that vision has come to fruition and visitors can enjoy delicious ripe walnuts in the fall. Next to the pool, a large catchment basin was dug. Muddy soil that forms there during the rainy season provides a good habitat for 'narcissus among the thorns,'" Teitelbaum points out.

The pool, called appropriately the "Pool of Solomon" reflects the tall date palms planted beside it, as well as the cedars growing on top of the adjacent hill; the majestic trees that appear together in the lovers' words in the Song and in Psalm 92: "The righteous will flourish like the date palm, and grow tall like the cedar of Lebanon. And quite naturally, this is the setting for wedding ceremonies at Neot Kedumim," Teitelbaum concludes.

Neot Kedumim is located on Route 443 near Modi'in and the Ben Shemen Forest, only 10 minutes by car from Ben Gurion Airport and 30 to 45 minutes by car from Jerusalem or Tel Aviv. Visiting hours are Sunday to Thursday, 8:30 to sunset, Friday and Jewish holiday eves 8:30 a.m. to 1 p.m. It is closed Saturdays and Jewish holidays. Special arrangements may be made to open the reserve as early as 6 a.m. to accommodate early morning incoming flights. The international phone number is 972-8-977-0777 and the fax number is 972-8-977-0766. Email information is info@neot-kedumim.org.il and their colorful website, one of my favorites biblical garden sites, is www.n-k-org.il. On that website we can all enjoy a virtual walk into biblical history.

Until a biblical village hotel is built at Neot Kedumim (one is on the planning board), it is best to stay in Jerusalem or Tel Aviv hotels. Travel agents can provide details about trips to the reserve and elsewhere in the Holy Land, as can Israel's national airline, El Al. As part of its educational work, Neot Kedumim holds seminars and tailor-made tours for special interest groups.

The best way to get information in North America is from American Friends of Neot Kedumim, a U.S. 501(c) (3) tax deductible charitable organization supporting the Reserve. Their address is P.O. Box 236, Howes Cave, NY 12092. They also have copies of Nogah's books available for sale. The telephone and fax number is (518) 296-8673 and e-mail is tikvah4afnk@yahoo.com

As the olive branch stands for peace, may Neot Kedumim continue to grow and encourage more biblical gardens to sprout and thrive in peace around the world in keeping also with the theme of this book: Let's grow together.

## Chapter 9

# Biblical Gardens Around the World

I n Jerusalem there is another garden, but unlike any you may have visited. This World of the Bible Gardens has full-scale archeological replicas that help interpret the Scriptures. There is a goat hair tent, a real sheepfold, a stone manger, and a well from which visitors can draw water. There also is a watchtower, wine press, a threshing floor, and olive press too. At the stone quarry, visitors can learn about ancient building methods. The Scripture Garden is located in Ein Karem, Jerusalem, Israel, and offers classes and even has authentic biblical meals.

The Garden of Gethsemane is another special garden in the Holy Land worth noting. It is located at the western base of the Mount of Olives. Within the walled perimeter of the Church of All Nations, you can find a small grove of ancient olive trees. The historic Garden of Gethsemane holds a place in the hearts of all Christians as the site where Jesus prayed the night before He was taken captive as described in Mark 14:32-50. In this churchyard, local tradition date these ancient trees back to Biblical times, but that is unlikely. More probable is that the gnarled and twisted olive trees may be descendants of the original ones. They are undoubtedly

**More biblical gardens seem to be taking root every year. Here are some biblical gardens growing around the world:**

Yad-Hasmona Biblical Gardens, Israel

Biblical Garden, St. George's College, Jerusalem, Israel

Biblical Garden, Brickman's Country Gardens, Ontario, Canada,

Bible Garden Memorial Trust, Palm Beach, New South Wales, Australia

Biblical Garden, St. Paul's Cathedral, Sydney, New South Wales, Australia

Biblical Garden, Rockhampton Botanic Garden, Queensland, Australia

Biblical Garden, Rutland Street Chapel, Christchurch, New Zealand

Biblical Garden, Holy Trinity Parish Church, Sheen Park, Richmond, Surrey, England

Millennium Bible Garden, Woodbridge, Suffolk, England

Biblical Garden, Royal Botanic Gardens, Kew, Richmond, Surrey, England

Millennium Bible Garden, St. Mark's, Isle of Man, England

Biblical Garden, Sternberg Centre for Judaism, the Manor House, London, England

Biblical Garden, Bangor Cathedral Close, Bangor, Caenaarvon, Wales

Biblical Garden, Elgin, Scotland

Biblical Garden, St. Benedict's Priory, the Mount, Cobb, Co. Cork, Ireland

Biblical Garden, Ara Virdis Project

Franciscan Center of Environmental Studies, Rome, Italy

Biblical Garden, Amsterdam Free University, Amsterdam, Holland very old. Although not a typical biblical garden, this unique spot deserves its place in this book as a special garden landmark in the Holy Land.

For those who wish to wander around the world to visit other fine biblical gardens, here are some that I've located during my research for this book. You'll find additional information in the reference section at the end of this book.

# Chapter 10

# Growing Adventures with Children

J esus thoughtfully advised His Disciples to let the children come to him and forbid them not. This admonition should guide us all as we garden with our families and encourage children to dig in with us, plant, and tend the good earth and learn how to make it productive.

A valued friend, Rev. Marsh Hudson-Knapp, wisely included a children's garden in the Biblical Garden at the Fair Haven church which he leads as pastor. It has become one of the highlights of that garden, for good reasons. The children have their very own garden they can plant, tend, and harvest. It also encourages growth in relationships with each other and with God as they all work together to grow the flowers and foods of the Scriptures.

With thanks to the inspiration from Rev. Marsh when I visited with him, here are some thoughts for your gardening pathways.

Plant three rows of peas for:

Peace of mind
Peace of heart
Peace of soul

Then, four rows of squash to:

> Squash gossip
> Squash difference
> Squash grumbling
> Squash selfishness

Try four rows of lettuce:

> Lettuce be faithful
> Lettuce be kind
> Lettuce be patient
> Lettuce love one another

And finally, take some thyme:

> Thyme for each other
> Thyme for family
> Thyme for friends
> Thyme for God

Just a few rows of thoughts to cultivate as you grow with God in your garden. Truly, God speaks to us often through the minds of marvelous people.

Here is Rev. Marsh's prayer guide to the children's garden he and his church congregation so faithfully tend in Vermont.

"Welcome to the garden! Young or old, we invite you to pray around the garden today. As you read about and pray about each plant, you might want to stop and look at the little creation of God. You may want to use our diagram to help you find them. Join me now in this reflection and prayer inspired by the plants God has given us to grow in our vegetable and herb garden.

"I am the lentils tricky young Jacob made into a soup. When his hungry brother Esau came home, Jacob talked hungry Esau into trading his special blessing for my soup. Thank you, God, for lentils that still feed US when we are hungry.

"I am the hyssop that grew in Egypt. When the Hebrews slaves cried to God to free them the Lord sent plagues to convince Pharaoh to release them, and finally the angel of death. God told the Hebrews dip my hyssop branches in blood from an innocent lamb and spread it over their doors.

Covered by the blood of the lamb, death passed over them and a grieving Pharaoh released them. Thank you, God, for the blood of Jesus that saves us from death.

"I am the coriander whose seeds reminded people of the manna God provided to feed the Hebrews during their years in the wilderness. When no one could find food, God fed the people just as God feeds you. Thank you, God, for caring for us when we are in the wilderness.

"I am the cantaloupe that grows in Egypt. The Israelites loved my juicy sweetness. When they left on the Exodus they missed me. They whined, complained, and sometimes wanted to turn back for me and their safe, though terrible, existence as slaves. Help us, God, when we choose slavery over the new life you offer us.

"I am the myrtle whose branches help form the shelter for the Feast of Tabernacles. When our ancestors the Hebrews lived in the desert they huddled in fragile huts made from branches, yet it was GOD who truly kept them safe. Thank you, God, for homes and friends whom you send to shelter us.

"I am the barley that grew in the fields of kind Boaz. When the workers harvested the crop they left lots of my stalks behind for the poor and hungry to harvest and eat, including Ruth and Naomi. Help us, Lord, to share with others who are in need.

"I am the broad beans from which the people of Manahaim made stews to feed King David's loyal soldiers when David's power-hungry son Absolom and his men sought to overthrow his dad. Use us, God, to make help people who try to do good.

"I am the pomegranate whose hundreds of seeds remind people of the Lord's innumerable blessings. When the priests made offerings to God at the temple in Jerusalem, they decorated their robes with picture of me. Remind us, O God, of the countless blessings you place in our hands.

"I am the chick peas who are soaked and salted as a nut-like treat. Prophet Isaiah promised that when God rules the earth, life will be good for all of creation. Even the donkeys will receive special treats. Thank you, God, for the promises you give to us!

"I am the cumin that must be harvested with tender care. The prophets promise that God also will care for us tenderly at our harvest time. Thank you, God, for your tender kindness to us.

"I am chamomile, one of the lilies of the field. I can do no work, but Jesus says that God still makes me beautiful and cares for me. So why do

YOU worry if you are good enough for God to love? Teach us, O God, to find our value by looking into your eyes.

"I am the violet whose tender blooms last but a short time in the hot sun. The prophet Isaiah reminds me and you that we will wither and fall, but God will abide forever. I will put my trust in God, not in my strength. Teach us, O God, to trust in you alone.

"I am the dill and mint and rue. Anyone would give God ten percent of these unimportant herbs. But when it comes to what is important, to money, power and possessions, we hesitate to offer those to God. Teach us, O God, to give like you give.

"I am the wheat and barley from which a small boy's mother made five tiny loaves of bread and sent him off with them for lunch. Little did she know that her son would share them with Jesus and he would feed five thousand folks with her son's trusting gift of everything he had to eat. Teach us, O God, to grow in faith by giving!

"I am the poppies who bound up with hope and color even in the driest, most deadly times. Like the angel at Jesus' empty tomb I tell the world, Jesus lives! Trust in him. Nothing can hold back his power! Teach us, O God, how to rise in victory over death every day.

"I am the earth formed by the word and hands and love of God. I nourish and sustain everything that grows in this garden of God. I sustain your very lives. Hold me in your hands. Smell my richness. Love me and care for me, for if you destroy me you will destroy yourself and your children. If you cherish me I will nourish humanity and all creation till the end of time. Teach us, loving God, to cherish and tenderly care for your earth!"

That is the worthy welcome to the Biblical Garden at First Congregational Church of Fair Haven in Vermont. It is truly worthy of heartfelt focus as we go about planting and growing our biblical gardens and guiding the lives of those around us, especially the children.

The reactions of children to their biblical growing experiences is noteworthy. As Rev. Marsh reflects, "Children have always been important to us in our biblical garden, both the young children of our church and community and the child within us all whose heart leaps when we taste the first sweet slurp of our garden-grown watermelon!"

These bits of advice will enable you to integrate children into the garden at your church or temple and grow with them and God. Study the material on biblical plants and start planting a few plants, trees, or shrubs around your church and or home. Many already grow there! Learn and tell their Bible stories. The plant lists in this book will give you a start.

Involve the children in some of the planting, with adults overseeing so that your garden doesn't turn into chaos. It takes a lot of advanced planning to order seeds from the various locations and sources. And, it requires concentration to plan and mark what will be planted where, and to get each adult to become familiar with how they will plant their seeds, started seedlings, and plants. The reward is that this makes a great multi-generational project. You can build benches near the gardens for observers as well as workers.

Also involve children in watering, weeding, and caring for their plants and keep telling them stories. Add Bible stories, life stories, and listen to their life stories too! They learn about caring and receiving care by working with you in the garden and in life!

Each Sunday during the growing season tell a story with the children in your church and bring in plants, blooms, and God-willing, fruit to explore! The brief reflections in the plant guide, the Bible references, and the articles about water gardens and vegetable gardens provide a worthwhile starting point. Then, you can decorate the communion table and worship areas in church school rooms with plants and their products and use them as starters for exploring biblical stories.

Try this idea, too. Draw and paint the plants and fruits of the gardens. Cindy Hudson-Marsh has taken the children outside to draw on nice days and brought in plants on yucky days. A few snacks of biblical foods, such as grapes, dates, cucumbers, melon, nuts, etc. can make the creating more fun and give a break to tell more stories.

In the process of more fully utilizing their biblical garden, Rev. Marsh and his church youth leaders are working on a calendar or booklet featuring the children's drawings, which they may publish. The children have done marvelous work and they feel proud and come to believe in themselves as they create and are affirmed by adults.

You may even choose to have an art sale for missions with the children's artwork. A few years ago their children did watercolors of Bible stories, displayed them during fellowship time and adults bought them, making contributions to the Heifer Project.

As gardens produce food, another idea sprouted at Fair Haven. They bring in food to share from the gardens during the summer and insist that people without gardens take home fresh vegetables. They also hand out goodies on the way out of worship. Children can help make the deliveries.

You too can take advantage of these ideas and teach adults and children to love the earth and to care for her as stewards. Another idea may sound odd, but it too has a purpose. On one Sunday a year they put a bag of garbage next to the communion table. Children help sort out all of the recycling, compost, and reusable materials, leaving very little to dump back into our earth! Then, each child does an environmental survey to evaluate how well they are doing in caring for our earth. Gardening and earth stewardship go hand in hand.

Being ecumenical helps too. After all, Jesus was a Jew and lived his life according to the biblical teachings of His time. At Fair Haven, a neighboring Rabbi, Sol Goldberg, taught the whole church how to celebrate the Sabbath. During the month they made items to use on their "family tables." The children from each "family," which was made up of random groups of people, hosted their table.

Another year they expect to engage the rabbi in teaching how to celebrate the Passover seder meal with its biblical herbs and foods and even make prayer shawls from wool or flax, which is another biblical plant, for all in the congregation and learn to prayer with them under the rabbi's instruction.

Other churches and temples have focused on serving foods of the Bible at snack time or a class picnic to help the children understand when, where, how, and what the people of the Bible ate and drank. It is important to note that in Jesus' time, the two main meals were at noon (Genesis 43:16) and in the evening (John 13:2). Also, there usually was no dining table or formal place for meals. Typically, people were sitting on the ground. An animal skin or piece of leather was used to cover the ground. The food was placed in the middle of the skin or on a piece of leather or wood. The Bible does not say whether people used knives, forks, or spoons when eating a meal. It does refer to eating bread which had been dipped into the food (John 13:26). It is likely that everyone at the meal dipped their bread into a common pot that held the stew, beans, soup, etc. Kids like to know this and will happily dip their bread into a pot or enjoy eating with their fingers. It was indeed the way people ate in the Holy Land when Jesus and His Disciples lived there, so introduce children to the authentic "dining" delights.

Don't stop yet. There are other ways to use biblical gardening in services. Flowers and greenery can grace the tables. Mint adds flavor to the tea. Think widely. These are just a few ideas for integrating creative, edible, active, earthy learning.

Rev. Marsh notes that their biblical gardens, and especially the water garden, has brought another blessing. People of all ages stop day after day at the gardens to watch things grow, to hunt out the frogs, to listen to the waterfall gurgle, to feed the fish and hunt for the one they have named . . . Young and old and teens end up listening to and talking with each other. The water garden especially seems to draw people together as a community.

# Teaching

As we begin growing with children, we would do well to learn more about the geography and history of the Holy Land. Here are some brief notes about that land, which is most likely far different from where you live. In the Holy Land, there are substantial differences of elevation with mountains 10,000 feet above sea level and many gradations of altitude within less than 200 miles. Valleys wind through the highlands, producing a wide variation in topography. Even today you'll find cultivated land side by side with patches of desert. The soil is often of clay or clay mixed with lime. However, you'll also find sandy areas and surface rock of soft limestone and basalt.

There also are variations of climate, influenced by changes of altitude and geographical position. These factors allow forms of vegetation which elsewhere grow far apart to thrive side by side within the narrow limits of the Holy Land. Vegetation along the west coast is like that of Spain, southern Italy, and Algeria; characteristic Mediterranean flora. Near the snows of the northern peaks are familiar plants of alpine and sub-alpine regions. Curiously on the eastern slopes of the northern ranges you'll find the vegetation of the steppes but by contrast, the peculiar climate conditions prevailing along the Dead Sea support a sub-tropical flora including species resembling those that thrive in Abyssinia. Considering that the Holy Land is only about the size of New Jersey, this is a surprising range of flora.

There are more than 3,000 species of Palestinian flora. However, what one sees in the Holy Land today, 2,000 years after the life of Christ, only provides an imperfect idea of what it was in His lifetime. Indeed, the hill-country of Juda and the Negeb are still basically grazing lands for goats and sheep. We know from archeology and historic records that groves, woods, and forests once flourished everywhere, including the famed cedars of Lebanon. Today few traces remain. The cedar forests of Lebanon are dramatically mentioned in the Scriptures as furnishing vital building materials for temples and homes. Most important to those who lived there, the arable land was available for growing their food.

Ancient records reveal that nearly every Jewish peasant had his own garden which provided vegetables and fruits for the table, flowers, and also herbs for flavoring, preserving, and as medicinal plants. We realize that some 130 plants are mentioned in the Scriptures. Most ordinary people are interested only in a few, whether ornamental or useful. Of the plants mentioned in the Bible, the most common varieties may be identified either with certainty or near probability. During my extensive research, it became clear that a large proportion of biblical plant-names are generic rather than specific. For example, we read about flowers of the field, briars, grass, nettles, but just what specific plants are meant is nearly impossible to determine. Biblical and botanical scholars through the centuries have focused on trying to determine which plants are meant by the scriptural references.

Reviewing many different translations and versions of the Bible, it was possible to assemble a composite and fairly complete list of the foods of the scriptures. Here's that basic list. It forms the foundation of this book about foods of the Bible. Then, with thanks to many accomplished and dedicated biblical gardeners all around America and in other countries as well as in the Holy Land, you'll find other information about specific foods and how to grow them in appropriate chapters in this book.

In addition, because there were other foods growing in that land in ancient times, we have dug deeper and traced many from different historic documents and archeological records. Those too are included to give you all a more "balanced" diet as was available from that land more than 2,000 years ago.

# Foods of the Bible List

Here's an alphabetical list of the basic plant names found in most commonly used English versions of the Bible.

**Almond tree**—Almonds are considered one of the best fruits in the Orient, and the tree has always been cultivated there. Several varieties grow wild in districts such as Lebanon, Carmel, and Moab.

**Apple tree**—still a matter of debate among botanists and biblical scholars as a true biblical plant.

**Barley** was cultivated as feed for horses and asses and also as a staple food among the poor and the people at large in times of stress. The grain was either roasted or milled, and cooked in ovens as bread or cake. Barley, being the commonest grain, was considered next to worthless.

**Beans**, especially the horse-bean or fava bean, was an ordinary food, extensively cultivated in the Middle. East.

**Bramble**, translated from Hebrew in Judges and in Psalms has been considered by many botanists to be different types of berried fruits.

**Corn** has been understood to be a general word for cereals in English Bibles, and most key references are to wheat, barley, and millet.

**Figs**, the fruit of the fig tree, grow wild and are cultivated throughout the Holy Land.

**Garlic** is a favorite food in the Middle East.

**Grapes** are widely mentioned in Scriptures as is wine, a favored drink in the time of Jesus among the people. Water was usually considered unhealthy since it could easily be contaminated.

**Herbs**, with the term bitter applied, includes, according to scholars, both wild lettuce and other plants eaten with the paschal lamb. Five species are indicated: wild lettuce, endive, chicory, plus millet and bitter coriander.

**Leeks**, also called grass, are considered one of the biblical vegetables.

**Lentils** are one of the biblical grains.

**Melons** include, scholars believe, both watermelons of old Egypt and other melons, most likely cantaloupes.

**Millet** is one of the grains of the Scriptures.

**Mustard** includes several kinds that grow naturally in the Holy Land, either wild or cultivated. We have all heard the often used reference comparing the kingdom of God to a mustard seed from Matthew 3:1–2, a familiar term to mean the tiniest thing possible.

**Oil tree**, which translates to olive tree. The olive tree, *Olea europæa*, is one of the most characteristic trees of the Mediterranean region, and universally cultivated in the Holy Land. scriptural references are numerous, the olive tree was considered the symbol of fruitfulness, blessing, and happiness, the emblem of peace and prosperity.

**Onions** are cultivated as an important part of the diet in the Middle East.

**Palm tree** means the date palm which flourishes now only in the maritime plain. In the past date palms grew in the Jordan Valley and other areas were renowned in antiquity for their palm groves.

**Pomegranates** are a great favorite in the Orient, and very plentiful in the Holy Land, with many references in the Bible. Pomegranates were frequently used as a model of ornamentation and several places of the Holy Land were named after the tree.

**Vine**, meaning the ordinary grapevine. Many varieties are cultivated and thrive in the Holy Land. In Old Testament times vine and wine were so important and popular that they are constantly mentioned in Scriptures.

**Wheat** also has been translated as "corn" and is applicable to all cereals according to biblical scholars. There are two types in the Holy Land: summer wheat and winter wheat.

# Seeds Are the Promise of Life

Seeds, especially the tiniest ones, can be used to teach valuable lessons. Seeds are the beginning and the end, miniscule miracles that contain all that's needed to produce a melon, a head of lettuce, or other biblical foods as well as beautiful flowers of the Scriptures and even trees.

Together you can watch these seemingly lifeless objects burst forth with growth to capture the imaginations of most kids. Here are more ways to explore the wonder of seeds beyond just planting them. Try some of these questions and see what children answer.

- What is the only fruit with seeds on the outside? The strawberry. On average, there are 200 tiny seeds on the outside of a strawberry.
- What are the largest seeds? The coconut—the seed of the coconut palm tree is the largest seed, sometimes weighing as much as a bowling ball.
- Do seeds know which way is up? Even if seeds are planted upside-down, the roots will grow down and the shoots will grow up. Gravity exerts its pull on the roots; and the shoots, seeking light, always grow upwards.
- Do large seeds produce large plants and vice versa? Surprisingly, the size of the seed has no relation to the size of the plant it can produce. The seed of a giant sequoia tree, for example, is smaller than a milkweed seed.

Try exploring some of the mysteries of seeds, too. Ask children to search the pantry and refrigerator for any seeds they can find, such as lentils, dried beans, melon seeds, and so on. Plan a "seed snack day" in which each food item has to contain seeds in some form. What would they like to make?

Then, challenge kids to grow some of those pantry seeds to see what happens. Encourage your kids to think big. Some tree seeds can be successfully germinated indoors and later planted in the back yard. They may not be biblical trees, but some of the easiest ones to grow are: red pine, Douglas fir, Colorado spruce, red and silver maples, black walnut, American chestnut, white oak, and apple. You also can try apricot, almond, and others that do have scriptural roots.

Children love handling seed packets. Veteran gardeners lovingly save heirloom seeds and you can teach children to do the same. Of course, avoid hybrid varieties for this project. Instead, save seeds from old type heirloom varieties. Encourage them to create their own seed company name and logo and seed packet. Help them decide what information needs to be included, such as planting tips and growing conditions. In the process, read about the work and experiments of Luther Burbank, a keen observer and curious scientist who explored how to produce better plants and tastier fruits and vegetables by saving seeds from selected plants.

There are many other growing projects to stimulate children as they begin what can be a lifetime love of gardening. Try making seed tapes. These are simply seeds fastened to a thin biodegradable paper with a glue that dissolves easily. They are fun to make, and they provide a handy way for kids to plant their seeds the appropriate distance apart. They also cut down on the chance of seeds being accidentally spilled onto the ground.

To make seed tape you'll need seeds, corn starch, paper towels and a small plastic bag with sealable or zip lock top. Then, follow these five simple steps:

1. First, dissolve 1 tablespoon of cornstarch in 1 cup of cold water. Cook over medium heat, stirring constantly. Once the mixture starts to boil and turns into a gel, remove from heat and allow it to cool to room temperature.

2. When mixture is cool, put a few spoonfuls into a small plastic bag and seal the top.

3. Take three or four paper towels, fold them at the perforations, and cut them into 1-inch strips. Unfold and lay them on a flat surface.

4. Refer to the seed packet to note how far apart the seeds should be spaced. Using a ruler and pen, make dots on the towel strips at the appropriate spacing.

5. Snip off the corner of the gel-filled bag and drop a little glob of gel on each of the marked spots. Place a seed on each drop of gel. The seeds will be firmly attached when the gel dries.

6. Lay the seed tapes in the soil at the preferred planting depth, cover with soil, and water.

Gardeners are sharing people and many began gardening when they were young so they know the joys they experienced as they and their gardens grew. Check with other veteran gardeners in your neighborhood and community. Often they'll provide ideas, advice, and even help as you work with youngsters.

Children need kid-size garden tools. High-quality small-scale kid gardening tools such as a trowel, rake, and hoe are available in chains and via mail order firms.

To cultivate interest among children, try walking around your garden area with them. Select a special area where a child can do as he or she pleases rather than planting in part of your garden. They like to have "ownership" of their very own garden spot. Although you want to focus on biblical foods, let children decide what they want to grow. It may be plants they recognize, such as pumpkins and sunflowers. Suggest growing foods they like, maybe a "pizza" garden containing tomatoes and peppers plus herbs such as basil and oregano.

Make gardening fun, not work. Crawl around with kids so you see the growing ground and plants from their viewpoint, down near the good earth. Offer encouragement and how-to, know how. When kids see you tending the garden, they'll most likely want to imitate what you do. Setting examples is the best way to teach.

There's help for you online. The National Gardening Association launched their GrowLab Science Program to help children learn through gardening. That award-winning program has proved the power of plants to teach. Children learn fundamental science concepts better through the cultivation, care, and nurturing of plants than through just getting disconnected facts in the classroom.

Ask around and volunteer at schools and in your neighborhood. Lend a hand and your experience to help build gardening projects in your community. The innovative NGB program teaches children that an understanding of the natural world is required so future generations will be able to feed themselves and the rest of world. Second, understanding of how to care for the environment begins with the care of one plant. Thirdly, and of special importance today when faced with television, video games, and Internet surfing, hands-on real life gardening teaches the interconnectedness of the earth, plants, and people.

The National Gardening Association has developed a School Garden Registry to document and highlight notable school garden projects and enable schools to contact one another about their gardens. To learn more, write to NGA at 1100 Dorset St., South Burlington, Vermont 05403, or call them toll-free at 888-538-7476.

Gardening also teaches basic lessons of life. City kids often have no idea where food comes from, except the supermarket. Start some melons indoors in pots well before you can begin outdoor gardening. It's a treat to watch the enthusiasm as seeds sprout, plants grow, and kids build enthusiasm for getting into their own garden spot outdoors. Eat a store-bought melon and ask them to guess how many melons they can grow on their vines. Watermelons and cantaloupes trace their roots to the Holy Land. Both were foods in ancient Egypt for the Pharaohs.

As you plan your gardens with children, tap into the knowledge available to you at several sources.

American Society for Horticultural Science
7931 East Boulevard Drive
Alexandria, VA 22308-1300

National Youth Gardening Symposium
International Reading Association, Special Interest Group
Gardeners and Readers Develop Naturally
RT. 1 Box 1038
Ellensburg, WA 98926

National Gardening Association
1100 Dorset St.
So. Burlington, VT 05403

The American Horticultural Society is at www.ahs.org and has information on educational programs including their annual Youth Gardening

Symposium. To excite kids you can try the Butterfly Garden Webster at www.mgfx.com/butterfly for discussions and how-to projects. You'll find Discovery Gardens at www.mindspring.com with a wealth of info on designing and maintaining indoor and schoolyard gardens plus landscapes for kids. Gardening Education for Youth at www.pierce.wsu.edu/tex/proggwp.html has early elementary studies and growing with plants garden and nutrition details. Let's Get Growing at www.letsgetgrowing.com is another net source for gardening education products and ideas.

Of course, the basic and major resource is National Gardening Association with their Kids Gardening material. NGA has long been recognized as a national leader in garden-based education. Their Youth Garden Grants program, begun in 1982, already has helped more than 1.2 million youngsters reap the rewards and lessons that green oases provide. With support from industry sponsors they offer grants and awards that recognize exemplary school and community garden projects and leaders and that help launch new programs. Since 1990, their award-winning GrowLab Science Program has been implemented in 25,000 classrooms. Details are available via NGB by phone at (802) 863-5251, or FAX at (802) 864-6889 and via their websites: www.garden.org and www.kidsgardening.com.

You'll find other ideas, no doubt, in the other chapters of this book. Look for good ideas as you visit biblical gardens on the Internet. Gather your children and their friends together at your home or church grounds, dig in, and get growing together with them and God.

# Chapter 11

# Biblical Food Celebration Service

"**I**n the beginning, God created the earth and the waters; and then He created the plants on the third day. Let the earth bring forth grass, the herb yielding seed, and the fruit tree yielding fruit after his kind, whose seed is in itself, upon the earth: and it was so. And the earth brought forth grass, and the herb yielding seed after his kind, and the tree yielding fruit, whose seed was in itself, after his kind: and God saw that it was good" (Genesis 1:11–12).

Reading these marvelous describing the creation, we discover the earliest references in scriptural passages to plants of the Bible. This led me to think about how plants of the Bible and especially foods of the Scriptures from Jesus day might be woven together into a celebration service that could be utilized in church. Talking with minister friends and other dedicated people at biblical gardens around our country, the idea for a special "foods that Jesus ate" celebration service took form. You'll find a basic service here. From your own experiences, and adding your own words, you can present a special meaningful service at your own house of worship. Basically, what follows is designed so that both clergy and lay leaders as well as gardening experts in your local congregation can work together to motivate, encourage and inspire children and families to dig in and grow together in many ways.

Throughout history, men and women have found both food and beauty among the plants of our good earth. Please use this Let's Grow Together Celebration Service about plants of the Bible to encourage everyone to read the Scriptures about the plants of the Bible and then actually dig in, plant them, cultivate and enjoy them and have many rewarding growing adventures together. That can include growing foods that Jesus ate, faithfully tending the garden until harvest time, then picking, preparing, cooking and enjoying those foods.

This growing project is being done in collaboration with my long-time friend, Rev. Lamar Robinson, who was the minister of Christ Church in our home town for 28 years. We wanted to celebrate God's gifts from the earth and the miracle of plant life whether from seed or bulb or root to growth and bountiful harvest. We also wanted to help make the Bible come alive by showing that we share some of the identical plants that our spiritual forefathers did, especially Jesus and His Disciples in the Holy Land. Another goal was to reduce the distance between Bible lands in history and geography today. By focusing on these biblical foods, we could reveal that we all can grow together with the plants of the Scriptures in home garden, church yard, school yard, and elsewhere around our communities.

In this service program, the focus has been that as you sow your seeds and flower bulbs, plant your foods and fruits and trees, you too are part of the continuing creation of life and beauty. We are all, in fact, gardening with God and as importantly, growing with God.

Plants of the Bible are thriving today much closer to home than many of us sometimes may realize. Perhaps with Biblical Plant Celebration Services you too can cultivate the blooming beauty and enjoy the fragrance of these flowers and the wonderful taste of vegetables, fruits, and herbs wherever you live.

As you consider doing this program, adding your own special touches to it for your house of worship, I trust that you will include others in this worthwhile project: your extended family, your group of friends and neighbors, plus members of your church and community. By digging in together, we can truly all learn to grow and enjoy the fruits and vegetables, herbs and trees for their beauty, nutrition, taste and the pleasure that they give us from their special meaning as plants of the Bible, deeply rooted in the Holy Land and the Scriptures.

The first Biblical Plant Celebration Service that you'll find here sets the theme: let's grow together. You can use this basic service to design others yourself, with the help of members in your congregation. Other services could focus on biblical flowers, herbs, and vegetables, fruits and trees with appropriate music that lifts hearts in song and praise. It helped to have a dedicated wife who was the choir director of our local church for twenty-five years. With her help I was able to focus on some of the most appropriate hymns and musical selections that would fit with plants that we can grow. You'll find some of those here and can add other hymns as you wish in your own special Celebration Services.

In each service, the aim is to have scriptural references about the many different plants of the scriptures and easy-to-follow, timely tips, ideas and advice about how to grow them. As we dig into the good earth together, here's a worthwhile pledge I still recall from my days as a 4-H Club member in the Garden State of New Jersey. It is worth repeating today.

"I pledge my head to clearer thinking, my heart to greater loyalty, my hands to larger service and my health to better living, for my community and my country."

I welcome you to enjoy a new growing experience today and tomorrow as we all plant and tend our gardens and also protect and preserve God's world wherever we live. Talk with your church leader today and your worship committee members. Ask about being able to present some special services based on biblical plants and their places in the Bible. Contact avid gardeners who can participate by sharing their expertise about growing biblical plants and using them in services. Ask for volunteers to help plant and grow a small biblical garden at your house of worship or elsewhere in the community. Dig in and get things growing. You'll be amazed how many people may respond and help with this new dimension in worshipping God.

# A Celebration Service of Plants of the Bible

## Silent Prayer

Prelude: "With Verdure Clad," Haydn Call to Worship

Opening: Today, in this Special Celebration of Plants of the Bible, we wish to celebrate God's gifts from the earth; to behold with wonder the miracle of seeding time and harvest. Today, with the same reverent attitude which characterized our spiritual ancestors of biblical times, we marvel at the orderly process through which God brings forth from the earth both food for our nourishment and beauty for our enjoyment. Today, as we realize that many of the plants that we can grow in our home grounds and gardens have ancestors rooted in our biblical heritage, we may closely identify with those people through whom God spoke his eternal message to all the succeeding generations.

Leader: The earth is the Lord's in all its beauty, the world and all who make their home upon it.

People: For God has made the earth, with its fertile valleys and mountain peaks, its green forests, fields, plains, its wide seas and great rivers, its infinite variety of life.

Leader: Who shall take his rightful place among all that God has created? To whom shall God say, "You are a faithful keeper of my earth?"

People: Those who appreciate the world God has given us. Those who use, but do not waste its resources, who enjoy but do not spoil its beauty, who are wise and thoughtful tenants.

Leader: Blessed are those who know the earth is not theirs, but belongs to God, who has given it for the benefit of all.

People: Let us praise God and be joyful; let us rejoice in the green earth, the warm sun, winter's fierce breath and the gentle touch of spring; all living, growing things. Let us rejoice and be glad for the earth is the Lord's in all its beauty, the world and those that make their home upon it.

HYMN: "Morning Has Broken"

Leader: Lord, today our thoughts go far beyond these four walls. We think of your garden we call the earth and its orderly process of seed and harvest; the cycles of night and day, sun and rain; winter, spring, summer, fall. We rejoice in the blooming beauty of flowers, the productiveness of vegetable gardens, the spicy smell of herbs, the gracefulness of trees. We think of the good earth you have given us to enjoy, use, protect and preserve. When we reflect upon these things, we are grateful, we are joyful, we are glad, and with the Psalmist we say, "The world is filled with the glory of God."

HYMN: "For the Beauty of the Earth"

# Reflections About Biblical Flowers

Leader: "Hyacinths and biscuits" wrote the poet. Beauty and utility. Who is to say we need hyacinths less than biscuits, if our soul is to soar and our spirit to flourish?

Beauty is not God, but surely one of the attributes of God is beauty. God gives us beauty in many ways, the glorious sea in its splendor, rugged mountain peaks, white rushing streams, gleaming church steeples pointing to the heavens, and the glory of a simple flower in your backyard, lifting up its face to the sun.

"What good is it?" the strict pragmatist may ask gruffly, looking at a lily. The whispered answer: "To show forth the glory of God."

"Oh," he slowly replies, seeing for the first time every a new dimension in God's world and in his own life.

A free-verse poem by Alfred, Lord Tennyson, says what a lot of us think, not only about flowers, but all growing plants and trees. He wrote:

Flower in crannied wall,
I pluck you out of the crannies.
I hold you here, root and all, in my hand.
Little flower, but if I could understand
What you are, root and all, and all in all,
I should know what God and man is.

Gardener: The Bible is alive with mentions of flowers as they grew in the Holy Land. [Here, select several scriptural references you prefer for the day. You'll find many in this book, my earlier three books and the bible as you wish.] You can grow many of these glorious flowers right in your own yard. Because of the two season climate of the Holy Land, wet and dry season, most of the flowers grow from bulbs. You probably already know many of them. The crocus, anemone, hyacinth, daffodil, lily, iris and others. [As you create your own special biblical plant service use scriptural references and how-to-grow tips.]

# Reflections About Biblical Vegetables

Leader: During the past decade, millions more American families have dug in and begun enjoying the rewards of growing vegetables. Many of you probably are vegetable gardeners, even if it is only a row of lettuce, a hill of cucumbers or squash, a few tomato plants. There is something almost spiritual about getting our hands down in the good earth; in planting, tending, cultivating your crops. What can compare with the satisfaction of bountiful harvests?

You have been a co-worker with God. Your dinner time grace will have a new meaning when the vegetables have come from your own work in your own garden. You may even wish to offer the words of one of the most ancient of Hebrew blessings; a part of the ritual of Passover: "Blessed are you, O Lord God, who brings forth food from the earth."

Gardener: In Genesis, we read about the creation [Use your own choice of references]. And later, as we read our bibles, we find references to the vegetables: cucumbers, melons, leeks, onions and other foods. All of these plants are deeply rooted in the Bible and Holy Land. Happily, we can trace their roots and plant them, grow them and harvest tasty cucumbers, melons and other vegetables from our own gardens. [Gardener then adds more how-to tips growing them.]

# Reflections About Biblical Herbs

Leader: What is an herb, but a plant with a flavor and a smell all its own, which when used in the right proportions, improves in a delightful way the food with which it is cooked! It is as if God wished to let us "spice up" our life a little, and gave us herbs we may use in order to add flavor and variety to our cooking. A woman who teaches at a famous hospital had a story about herbs that bears retelling. She had taken several ill mental patients to a garden where herbs were growing. Several times she had seen patients who had retreated far from the world that they didn't even talk, but who began to speak again after smelling certain herbs with which they had good associations in their earlier lives. Perhaps it reminded them of their mother's kitchen in their early childhood, in the age of innocence, before the complexity of the world overcame them. The patients would sometimes ask if they could bring a leaf back with them to their rooms. It was sometimes the first, small but crucial step on the road to their recovery. There is power and mystery in herbs, now as in the days of our spiritual Holy Land ancestors. Herbs are one of God's gifts from the good earth.

Gardener: We find the first mention of herbs in Genesis [select the specific quotations that you prefer]. Often again, through many passages and pages in the Bible. Several of them are easily and tastefully grown in our own gardens: dill, sage, rosemary, etc. [Gardener then adds more tips for growing herbs from personal experience].

# Reflections About Biblical Fruits

Leader: We have all ready and know about the fruits of the Holy Land: dates, figs, olives, grapes. We may not know how they grow or be able to grow many of them ourselves, but we can enjoy their good flavor. Life is like that. Everyone doesn't have to know it all. Everything doesn't have to grow everywhere. There is an inter-dependence in life which is wholesome, and we can see and appreciate it even in something as basic as the geographical distribution of fruit trees and. In biblical literature, vineyards and olive groves are symbols of the well-being of the people. They are often used to express, symbolically, the bountifulness of God's favor, and the graciousness of God's gifts. Let us reflect, that while dates and olives are right for growing in other lands and places, we can see revealed and enjoy the fruitful abundance of that other popular plant of the Holy Land, grapes, hanging in abundance from our own backyard arbor, as we reflect on this fruitful gift that God has given us.

Gardener: Grapes are one of the most often mentioned plants in the Bible, if you include the many references to wine, which was one of the common beverages of that era. Today, we all can enjoy many types of grapes: green, red, yellow that offer tasteful bounty from arbors in our own backyards. [Add some scriptural references and how-to-grow tips.]

# Reflections About Biblical Trees

Leader: There is a special quality about trees which is sometimes difficult to put into words. If you have stood beside a giant California redwood, remember that it was a sapling when a man named Jesus walked with his disciples along the Sea of Galilee. That same tree was quite mature when a man named Columbus was believed to be crazy for thinking that the world was round. The tenacity of trees just below timberline in the mountains is really remarkable: hanging on doggedly against the odds, fighting the cold of winter, the dry heat of summer, conditions of severe wind and space and rocky soil.

Or, of cypress trees with their bases hidden beneath the dark waters, their knees protruding up as if for a breath of air. We can all enjoy the sights of trees and the scents of them too; the distinctive aroma of olive wood from the Holy Land or the heady scent of cedar. Who doesn't appreciate the strong, sweet smell of balsam firs during the holidays or the pungent smells of a pine grove after a rain?

Trees are a glorious expression of God's graciousness as creator. As we look at the trees in our yards, around our town and in the woods where we camp on vacations, we too may see them as messengers of God's greatness and goodness.

Gardener: Many different trees are mentioned in many passages in the bible; poplar and cedar among them. [Add more references as you wish.]

You can enjoy the sight of some of them, that you can plant and grow in your own landscape. Poplar, cedar, pine . . . these are all related to the trees of the Holy Land and will thrive. (Gardener gives more details, how-to tips, ideas, advice.)

Leader: Let us reflect on the flowers, the herbs, the vegetables, fruits and trees which we can plant and enjoy, as we refocus on learning to grow together better, here in God's world today and for the many good years ahead.

HYMN: "This Is My Father's World"

Closing: Thoughts, Reflections, Benediction.

## Some Possible Hymns with Gardening and Plant Themes

"All Creatures of Our God and King"
"All Things Bright and Beautiful"
"America"
"America the Beautiful"

"Come Ye Thankful People"
"Faith of Our Fathers"
"Faith While Trees Are Still in Blossom"
"For the Beauty of the Earth"
"For the Fruits of this Creation"
"Hymn of Promise"
"In the Garden"
"Let Us Break Bread Together"
"Morning Has Broken"
"Mountains Are All Aglow"
"O Food to Pilgrims Given"
"Sheaves of Summer"
"This Is My Father's World"

# Chapter 12

# Gardening Sources—Web Sites and Know How

I t is nice to know there's lots of help available whenever you need it. While writing this book, I've compiled my best gardening information sources for you from all across America and around the world. Naturally, in any focus on growing the foods that Jesus ate, sources in the Holy Land are especially helpful.

Equally important, you can tap top gardening talent at dozens of colorful, informative Websites on the Internet and print out selected pages of valuable garden ideas, tips, and advice. There are bushels of useful information and hundreds of free pages about every aspect and type of gardening.

When I first began gardening, as a 4-H Club member during the Victory Garden era, we had to learn from our neighbors. Other reliable sources were the County Agricultural Agents and our State Extension Service and agricultural colleges. They are still there to help. County Agents are located in every county seat and are at your service to answer questions and guide your gardening efforts as you need help. They also can tap the expertise of state horticulturists at each state's agricultural college. Their job is to help farmers and citizens.

The Mailorder Gardening Association is the world's largest group of companies that specialize in providing garden products via mail-order and online. They have more than 130 members who offer colorful, illustrated catalogs packed with tips and ideas. It pays to look them up and order some of the free catalogs. The companies that develop new and improved plant varieties provide more than just sales data. Many catalogs provide valuable down to earth good growing knowledge that you can put to use in your garden.

At MGA's Web site, www.mailordergardening.com, you also can find a glossary of gardening words and phrases. Perhaps the best thing about this site is the impressive list of member companies. They're categorized by the types of products they provide: annuals, perennials, fruit trees, garden supplies, fertilizer, and other categories.

The National Gardening Association, www.garden.org, publisher of the *National Gardening* magazine, has one of the most comprehensive and useful sites on the Web. You can read from the magazine, find out about the NGA's Youth Garden Grants program, search their extensive NGA Library for data on a wide variety of gardening topics, and even check out a seed swaps section. If you want more knowledge, you can subscribe to a free e-mail newsletter or ask gardening questions. Actually, 16,000 questions have already been answered, so there's a good chance that the information you want is already there.

If you can't find just the right tool or piece of equipment locally, check the Gardener's Supply Company site, www.gardeners.com. This site is primarily devoted to fine merchandise found in their printed catalogs and periodically includes bargains not in the catalog. In addition, you can search an extensive Q&A library of gardening information.

For biblical gardening, you can look up dozens of wonderful biblical gardens at their websites. You'll find my list of favorite biblical garden Web sites in a separate section in this book, combined with a list of biblical gardens to visit with their mailing addresses and other contact information. Many avid, dedicated, faithful gardens are devoted to growing with God. They gladly share their knowledge with others. Gardeners are a sharing group of people. There seems to be something about gardening that draws people together and encourages sharing ideas, tips, advice, and knowledge of all types. Tune in, ask for advice, and also for sources for biblical plant seeds. You may indeed want to expand your garden to include biblical flowers, herbs, or trees. You'll find sources in this book, and you can obtain a variety of free mail order catalogs each year for ready reference.

To preview biblical gardening pleasures, go to the web or have a computer-savvy friend take you to the Holy Land. It's an easy trip. You can wander the biblical plant world at a 625-acre Biblical Garden Preserve in the Holy Land at www.neot-kedumim.org.il. Neot Kedumim is a labor of love, recreating an extensive preserve with the flowers, herbs, vegetables, fruits, trees and also some of the fauna mentioned in Scriptures. This is the world's largest biblical garden, well worth visiting by Internet and 'walking' their trails to see glorious plants blooming and growing in their natural sites. You'll find an entire chapter about Neot Kedumim in this book that will give you special insights.

For organic gardening information, check out www.organicgarden.com. They're America's experts and advice is plentiful. From that site you'll find others about natural gardening. Today, in this marvelous "Internet World," there are a multitude of gardening sources. It pays to explore some each week or month, especially during winter as you plan your gardens. Then, copy and print out the best advice for your own gardening guide.

Since I first began crawling along vegetable garden rows as a 10-year old apprentice gardener, I've kept notebooks full of useful advice for reference. Today, finding information is much easier. Here's my list of key sources.

# My Favorite Garden Catalogs

Appalachian Gardens, PO Box 82, Waynesboro, PA 17268 (Rare trees/ shrubs)

Bluestone Perennials, 7211 Middle Ridge Road, Madison, OH 44057 (Nice variety)

Burpee, 300 Park Avenue, Warminster, PA 18974 (Seeds/bulbs/plants)

Burgess Seed/Plant Co., 904 Four Seasons Rd., Bloomington, IL 61701 (Bulbs, seeds)

Clyde Robin Seed Co., PO Box 2366 Castro Valley, CA 9454 (Wildflowers)

Crystal Palace Perennials, PO Box 154, St. John, IN 46373 (Water Garden plants)

Drip Rite Irrigation, 4235 Pacific St. Ste. H, Rocklin, CA 95747 (Irrigation supplies)

Dutch Gardens, PO Box 200, Adelphia, NJ 07710 (Dutch bulbs)

Ed Hume Seeds, Inc., PO Box 1450, Kent, WA 98035 (Short season varieties, plus)

Flowery Branch Seeds, Box 1330, Flowery Branch, GA 30542 (Rare, heirloom, medicinal)

Forest Farm Nursery, 990 Tetherow Road, Williams, Oregon, 97544 (Good source)

Gardener's Supply Co., 128 Intervale Rd., Burlington, VT 05401 (Many gardening supplies)

Gardens Alive, 5100 Schenley Pl., Lawrenceburg, IN 47025 (Organic gardening source)

Harris Seeds, 60 Saginaw Dr., Rochester, NY 14692 (Old line seed firm)

J. L. Hudson, seedsman, Star Rt. 2, Box 337, La Honda, CA 94020 (Biblical plants)

Johnny's Selected Seeds, RR 1, Box 2580, Albion, ME 04910 (Seeds, wide variety list)

Klehm's Song Sparrow Perennial Farm, 13101 East Rye Rd. Avalon, WI 53505 (Specialities)

Lilypons Water Gardens, PO Box 10, Buckeystown, MD 21717 (Great water garden source) Mantis, 1028 Street Road, Southampton, PA 18966 (Tillers and tools)

Mellinger's, 2310 W. South Range Road, North Lima, OH 44452 (Variety)

Miller Nurseries, 5060 West Lake Rd, Canandaigua, NY 14224 (Great berry/fruit tree source)

Nichols Garden Nursery, 1190 N. Pac.Hwy.NE, Albany, OR 97321 (Many Asian, Int'l)

Northwoods Nursery, 27635 S. Oglesby Rd., Canby, OR 97013 (Rare fruits, nuts, others)

One Green World, 28696 S. Cramer Rd., Modalla, OR 97038 (Rare Int'l plants)

Park Seed, 1 Parkton Ave., Greenwood, SC 29647 (Major US Seed and plant firm)

Quality Dutch Bulbs, 13 McFadden Road, Easton PA 18045 (Many bulb flowers)

Roris Gardens, 8195 Bradshaw Rd., Sacramento, CA 95829 (Iris specialists)

Royal River Roses, PO Box 370, Yarmouth, ME 04096 (Rare, hardy, old time roses)

Seeds of Perfection, P.O. Box 86, Station A, Toronto, ON, Canada M9C 4V2 (Unique)

Select Seeds Antique Flowers, 180 Stickney Rd., Union, CT 06076 (Heirloom seeds, plants)

Stokes Seeds, Box 548, Buffalo, NY 15240 (Many varieties)

Stokes Tropicals, PO Box 9868, New Iberia, LA 70562 (Exotic tropical plants)

The Cook's Garden, PO Box 535, Londonderry, VT 05148 (Special salad/veggie varieties)

Van Bourgondien, PO Box 1000, Babylon, NY 11702 (Major Dutch bulb specialist)

Vessey's Seeds Ltd,. PO Box 9000, Calais, ME 04619 (US/Canadian varieties)

Wayside Gardens, Hodges, SC 29695 (Major plant source)

White Flower Farm, P.O Box 50, Litchfield, CT 06759. (Specialists in rare bulb flowers) Wildseed Farms, 525 Wildflower Hills, Fredericksburg, TX 78624 (Wildflower specialists)

Here's a handy list of biblical plant suppliers I've dealt with over the years and found reliable. You may have to hunt around among various suppliers to find the specific plants you want. No one place has them all.

Jim Johnson, www.Seedsman.com, 3421 Bream Street, Gautier, MS 39553 writes on his Web site. "At the request of many of our customers, we have created a list of seeds for plants that are listed in the Bible. We have only listed seeds for plants that will do well in a wide variety of climates and conditions, if there is a plant mentioned in the Bible that is not listed here, it is probably because the plants will only grow well in a certain region, or because seeds for these plants are not commercially available."

Others include:

*PlantFinder*, a magazine, is based in Hollywood, FL 33024. http://www.hortworld.com. Bluestone Perennials, Madison, OH 44057 has lovely, reasonably priced plants. http://www.bluestoneperennials.com/.

Gurney's is economical and offers both common and unusual plants. http://www.gurneys.com.

Meadowsweet Herb Farm, North Shrewsbury, VT 05738. 802-492-2565.

Miller Nursery, Canandaigua, NY. Reasonably priced, healthy, hardy fruit, nut, and foliage trees and shrubs. 800-836-9530.

Mountain Valley Growers in California sells many biblical varieties of plants by mail order. http://www.mountainvalleygrowers.com/bibleherbgarden.htm.

Park Seed Company, Greenwood, SC 29647 has many seeds of less available varieties. http://www.parkseed.com.

Territorial Seed Company. Their catalog is a treasure trove of information! Good seeds also. http://www.territorial-seed.com/.

Wayside Gardens. High quality plants of hard-to-find species. http://www.waysidegardens.com.

# Mail Order Shopping Tips

Gardening continues to be America's most popular leisure activity. According to a recent survey, approximately 74% of America's 100+ million households participate in lawn and garden activities. Many depend on mail order catalogs to deliver the quality gardening products they demand. More than $2 billion is spent annually on gardening supplies by mail order. There's good reason for this.

Catalogs offer more gardening choices than typical local stores. Also, shopping by mail is convenient, fun, and virtually risk-free, considering the guarantees most firms offer today. Mail order gardening is deeply rooted in America. Each year I would enjoy lunch with David Burpee at Fordhook Farms in Doylestown, Pennsylvania. For decades Burpee was America's foremost mail order seed firm. Today the selection of companies and their specialty seeds, plants, and products is wider than ever. The Mail Order Gardening Association likes happy customers, so they have provided these worthwhile guidelines that can help as you shop by mail and when you receive your orders.

1. Buy selections appropriate for your climate and garden setting. Most catalogs provide zone ranges for each plant. Some may provide a map showing zones so you can determine which zone your home is in. If not, check with the company or your local County Extension Service to determine your zone.

2. Be ready when your order arrives. Have the bed or ground tilled and ready for planting because the quicker you can get live plants into the ground, the better. We're all busy, but plants need immediate attention on arrival. Most mailorder firms ship plants and bulbs to arrive at the appropriate planting time for your region. Also, you should plant seeds when appropriate for your area.

3. If you need help or have questions, call and ask. Most mail order companies have customer service people to answer questions. They can be very helpful and are ready to serve you. Also, access the websites I have provided and contact telephone numbers and usually email addresses too. Some have most asked Q&A already posted to help solve basic problems, as well as more tricky ones.

4. Order early to avoid sold out notices. Because seeds and planting stock are produced at least a season in advance, quantities often are limited so it pays to order early, especially when a sale catalog arrives.

5. Many mail order firms may substitute a similar item for one that is sold out. Usually there is a place on the order to check if you prefer no substitutions. That may be truer for those of us seeking special biblical plants or closest related plants. Be sure to specify clearly on the order form that you do not want substitutions made, unless you are more flexible and willing to accept them.

6. Keep a record of your purchases: names, item numbers, prices and dates to facilitate communications between you and the company regarding an order. Mail order companies receive thousands of orders each week during peak season, so they need your help to track your specific order if a problem occurs.

7. Here's a sample record keeping form to copy and use for your mail ordering.

Company Name _____Date of Order _____

Catalog/Brochure # _____Ordering Phone # _____

Customer Account # _____Customer Service Phone # _____

Items Ordered:

Item #_____Name_____Quantity_____Price _____

Item #_____Name_____Quantity_____Price _____

Item #_____Name_____Quantity_____Price _____

Item #_____Name_____Quantity_____Price _____

Shipping and Handling Charge $_____Total $_____

Discounts or coupons applied _____

Check # _____Card used_____

Date Order Rec'd. _____ Invoice # _____

Guarantee cut off date _____

Condition of plants and notes _____

_____

_____

8. Most firms offer outstanding guarantees. Usually there is a cut-off date by which a company must be notified of problems or plant failures. The date is generally set late enough to allow you sufficient time to plant your order and observe growth. Be sure to inform the company of plant failures or problems before this date.

9. Order appropriate fertilizers and supplies with your plants. That way you'll have them on hand when planting. Using the right starter fertilizer and soil amendments from the beginning ensures that plants have the best chance of taking root well and prospering.

10. Finally, as you review the myriad of marvelous mail order catalogs available, look for tips and ideas to help you make the best choices. Most gardening catalogs also offer useful tips for growing plants, especially to guide your to success with the more difficult ones. Take advantage of the catalogs' expertise to create a healthy, beautiful, and bountiful garden.

# To Do's When Your Order Arrives

This part may seem silly, but it is one area many people overlook to the detriment of the plants they order, which adversely impacts gardening success. With thanks to NGA, here are their worthwhile bits of gardening wisdom. Although this book is about biblical foods, most gardeners do grow flowers, shrubs, and other type plants. Since these tips are for all gardeners, I've included them here as a reference.

1. Open the package and make sure your order is complete and correct. Check your order form to make sure all of the seed varieties, plants, supplies, and other items have arrived. There may be a note stating that other packages will arrive later. Open any plants wrapped in plastic to allow air circulation. Don't be alarmed if you see dried foliage on dormant plants. Because they are dormant, dried foliage from the prior year is natural and will soon be replaced by new growth.

2. Look for instructions for temporary handling. These are usually included as part of the planting instructions. Handling will vary from plant to plant, but you'll find a few general rules for different types of planting stock here, courtesy of my mail order garden friendly advisors.

3. Plant as soon as possible. Until you do, give the planting stock proper care to maintain its viability. Follow the instructions provided with your shipment. The company's experts have experience from years in the business and they want you to be well pleased when you follow their useful advice.

Follow these rules for temporary handling of seeds. Simply store your seeds in a cool, dry place until it is time to plant outdoors, or start them indoors in pots and trays if you wish.

For bulbs, corms, rhizomes and tubers follow these tips. Keep bulbs such as tulips and daffodils in a cool, dry spot with good air circulation until they can be planted. Remove them from the packaging and spread them in a single layer. Keep them dry and avoid temperature extremes. The ideal time to plant such bulbs is in the fall, after temperatures have permanently cooled and before the onset of winter freezes harden the ground. You don't want to plant them too early, nor wait until the ground is unworkable. Remember, always plant bulbs pointy end up.

In contrast, lilies and other bulbs that are not winter hardy should be stored in the dark in a closed box and lightly sprayed with water occasionally to keep them moist until planted. Rhizomes, such as irises, can be kept in their packaging material as long as the shipping carton is open. Store them where they receive some light, but are not exposed to direct sun or wind.

Bareroot stock is standard for mail order shipping. Many perennials, shrubs, and even trees are shipped barefoot, without soil, in a dormant state. Until planting, keep the roots in their protective wrapping of plastic, newspaper, burlap, and wood shavings, in which they were shipped. Moisten them frequently and keep them from exposure to direct sun. The greatest danger is excessive drying. Before planting roses, shrubs, and trees, soak their roots in water for a few hours. Carry them to the garden in their water bucket and plant them directly from the water to avoid any drying prior to planting.

If you are unable to plant for a longer period, a week or more, it is advisable to "heel in" bareroot plants. Heeling-in is a form of temporary planting. Dig a V-shaped trench deep enough to hold the roots. Place the plants in a trench so they are sitting at about a 45 degree angle, and cover the roots with an equal mix of builder's sand and peat moss. If soil is workable, you can use it instead of the sand-peat mix. Keep plants well watered, especially if temperatures are warm, until you are able to uncover and plant them where they will grow in your garden or landscape area.

Green plants need special attention. Green plants in nursery pots are in their growth cycle and require the most careful handling. Remove them from their packaging, water them, and place them where they receive the proper amount of light according to specific instructions, and the proper range of temperatures, especially if they are tender plants.

Stock in small pots can dry out quickly, so keep close watch on them and plant as soon as possible. For container stock planted at mid-summer, cut back tops by one-third to prevent die-back.

You can apply these tips to bulbs, roots, and plants you buy locally, of course, if you are faced with a tight work schedule and can't get into the garden ground immediately. Too often many gardeners have a variety of ongoing projects that require attention. These tips will help you have more success with each of them.

# Favorite Garden Websites

As a garden writer I've found great growing ideas, tips and advice on many garden websites, so gladly share these with you. Some may change. To update use Google and enter a company's name to find them and save their website. Good growing !

| | |
|---|---|
| All America Roses | www.roses.org |
| All America Selections | www.all-americaselections.org |
| Antique Flowers | www.selectseeds.com |
| Bartlett Tree Company | www.bartlett.com |
| Bluestone Perennials | www.bluestoneperennials.com |
| Burpee | www.burpee.com |
| Carnivorous Plants | www.peterpauls.com |
| Charley's Greenhouse Supply | www.charleysgreenhouse.com |
| Cook's Garden | www.cooksgarden.com |
| Clyde Robin Wildflower Seeds | www.clyderobin.com |
| Drip Rite Irrigation | www.dripirr.com |
| Dutch Gardens | www.dutchgardens.com |
| Gardens Alive | www.GardensAlive.com |
| Gardener's Supply Company | www.gardeners.com |
| Garden to the Kitchen | www.gardentokitchen.com |
| Gardenscape Tools | www.gardencapetools.com |
| Harris Seeds | www.harrisseeds.com |
| High Country Gardens | www.highcountrygardens.com |
| Johnny's Selected Seeds | www.johnnyseeds.com |
| Lilypons Water Gardens | www.lilypons.com |
| Mantis Tools | www.mantisgardentools.com |
| Miller Nurseries | www.millernurseries.com |
| Mail Order Gardening Assn | www.mailordergardening.com |
| Monticello | www.monticello.org/shop |
| National Garden Bureau | www.ngb.org |
| Neot Kedumim Biblical Gardens | www.neot-kedumim.org.il |
| Nichols Garden Nursery | www.pacificharbor.com/nichols |
| National Gardening Association | www.garden.org |
| Nichols Garden Nursery | www.pacificharbor.com/nichols |
| Organic Gardening | www.organicgardening.com |
| Park Seeds | www.parkseed.com |
| Raintree Nursery | www.RaintreeNursery.com |
| Seeds of Distinction | www.seedsofdistinction.com |
| Stark Bros. Nurseries | www.starkbros.com |
| Stokes Tropicals | www.stokestropicals.com |
| Territorial Seed Co. | www.territorial-seed.com |
| Van Bourgondien Bulbs | www.dutchbulbs.com |

| Water Gardens | www.watergarden.com |
| Wayside Gardens | www.waysidegardens.com |
| White Flower Farm | www.whiteflowerfarm.com |
| Wildseed Farms, Ltd. | www.wildseedfarms.com |

# Chapter 13

# Foods of the Bible Quiz

**H**ow many foods named in the Bible do you remember? Here's a fun quiz you can try out on friends as you read this book and study the Bible. The answers to the following statements are the names of foods found in the Bible. As a hint to give you a bit of help, the number of letters in the word of each answer is given in parentheses. The answers generally use the singular form of the word unless designated "pl.," ie. plural.

Sometimes there is wide variation among different Bible translators as to how to render some of the plant and animal names. For consistency, the names used in this quiz are taken from the New World Translation of the Holy Scriptures. The quiz for this book can be done from the King James Version or NIV.

1. When the voice of this bird was heard in the land of Palestine, it signaled the arrival of spring. (10)
2. Bread made from this grain figured in a dream about striking down a tent in the war camp of Midian. The five loaves of bread that Jesus multiplied were also made from this grain. (6)
3. This was one of the foods that Abraham set before the three "men" who visited him when he was tenting among the big trees of Mamre. (6)

4. These bitter vegetables eaten at Passover—possibly endive and chicory—were designated only by what generic name in the Bible? (6 pl.)

5. This red stew figured in a bargain between twins that ultimately had to do with a Bible prophecy regarding the Messianic lineage. (6)

6. Both of these herd or flock animals were considered permissible to eat under the Mosaic Law. Jesus, however, put one of these animals into a good category and the other into a bad category when he used them in a pictorial way to explain how people of the nations would be separated either to life or to death. (5, 5 pl.)

7. The Israelites, who had eaten a tasty variety of this food when they were captive in Egypt, longed for it in the wilderness. (8)

8. This well-known drink was sometimes used for medicinal purposes. (4)

9. Jacob (Israel) sent these nuts with his sons as a gift when they returned to the land of Egypt. (9)

10. These sometimes plague-like insects were on John the Baptist's wilderness food menu. (7 pl.)

11. This non-grain ingredient was included in Ezekiel's bread. (5 + 5 pl.)

12. The shepherd companion of the Shulammite maiden compared her breath to the fragrance of this fruit. (5)

13. The sons of Israel and the mixed company from Egypt who were eating only manna longed for these three botanically related plants they had eaten in Egypt. (5 pl., 6 pl., 6)

14. This male animal, which was used as a draft animal by the Israelites and was permissible for them to eat and to sacrifice under Mosaic Law, was worshiped as a god by the Egyptians and some unfaithful Israelites. (4)

15. The prophet Isaiah said that the unfaithful of Zion had diluted this alcoholic drink. (5 + 4)

16. King Saul's oath nearly caused the execution of his son Jonathan when Jonathan innocently ate some of this food. (5)

17. Although this animal was forbidden as food for the Israelites under Mosaic Law, some apostate Israelites ate it anyway. (3)

18. Job said the slimy juice from this plant was tasteless. (11)

19. This "bread of powerful ones" tasted like "flat cakes with honey." (5)

20. The fruit that comes from this type of sycamore tree has to be "nipped" or pierced with a sharp instrument while it was premature in order to make it ripen into edible fruit. (3 + 8)

21. Gideon was threshing this grain in a winepress so that he would be out of sight of the Midianites. (5)

22. This adult male animal's ability to climb steep places easily was used to illustrate a future cure for lame persons. (4)

23. In one of Jesus' illustrations, the hungry prodigal son desired to eat some of the pods that came from this tree. (5)

24. The Israelites said they had eaten this animal food for nothing when they were captive in Egypt. (4)

25. This drink can be life-saving or death-dealing. (5)

26. The blossoms of this nut tree were used by Solomon to picture the white-headedness of old age. (6)

27. This "fattened" bird, considered a delicacy by the ancient Romans and even today in Italy and Greece, was one of the meats provided for King Solomon's table. (6)

28. A person who took the vow of Naziriteship could not eat this fruit either fresh or dried. (6 pl.)

29. Job said this plant (thought by some to be sea purslane or orach) was eaten by those of little account, whose fathers Job "would have refused to place with the dogs of his flock."(4 + 4)

30. The shepherd companion of the Shulammite maiden likened her two breasts to young twins of a female of this gracefully beautiful game animal. (7)

31. According to the Mosaic Law, everything offered on the altar to Jehovah must have this item added to it. (4)

32. The Shulammite maiden's skin was compared to "a paradise of" these Middle Eastern fruits, but the prophet Joel spoke of a time when the trees from which this fruit comes, along with apple, fig, and palm trees, would dry up. (11)

33. The prophet Isaiah said the sons of Jerusalem would be as helpless in resisting the Babylonian invaders as this game animal would be when caught in a net. (4 + 5)

34. In the seventh plague on Egypt, wheat and what other grain were not struck by hailstones due to being seasonally late? (5)

35. The prophet Jonah was named after the bird that performed three reconnaissance flights for Noah. (4)

36. The land that flowed with these two liquid foods was blessed with prosperity. (4, 5)

37. In the first century, a couple of these birds sold for a pittance. (8 pl.)
38. The Shulammite maiden's shepherd companion had locks of hair like clusters of this fruit. (5 pl.)
39. Solomon compared the wife of one's youth to a "charming" one of these game animals. (8 + 4)
40. One tiny grain from this vegetable plant figured in one of Jesus' illustrations about faith. (7)
41. This small goatlike antelope, acceptable for food under the Mosaic Law, frequented high places and is known for its agility and surefootedness. (7)
42. The Israelites used to eat this sweet fruit while captive in Egypt, and they longed for it after they left Egypt. (10)
43. Jesus asked what father would hand his son a scorpion if his son asked for one of these. (3)
44. This grain was included in Ezekiel's bread. (6)
45. This game animal resembling a gazelle appeared on King Solomon's table. (7)
46. Jesus pronounced woe to the hypocrites who gave a tenth of these three herbs, yet disregarded justice and mercy and faithfulness. (4, 4, 5)
47. The Pharisees in Jesus' day gave a tenth of this herb. (3)
48. The tree from which this valuable fruit comes was often planted in groves. (5)
49. Many people of Israel died as they attempted to eat this meat at Kibroth-hattaavah. (5)
50. To sit under the tree that produced this food was considered a symbol of a person's security.

# Foods of the Bible Quiz—answers

1. (10) TURTLEDOVE (Song of Solomon 2:12)
2. (6) BARLEY (Judges 7:13; John 6:9, 13)
3. (6) BUTTER (Genesis 18:1, 2, 6–8)
4. (6 pl.) GREENS (Exodus 12:8)
5. (6) LENTIL (Genesis 25:23–34)

6. (5, 5 pl.) SHEEP, GOATS (Deuteronomy 14:4, 5; Matthew 25:31–46)
7. (8) CUCUMBER (Numbers 11:4, 5)
8. (4) WINE (Luke 10:34; 1 Timothy 5:23)
9. (9) PISTACHIO (Genesis 43:11)
10. (7 pl.) LOCUSTS (Matthew 3:4)
11. (5 + 5 pl.) BROAD BEANS (Ezekiel 4:9)
12. (5) APPLE (Song of Solomon 7:8)
13. (5 pl., 6 pl., 6) LEEKS, ONIONS, GARLIC (Numbers 11:4, 5)
14. (4) BULL (Exodus 29:10–14; 32:8; Numbers 14:4, 5; Leviticus 22:23, 24; 1 Kings 19:21; Psalm 106:19, 20)
15. (5 + 4) WHEAT BEER (Isaiah 1:21, 22)
16. (5) HONEY (1 Samuel 14:24–30, 41–45)
17. (3) PIG (Deuteronomy 14:8; Isaiah 65:4; 66:17)
18. (11) MARSHMALLOW (Job 6:6)
19. (5) MANNA (Exodus 16:31; Psalm 78:25)
20. (3 + 8) FIG-MULBERRY (Amos 7:14; Luke 19:4)
21. (5) WHEAT (Judges 6:11)
22. (4) STAG (Isaiah 35:6)
23. (5) CAROB (Luke 15:16)
24. (4) FISH (Numbers 11:5)
25. (5) WATER (Genesis 7:11–24; Exodus 17:2, 3; Deuteronomy 8:7–9; Nehemiah 9:15)
26. (6) ALMOND (Ecclesiastes 12:5)
27. (6) CUCKOO (1 Kings 4:22, 23)
28. (6 pl.) GRAPES (Numbers 6:3)
29. (4 + 4) SALT HERB (Job 30:1–4)
30. (7) GAZELLE (Song of Solomon 4:5)
31. (4) SALT (Numbers 18:10; 2 Chronicles 13:5
32. (11) POMEGRANATE (Song of Solomon 4:13; Joel 1:12)
33. (4 + 5) WILD SHEEP (Isaiah 15:17–20)
34. (5) SPELT (Exodus 9:31, 32)
35. (4) DOVE (Genesis 8:11; Jonah 1:1 ftn.)
36. (4, 5) MILK, HONEY (Exodus 3:8)
37. (8 pl.) SPARROWS (Matthew 10:29)
38. (5 pl.) DATES (Song of Solomon 5:11)
39. (8 + 4) MOUNTAIN GOAT (Proverbs 5:18, 19)

40. (7) MUSTARD (Matthew 13:31)
41. (7) CHAMOIS (Deuteronomy 14:5)
42. (10) WATERMELON (Numbers 11:5)
43. (3) EGG (Luke 11:11, 12)
44. (6) MILLET (Ezekiel 4:9)
45. (7) ROEBUCK (Deuteronomy 14:5, 6; 1 Kings 4:22, 23)
46. (4, 4, 5) MINT, DILL, CUMIN (Matthew 23:23)
47. (3) RUE (Luke 11:42)
48. (5) OLIVE (Exodus 23:11; Judges 15:5; 2 Kings 5:26)
49. (5) QUAIL (Numbers 11:31–34)
50. (3) FIG (1 Kings 4:25)

And for those biblical gardeners with a down-to-earth sense of humor, here are some truly corny, but nicely clean veggie jokes. Share as you wish.

Q: Why did the tomato turn red?
A: Because it saw the salad dressing.

Q: What vegetable might you find in your basement?
A: Cellar-y.

Q: What is green and goes to a summer camp?
A: A Brussels' scout.

Q: What vegetable do you need a plumber for?
A: A Leek.

Q: Why do potatoes make good detectives?
A: Because they keep their eyes peeled.

Q: Where did the vegetables go to have a few drinks?
A: The Salad Bar.

Q: What is small, red, and whispers?
A: A hoarse radish.

Q: What vegetable can tie your stomach in knots?
A: String beans.

Q: Why is it not wise to tell secrets in a cornfield?
A: There are too many ears.

Q: When is a cucumber like a strawberry?
A: When one is in a pickle and the other is in a jam.

Q: What did the lettuce say to the celery?
A: Quit stalking me.

Q: What do you say to rotten lettuce?
A: You should have your head examined.

Q: Why did the tomato go out with a prune?
A: Because he couldn't find a date!

Boy Melon: Honey, dew you want to run away and get married?
Girl Melon: Sorry, I cantaloupe.

# Chapter 14

# Plan a Trip to the Holy Land

The best way to tour the Holy Land is to contact your local travel agent who can find packaged tours offered by professional tour firms. In the process, in keeping with the theme of this book, here are some ideas to guide your thoughts and help a travel agent focus on key elements that relate to foods that Jesus ate and the beauty of biblical plants there too. To enjoy the land at its most glorious blooming peak, keep these points in mind.

Remember, the growing season there begins in October as the first rains arrive and plants are awakened and regrowth is stimulated. It is most logical that the Jewish New Year, Rosh Hashanah, is in October. When October rains fall on mountain slopes, meadows and fields, the flowers of the well-designed bulbous plants begin their blooming cycle. Crocus and early wild narcissus begin to bloom with their whitish petals and orange crown in the center, a dramatic sight. Cyclamens spread their heart-shaped leaves among rocks and send their crown-like blooms up early and last longer than most others, especially in the Upper Galilee area.

With the encouraging rains, tulips display their showy blooms and anemones get ready for flowering. Anemones are found everywhere from the Negev Desert to the Galilee area. By late winter hundreds of red anemones blaze across fields. Wild flowers abound.

By November, rains will have worked wonders to awaken other dormant plants. Narcissi will be in their glory and cyclamen in dazzling beauty. Farmers will be busy in their fields with crops as they have been for centuries, guided by that growing cycle.

In December, berries and fruits including oranges, lemons, and grapefruit will begin maturing and ripen. During January, anemones continue their long, colorful display, adding their bright reds and purples to the landscape and irises will begin blooming alongside streams and waterways.

By February, more trees blossom along with wild iris, one of the striking flowers in the hills around Nazareth and in the northern Negev area. Botanists explain that there are several distinctive irises native to the Holy Land, but the typical Flag iris seems most common. The delightful anemones and hyacinths add color to the land and fragrance to the air. It is indeed one of the most beautiful times in the Holy Land.

In March and April, the large iris, tulip, lupine, and other colorful plants adorn the countryside. Patiently planted gardens respond to rains of winter and are reaching their prime. By May, poppies and thistles, lilies, and flowers that prosper with the warmth of summer begin their bountiful displays of beauty. By June, depending on the zone, late summer flowers appear. And, at last, it is harvest when vegetable and fruit crops mature from family plots, orchards, and farms alike.

In late July and August, warm, drying winds will regain their dominance. Plants will wither and the land returns to its natural dormancy. In September, many plants near their end. Seeds are set and dropped. New blooms and nutrients for next year's plant growth are safely deposited in the bulbs, corms, tubers, and rhizomes of flower plants. That is the natural cycle, blooming and then storing nutrients in the respective root areas for the coming year's plant.

Plants go into their waiting mode as perennial flowers do in North America and Europe during the winter season where cold weather is the factor that induces dormancy in flowers and plants each fall. In America and Europe, snow may blanket the ground, yet the bulbous flowers and roots of perennial plants lie safely tucked safely below. In the Holy Land, the roots and bulbs lie sleeping through the dry time.

With October's approach, the winter rains traditionally appear again as they have for centuries. With the rain, the growing cycle begins anew, encouraging the land to once more sprout into greenery, bloom, and bear. And thus is the growing cycle in the Holy Land, from whence have sprung the plants of the Scriptures.

From that understanding of the growing seasons of the Holy Land you can plan the best time to see the glory that God has placed there for all. Here is a possible itinerary that friends who have traveled there extensively have suggested. Modify this as you and your travel agent wish to see the areas in which you are most interested.

# Guideline for Holy Land Tour

**Day 1**—Depart USA

Begin your journey to the Holy Land with an overnight trans-Atlantic flight

**Day 2**—Arrive Tel Aviv, Israel.

Arrive in Tel Aviv, one of Israel's resorts on the Mediterranean coast, transfer to your hotel.

**Day 3**—Neot Kudemim Gardens

Travel to nearby Neot Kedumim, the amazing 625 acre Biblical Landscape Reserve that features the plants of the Bible in many displays that capture the spirit of the Holy Land from Jesus time. You'll enjoy appealing walks including: Trail A - The Garden of Wisdom and Literature to see ancient winepresses, cistern and ritual bath, the Sharon Forest and the Dale of the Song of Songs. Trail B – includes grain, wine, and oil: threshing floors, olive press, winepress, plus fragrant spices and incense, the Mosaic of Time, an interactive calendar and The Dale of the Song of Songs. Trail C - The Land of Milk and Honey includes a reconstructed water wheel and the Four Species of Sukkot. Trail D - Date palms in the Valley of Jericho, a watchtower in Isaiah's Vineyard and the Forest of Milk and Honey. Your meal there will include traditional foods that Jesus and His Disciples ate that trace their roots to ancient times and the Scriptures. In advance, read the chapter in this book about these famed gardens and view their colorful Website.

**Day 4**—Haifa/Tiberias

Next, enjoy a tour of Haifa beginning at the summit of Mount Carmel where you enjoy a breathtaking panoramic view of Haifa Bay and Western Galilee. Mt. Carmel is where lilies of the Scriptures were first found by modern botanists. Continue to Bahai Temple and its exotic Persian Gardens. Drive north to see the ancient Roman and Byzantine remains at Zippori, a small village that was the most important town in Galilee in Jesus' time. A church in Zippori, built on the ruins of an early Crusaders' church, now marks the birthplace of Mary, mother of Jesus. Then travel through the Golan Heights to see the former Syrian bunkers, Kuneitra and the ancient village of Katzrin, and on to Tiberias for the night. Along the way you'll see delightful native wild flowers.

**Day 5**—Tiberias/Capernaum/Jerusalem

This morning take a boat ride across the Sea of Galilee from Tiberias to Capernaum, an important city on the road from Syria to Egypt that Jesus made "the center of His teaching." On the way you'll see other glorious flowers that were mentioned in the Scriptures. Next visit Tabgha, a serene and beautiful area where you'll find the Mount of the Beatitudes and the sites of three of the New Testament's significant episodes: The Sermon on the Mount; the Multiplications of the Loaves and Fishes, and the post-resurrection appearance of Jesus. Next visit Nazareth and see Mary's Well, Joseph's Church, and the Church of the Annunciation. A stop at Beit Shean reveals vast excavations of a beautiful Roman-Byzantine city, Scythopoli, whose streets, public buildings, and temples have been unearthed. Later, continue through the Judean Hills to Jerusalem, admiring the beauty of the land along the way.

**Day 6 to 8**—Jerusalem

A Holy City for each of the world's three great religions Judaism, Christianity, and Islam, Jerusalem occupies a unique role in history. Enjoy a city tour that begins with a visit to Mount Zion, with the traditional tomb of David and the Room of the Last Supper. Enter the Old City and walk through the restored Jewish Quarter, visit the Roman Cardo, the Herodian Masion, and continue on to the Temple Mount and see the Western Wall. A walk along the Via Dolorosa brings you to the Church of the Holy Sepulcher. Finally, see Mount Scopus and Mount of Olives and enjoy a magnificent panoramic view of the old city.

On another day be sure to visit the modern side of Jerusalem including the Knesset, the Chagall Windows of Hadassah Medical Center, and other historic and contrasting modern sites. In this area pause to admire beautiful landscaping and gardens that are part of Jerusalem's appeal today.

Other visits could include the Qumran Caves where the Dead Sea Scrolls were discovered and Masada, the hilltop ruins rich in history. Consider a visit to the Dead Sea and a swim in it, the lowest body of water on earth.

**Day 9**—Return to USA

Whether you stay longer or just this short period, you'll absorb the wonder of the Holy Land in all its historic magnitude and scriptural significance. For biblical gardeners, a trip to where our faith began can be a lifelong inspiration.

# Appendix A

## Seeds from the Holy Land

Zeraim Seed Growers Co.
14 Haibilolm Street
Gedera, Israel

Agrexco
149-32 132nd St.
Jamaica, NY 11430
taly1@agrexco.com

Zvi Ben Schachar Seeds Ltd.
8 Petah Tikva Road
Tel Aviv, Israel

Bickel Flowers Ltd.
Weitman Street
Ra'anana, Israel
www.bickel.co.il

Hazera, Ltd.
Bar Yehuda Road, Box 15615
Haifa, Israel
972-4-8420865

# Appendix B

## Biblical Garden Directory

As I research my earlier three biblical garden books and this latest one, I e-mailed and snailmailed every biblical garden I could find, including new ones on the Internet. For ready reference, here are the updated contacts at all the key Biblical Gardens in the United States and those I have heard from and researched overseas.

Col. Hy Mandell
Chairman, Biblical Garden
Temple Beth Shalom
Jewish Community Center of Sun City
12202 101st Ave.
Sun City, AZ 85361
*www.goodnet.com/~tablespoonaz/body_index.html*

Bob Morgan, Biblical Garden Curator
Paradise Valley United Methodist Church
4455 E. Lincoln Drive
Paradise Valley, AZ 85253
*www.pvumc.org/about/biblicalgarden.html*

Betty D. Senter, Director
Plants of the Bible
Phipps Conservatory, Schenley Park
613 Oxford Blvd.
Pittsburgh, PA 15243
*www.phipps.conservatory.org*

Martha Finger, Director
Temple Beth-El Biblical Garden
1 Regency Plaza #1201
Providence, RI 02903

Curator, Biblical Garden
Temple Beth-El Synagogue
70 Orchard Avenue
Providence, RI 02903

Office of the Director
Magnolia Plantation and Gardens
3550 Ashley River Road
Charleston, SC 29414
*www.magnoliaplantation.com/gardens/index.html*

Director, Biblical Garden
Missouri Botanical Gardens
St. Louis, MO
*webmaster@mobot.mobot.org*
Tel: 314-577-9400
*www.mobot.org/hort/gardens/org/hort/gardens/bibleplants*

Scott Medbury, Dir. Strybing Arbo-
retum
Barbara Pitschel, Head Librarian
Golden Gate Park
San Francisco, CA
*www.strybing.org*

Paul Heimbach, Director
Warsaw Biblical Garden, Rt. 15
Warsaw Community Development
Corp.
P. O. Box 1223
Warsaw, IN 46580
*www.warsawbiblicalgarden.org*

Joseph Scott, Curator
Biblical Garden
Prince of Peace Lutheran Church
209 Eastern Ave.
Augusta, ME 04330
*www.poplink.org*

Betty Clement, Director
St. Gregory's Episcopal Church
Biblical Garden
6201 East Willow Street
Long Beach, CA 90815-2296
*www.stgregorychurch.com*

Irene Jacob, Director
Rodef Shalom Biblical Botanical
Garden
4905 Fifth Avenue
Pittsburgh, PA 15213
*www.rodefshalom.org/Garden/
initial/html*

Rev. Marsh and Cindy Hudson-
Knapp
Fair Haven Biblical Garden
First Congregational Church
19 West St.
Fair Haven, VT 05743
*hkfamily@sover.net*
Phone/FAX 802-265-8605
*www.sover.net/~hkfamily*

Charles Sourby
Therapeutic Biblical Gardener
Schervier Nursing Care Center
2975 Independence Avenue
Riverdale, NY 10463
*Csouby@bestweb.net*

Mrs. Henry Thompson, Chairman
The Biblical Garden
The Cathedral House
1047 Amsterdam Avenue
New York, NY 10025
*www.stjohndivine.org*

Curator or Director
Temple Sinai Biblical Gardens
11620 Warwick Blvd.
Newport News, VA 23601
*www.ujcvp. org/temple_sinai/
bulletin04-00*

Betty Burns, Director, Biblical Garden
St. John's Episcopal Church
PO Box 2088
Norman, OK 73070
*www.episcopalnorman.org/outreach.
htm#garden*

Curator or Director, Biblical
Garden
St. James Lutheran Church
110 Avenue Phoenetia
Coral Gables, FL

Director, Biblical Garden
Highlands- Presbyterian Church
1001 NE 16th Ave.
Gainesville, FL 32601
*www.gnv.fdt.net/hpc/garden/*

Director, Biblical Garden
Messiah Lutheran Church
5740 W. Holt Road
Holt, MI 48842

Biblical Garden of B'nai Shalom
74 Eckley Lane
Walnut Creek, CA 94596
*www.BiblicalGardens.com*

Tress Elizabeth Jones
Director, Biblical Garden
First Presbyterian Church
4815 Franklin Road
Nashville, TN 37220
*www.fpcnashville.org*

Mrs. C. Page McMahan
Director, Biblical Garden
Church of the Holy Spirit
9 Morgan's Way
Orleans, MA 02653
*www.diomass.org*

Stan Averbach, Co-Chair
Shir Ami Biblical Garden
Committee

Shir Ami - Bucks County Jewish
Congregation
101 Richboro Road
Newtown, PA 18940
*poppopstan@aol.com*
*www.vahc.org*

Director, Biblical Garden
First Congregational Church of
Vernon
Rt. 30 and Central Road
Vernon, CT

Joanne Russ
Director, Biblical Garden
Parkside Lutheran Church
2 Wallace Avenue
Buffalo, NY 14214

Jan McGarity
Concordia Lutheran Church
40 Pitkin St.
Manchester, CT 06040
*Bobmcgar@aol.com*

Director, Biblical Garden
Faith Methodist Church
Douglasville, GA 30134
Curator or Director, Biblical
Garden
Congregational Church
Charlotte, VT 05445

Director, Biblical Garden
Ojai Presbyterian Church
304 North Foothill Rd.
Ojai, CA 93023
*www.ojaipc.org*

Kathy Kulper, Biblical Garden
Church of the Wayfarer
Corner of Lincoln and 7th
Carmel by the Sea, CA 93921
*www.churchofthewayfarer.com*

Director, Biblical Garden
Alta Sierra Biblical Gardens
16343 Auburn Road
Grass Valley, CA 95945

Director, Biblical Garden
Biblical Resources U.S.A.
P. O. Box 1970
Bellaire, TX 77402
bruas@flash.net
Phone: 713-827-8001
*www.brusa.org/biblegardenpage.htm*

Mary Lou Froehle, Biblical
   Gardener
Rev. Edward Schneider, Rector
St. Peter & Paul Church Donald
   Haag, Deacon
711 Walnut Street
Petersburg, IN 47567-1447

Parkside Lutheran Church
2 Wallace Street
Buffalo, NY 14214

Pud Kearns, Biblical Gardener
United Methodist Church
2516 Park Street
Greenville, TX 75401
*KearnsPAD@aol.com*

Biblical Gardener
Liberty Presbyterian Church
7080 Olentangy River Rd.
Powell, OH 43017

Biblical Gardener
First Congregational Church
225 South Interlaken Ave.
Winter Park, FL 32789

Biblical Gardener
Missouri Botanical Garden
4344 Shore Blvd
P.O. Box 299
St. Louis, MO 63166

Zilker Garden
2220 Barton Springs Rd
Austin, TX 78746

Rick Jarvis, Biblical Gardener
St. John's Lutheran Church
Babbtown, MO

Rev. Ann D. Krugen
St. Mark's Church
111 S. Roanoke St.
Fincastle, VA 24090
*crgeiger@attglobal.net*

Bob Holladay, Biblical Gardener
St. Michael's Church
2025 Bellefonte
Lexington, KY 40503
*stmichael.@juno.com*
Tel: 859-277-7511
*www.saint-michaels.org/new*

Rev. Karin Wade, Rector
St. Mary's Church
24 Broadway
Rockport, MA 01966
*stmaryse@ma.ultranet.com*

Rev. Arthur Hadley
St. John's Episcopal Church
700 High Street
Worthingtonj, OH 43085

Rev. Elizabeth Moore
St. Thomas of Canterbury
5306 E. Arbor Road
Long Beach, CA 90808
*stthomas@worldnet.att.net*
Tel: 562-425-4457
*www.home.att.org/temple_sinai≈
    web/00038*

Rev. Robert S. Ervin, Rector
St. Thomas Church
5 Hale St.
Dover, NH 03820

Bob Puchra
Horticulture Department
Father Flanagan's Boys' Home
318 Bucher Drive
Boys Town, NE 68010

Director, Biblical Garden
Christus Gardens
510 River Rd.
Gatlinburg, TN 37738

# Overseas Biblical Gardens

Director, Biblical Garden
Brickman's Country Gardens
Ontario, Canada
*www.granite.sentex.net/!lwr/brick
    man.html*

Helen Frenkley, Director
Neot Kedumim
P. O. Box 1007, 71100
Lod, Israel
*www.neot-kedumim.org.il*

Director, Biblical Garden
St. George's College
PO Box 1248
Jerusalem, Israel

Director, Biblical Garden
c/o Bible Garden Memorial Trust
12 Mitchell Road
Palm Beach, New South Wales
Australia

Director, Biblical Garden
St. Paul's Cathedral
Sydney, NSW
Australia

Director, Biblical Garden
Rockhampton Botanic Garden
Queensland
Australia

Director, Biblical Garden
Holy Trinity Parish Church
Sheen Park
Richmond, Surrey
England

Nicholas Green, Director
Millennium Bible Garden
Woodbridge, Suffolk
England

Director, Biblical Garden
Royal Botanic Garden
Kew Gardens
Richmond, Surrey
England

Director, Biblical Garden
Robert Easton, Designer
Millenium Bible Garden St. Mark's
Isle of Man
England

Director, Biblical Garden
Sternberg Centre for Judaism
The Manor House
80 East End Road
London N3 2SY

Director, Biblical Garden
St. Benedict's Priory
The Mount
Cobb, Co. Cork
Ireland

Director, Biblical Garden
Ara Virdis Project
Franciscan Center of  Environmen
    tal Studies
Via del Serafico
1,00142 Rome
Italy

Daan Smit, Curator
University Hortus Botanicus
Amsterdam Free University
van de Boeschortstraat 8
Amsterdam, Holland

Director, Biblical Garden
Rutland Street Chapel
Christchurch
New Zealand

Director, Biblical Garden
Bangor Cathedral Close
Bangor, Caenaarvon
Wales

Director, Biblical Garden
Biblical Garden - Elgin Scotland
Elgin, Scotland

# Appendix C
## Biblical Garden Update Form

More biblical gardens are being planted at houses of worship, in communities and home landscapes all around our country. For future editions of this book I would like to include updates on gardens included here and know about other gardens that deserve to be added.

Please use this form to provide me with an update about your Biblical Garden, so I may salute your garden and many others in our country and around the world. Use as much space as you need. Please include your website and email address so that other gardeners may learn from your experience and also grow with God themselves. Thank you.

Name of Biblical Garden or Your Name if a private garden.

_____

Address _____

City _____ State _____ Zip _____

Curator or Contact Person: _____ Tel: _____

Email: _____ Website: _____

For an update please email or snail mail any corrections, additions, changes and be sure to include contact information so I can double check the information for accuracy to be sure you earn proper credit for your good work. For a new garden, please add as much material as you can. Copy this form, share with others, and be sure to print or write clearly. If you have printed literature, it would help if you could send a copy of it. Many thanks.

# Appendix D

## Concordances

As you study the bible and dig in to biblical gardening, there are several excellent sources to help you locate scriptural references about biblical plants. I used *Cruden's Concordance* in 1980 when I wrote *Your Biblical Garden*. Over the years I've used it regularly and have begun double checking against other sources, too. Here are key sources for you.

*Cruden's Concordance* is a concordance of the King James Bible (KJV) that was single-handedly created by Alexander Cruden. In the mid-1720s, Alexander Cruden took on a self-imposed task of Herculean proportions, Himalayan tedium, and inhuman meticulousness: he decided to compile the most thorough concordance of the King James Version of the Bible to date. Cruden worked alone in his lodgings, writing the whole thing out by hand. The KJV has 777,746 words, all of which needed to be put in their proper place. Cruden even wrote explanatory entries on many of the words, including a Bible dictionary as a bonus. He had no patron, no publisher, no financial backers: his only commission was a divine one. *Cruden's Concordance* has never been out of print. Some hundred editions have been published, and at a popular online bookstore today you can choose from 18 different in-print versions of *Cruden's*.

*Strong's Concordance*, strictly *Strong's Exhaustive Concordance of the Bible*, is a concordance of the King James Bible (KJV) that was constructed under the direction of Dr. James Strong and first published in 1890. Dr. Strong was Professor of exegetical theology at Drew Theological Seminary at the time. It is an exhaustive cross-reference of every word in the KJV back to the word in the original text. *Strong's Concordance* was constructed with the effort of more than a hundred colleagues. It has become the most widely used concordance for the King James Bible.

*Nave's Topical Bible*: Nave's Topics were produced by Orville J. Nave while serving as a U.S. Army chaplain after years of "delightful and untiring study of the Word of God." His topics were first published in the early 1900s, and consist of more than 20,000 topics and subtopics and 100,000 references to the Scriptures.

*Thompson Chain Reference* is drawn from over thirty years of Bible study by Dr. Thompson who examined every verse of the Bible to determine its exact meaning. He then arranged topical chains from the verses for easier, more in-depth study. *The Treasury of Scripture Knowledge* has provided a cross-reference resource for Bible students worldwide for generations. This highly respected and nearly exhaustive compilation was developed by R.A. Torrey from references in Thomas Scott's Commentary and the Comprehensive Bible. With nearly 500,000 cross-references it is the most thorough source available. *Torrey's New Topical Textbook* is published by Sword of the Lord Publishers, P.O. Box 1099, Murfreesboro, TN, 37133. *The New Topical Textbook* was published with 20,000 topics and sub-topics and 30,000 Bible references.

# Appendix E
## Sources and Resources for Biblical Gardens

*by Rev. Marsh Hudson-Knapp First Congregational Church of Fair Haven UCC*

**Biblical Gardening Books/Booklets:**

Hudson-Knapp, Rev. Marsh. *Selection Guide for Planning Your Biblical Garden: Revised and Expanded Edition.* The fruit of twenty years of study by the Rev. Marsh Hudson-Knapp, this book includes a thirty-two page chart covering 126 biblical plants, with additional background materials on planning your gardens, a USDA hardiness chart, and an index of common and botanical names of biblical plants, providing virtually all of the information you would want to select, plan, and care for your biblical plants. This simple and clear chart includes common name, botanical name of the plant we grow and the actual plant in the Bible, the Hebrew and Greek names, a brief biblical quote or background or life application note, growing zones, sun needs, color of blooms, soil and water needs, height and spread, care, and much more about each plant.

    The new edition includes five new indices that sort the biblical plants according to growing zone, sun needs, height, plant type, and times of blooming, as well as an expanded section on planning your garden. $12 postpaid. To order: e-mail your mailing address and quantity you would like to hkfamily@sover.net.

Hudson-Knapp, Rev. Marsh. *Plants in a Biblical Garden.* A journey through 100 of the stories of the Bible where plants play a key role, each of which have been grown in the Fair Haven Biblical Gardens. Illustrated with 19th century prints. $5 postpaid. To order e-mail your mailing address and quantity you would like to hkfamily@sover.net.

Hudson-Knapp, Rev. Marsh. *Prayer Guide to the Children's Vegetable and Herb Garden.* $3 postpaid. Includes: Children's garden layout, children's artwork depicting Biblical plants, prayers, and meditations about the plants in the children's garden. Adapted from dedication ceremonies at the gardens. Not copyrighted. Available to reproduce if you give proper credit. To order e-mail your mailing address and quantity you would like to hkfamily@sover.net.

Hudson-Knapp, Rev. Marsh. *Welcome to the Water Gardens at First Congregational Church of Fair Haven*, $2 postpaid. Stories, songs, poems, and prayers of plants in our children's gardens. To order e-mail your mailing address and quantity you would like to hkfamily@sover.net.

Hudson-Knapp, Rev. Marsh. *Signs for Your Biblical Garden*. 100 signs each with botanical name and commons name of Biblical plant, Scripture, and life application notes, information about soil, sun, water, feeding, and other care for your volunteer gardeners and visitors. 100 5 1/2"x7" signs on card stock, ready for you to laminate and mount on stakes. $20 postpaid. To order e-mail your mailing address and quantity you would like to hkfamily@sover.net.

We recommend the use of Parker Davis Nursery Marker Stakes. Order directly from them. Approximate cost for 100 corrugated cards (5 1/2x7") and galvanized stakes (8" high) is $46 plus shipping. Contact: Parker Davis Inc., 2310 North Tryon Street · Charlotte, NC 28206 · (704) 375-9111 or 800-438-0387 or www.parkerdavis.com/nursery.html

Hepper, F. Nigel. *Planting a Biblical Garden*. (Grand Rapids: Revell, 1997). A colorful, wise, enjoyable book with which to start. Out of print but see Finding Used or Out of Print Books below

Hepper, F. Nigel. *Baker Encyclopedia of Bible Plants*. (Baker Book House, Grand Rapids, Michigan, 1992). Extensive information about plants in the Bible and in Israel today. Colorful. Helpful lists of plant species. Out of print but see Finding Used or Out of Print Books below.

Krymow, Vincenzina. *Healing Plants of the Bible*. (Cincinnati, St. Anthony Messenger, 2002). A beautiful hardcover book with rich material about a range of biblical plants and wonderful reviews of biblical gardens around the world. Also includes meditations about many biblical plants. See a full review. Available from Amazon.

Swenson, Allan A. *Plants of the Bible and How to Grow Them*. (New York, Citadel, 1995) Great ideas for designing and planting your biblical garden and longer articles about a more limited number of plants and trees. A 2004 selection of the Crossings Book Club. Available from Amazon.

Swenson, Allan. *Flowers of the Bible: and How to Grow Them*. (Citadel, Spring 2002) This exciting book will take you to biblical flower gardens around the world and features wonderful photographs from Neot Kedumim, the biblical Landscape Preserve in Israel. It will offer horticultural and biblical background on a wide array of plants to bless your gardens. $12.95, paper, 288 pages. Available from Amazon.

Swenson, Allan. *Herbs of the Bible.* This book explores the wide array of herbs in the Bible and gardens hosting them. Also included is a fascinating look at monastery and convent gardens. $12.95 Paper, 220 pages. Neot Kedumim publications: You can see or order them in the U.S. from American Friends of Neot Kedumim Tel. (518) 296-8673.

Hareuveni, Nogah. *Nature in Our Biblical Heritage.* (Neot Kedumim Ltd., Lod, Israel, 1980, 1996) 144 pp. Color & b/w.

Hareuveni, Nogah. *Tree and Shrub in Our Biblical Heritage.* (Neot Kedumim Ltd., Lod, Israel, 1984) 142pp, color & b/w.

Hareuveni, Nogah. *Desert and Shepherd in our Biblical Heritage.* (Neot Kedumim Ltd., Lod, Israel, 1991, 2000) 160 pp. color & b/w.

Hareuveni, Nogah, in association with Helen Frenkley. *Ecology in the Bible.* (Neot Kedumim Ltd., Lod, Israel, 1974) 52 pp. color.

Hareuveni, Nogah, *The Emblem of the State of Israel: Its Roots in the Nature and Heritage of Israel.* (Neot Kedumim Ltd., Lod, Israel, 1988) 32 pp., color.

*Seder Tu B'shvat: A celebration of Israel's seasons & of ecology in the Jewish tradition.* (Neot Kedumim Ltd., Lod, Israel, 1998), double-sided, laminated, full color accordion pullout pamphlet.

Shir Ami: Bucks County Jewish Congregation. *Shir Ami Biblical Gardens..* This is a 48 page booklet telling about their gardens and recipes for biblical foods, with photos of plants from their newly established gardens. Cost: Donation. Contact Stan Averbach poppopstan@aol.com.

Patterson, John and Katherine. *Consider the Lilies: Plants of the Bible.* Anne Ophelia Dowden (Illustrator) (Clarion Books, 1998). Breathtaking illustrations. Short, beautiful reflections on each plant or series of plants. Especially for readers age 9 and up, yet beautiful for adults. Out of print but see Finding Used or Our of Print Books below.

Gilmer, Maureen. *Rooted in the Spirit: Exploring Inspirational Gardens.* (Dallas: Taylor, 1997) Visit gardens and shrines around the world that reach out to encounter the divine. Not only Biblical, but other religious or spiritual theme gardens. Inspiring ideas. Not exclusively Biblical. Out of print but see Finding Used or Out of Print Books below.

Zohary, Michael. *Plants of the Bible*. (New York: Cambridge University Press, 1982). Superb research and original reasoning to identify actual plants of the Bible. Many color photos to identify plants. Out of print but see Finding Used or Out of Print Books below.

**Gardening Books:**

Brickell, Christopher, Ed. *American Horticultural Society A To Z Encyclopedia Of Garden Plants* (New York: DK Publishing, 1997). This huge tome is a treasure chest of information including growing zones, many photos, and extensive information about growing and caring for many species and varieties of plants. Since many biblical plants are quite unusual, this is one of few books that can provide information about many of them. The growing zones are especially important in discerning whether you can winter or summer a particular species in your area.

Brickell, Christopher, Ed. *American Horticultural Society Pruning & Training*. (New York: DK Publishing, 1996). How do you prune each different tree or shrub as it grows? With many different plants in the Biblical garden, this encyclopedia is the only resource I've seen that explains and illustrates the unique care each plant needs.

**Finding Used or Out of Print Books:**

www.amazon.com
www.abebooks.com
www.alibris.com
www.bookfinder.com

**Biblical Garden Group:**

American Friends of Neot Kedumim
P. O. Box 236
Howes Cave, NY 12092
Tel: (518) 296-8673

**Finding the Unusual (to us) Plants of the Bible:**

PlantFinder (magazine) Hollywood, FL 33024. Also at http://www.hortworld.com/

# Bibliography

One goal of this book is to help promote planting and cultivation of more biblical gardens all across America and around the entire world. My focus has been not on one type of plant but the entire range of plants of the Scriptures and Holy Land. The more you and your family read and learn about this fascinating field of gardening, the easier it will be for you and your friends to become biblical gardeners and apostles for biblical gardens in your area.

Since 1981 when my first biblical garden book, *Your Biblical Garden* was published, I've assembled a useful set of favorite reference books. Today most are available from bookstores, Internet sources, and some from out of print book specialists. Other reference books are mostly out of print but can sometimes be found through state library search systems, horticultural libraries or rare book dealers. For your reading and biblical gardening enjoyment, here are my favorite and resource books focused on biblical gardening and the Holy Land.

They are listed by author name.

Hareuveni, Nogah, *Tree and Shrub in Our Biblical Heritage*, 1984, 146 pages illustrated.

Hareuveni, Nogah, *Desert and Shepherd in Our Biblical Heritage*, 1991, 160 pages illustrated.

Hareuveni, Nogah, *Ecology in the Bible*, 1974, 52 pages, 62 color photos.

Hepper, F. Nigel, *Baker Encyclopedia of Bible Plants, Flowers, Trees, Fruits, Vegetables*, -Ecology, 1992, 190 pages, well illustrated.

Hepper. F. Nigel, *Planting a Bible Garden*, 1987 and 1997, 92 pages illustrated.

Hudson-Knapp, Rev. M., *Plants in a Biblical Garden, Prayer Guide to the Children's Vegetable and Herb Garden, a Biblical Garden Database* via hkfamily@sover.net

King, E. A. *Bible Plants for American Gardens*, 1941 and 1975 revised edition.

Moldenke, H. N, *Plants of the Bible*, 1940, 135 pages.

Moldenke, H. N. and A. L. E., *Plants of the Bible*, 1952, 328 pages, reprint, 1986.

Swenson, Allan A., *Your Biblical Garden*, Doubleday edition, 1981. 220 pages.

Swenson, Allan A., *Plants of the Bible and How To Grow Them*, 1995, 220 pages.

Swenson, Allan A., *Flowers of the Bible and How to Grow Them*, 2002, 280 pages, Citadel Press of Kensington Publishing.

Swenson, Allan A., *Herbs of the Bible and How To Grow Them*, 2003, 220 pages, Citadel Press of Kensington Publishing.

Zohary, Michael, *Plants of the Bible*, 1982, 220 pages

# Other Biblical Plant Resource Books

Alon, Azaria. The Natural History of the Land of the Bible, 1969, 276 pages.

Crowfoot, G. M. and L. Baldensperger, From Cedar to Hyssop: A Study in the Folklore of Plants in Palestine, 1904, 204 pages.

Zohary, Michael, Flora of the Bible, Interpretors Dictionary of the Bible, 1962.

Zohary, Michael, The Plant Life in Palestine, 1962.

The American Horticultural Society's A-Z Encyclopedia of Garden Plants.

# Bibles for Biblical Scripture Comparisons and Plant Identifications

Bible, English. Holy Bible, Authorized King James Version, 1967.

Bible, English, Revised Standard Version translated from the original languages as the version set forth in 1611, revised 1946-1952 and 1971.

Bible, Authorized King James Version, translated out of the original tongues and with the former translations diligently compared and revised, Judson Press, 1942.

Moffatt, J. The Old Testament: a new translation. Volume I, Genesis to Esther, 571 pages, 1924. Volume II, Job to Malachi, 482 pages, 1925.

Bible, Good News for Modern Man, The New Testament in Today's English Version.

American Bible Society, 1966 Bible, The New English Bible, Standard Edition, Oxford University and Cambridge

University Press, 1970. Bible, Life Application Study Bible, New International Version, Tyndale House Publishers, and Zondervan Publishing House, 1997.

Moffatt, J., The New Testament: A New Translation Together with the Authorized Version. Parallel edition with introduction, 676 pages, 1922.

Phillips, J. B. The New Testament in Modern English, 1960 Goodspeed, Edgar J. Popular Edition, An American Translation, 1935

Bible. Various Translations, Versions at Bible Study Tools website www.biblestudytools.com.

*Young's Analytical Concordance* by Robert Young, LL.D. This concordance organizes plants and other words based on their Greek and Hebrew names.

*Cruden's Concordance* by Alexander Cruden, M.A., remains a valuable guide to the Scriptures of the Old and New Testaments of the King James Version.

A list of my favorite garden information Websites is included in the sources chapter of this book and provides a wealth of links to horticultural experts at major companies in the United States and also around the world. Tap their talents for great growing knowledge.

You'll also find a list of leading mail order gardening catalogs which off free, mostly well and full color illustrated catalogs you can order. Sign on, read their tips and ideas and get growing better.